On Your Own

A Widow's Guide to Emotional and Financial Well-Being

Sixth Edition

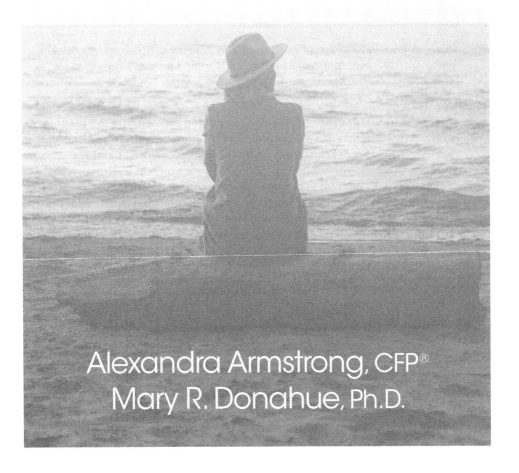

Alexandra Armstrong, CFP®
Mary R. Donahue, Ph.D.

Praise for Previous Editions
of *On Your Own*

" *Yours is the only book that truly approaches it from the woman's viewpoint and clarifies what is a mass of strange and threatening terms and tasks. You have done an important thing in a beautiful way. Thank you from my heart and my checkbook!*"

—A widow, Annapolis, Maryland

" On Your Own *is a wonderful book that manages to combine both the financial and emotional advice a widow needs in a helpful and supportive manner. If someone you care about is widowed, don't send flowers—send this book.*"

—Terry Savage, best-selling author

" *For all who have asked 'What do I do now?' or 'Who can help me...?' I recommend* On Your Own... *the authors lead the reader through important topics often thought to be too intimidating or too confusing for someone wrought with fear and sadness.*"

—Edward Jay Beckwith,
Estate Planning Attorney

" *I was a fan of the 5th edition of* On Your Own, *but the 6th edition is even better! The authors improved this essential guide in so many ways. It is packed with education and solid advice, while being easily accessible to every widowed person. I highly recommend the knowledge and learning in this comprehensive and helpful book.*"

—Amy Florian, speaker and author,
expert in life transitions

Dedications

*This book is dedicated to my mother, a widow who
taught me how to be a survivor by her example and
to my husband, whose encouragement, patience,
and advice helped me write these books.*
Alexandra Armstrong

*This book is dedicated to my parents, who, in an age when
it was not the norm, established for me the concept that it was
a woman's right to reach her potential, whatever it might be.
To my late husband, George, whose unconditional love and
support enabled me to expand my horizons and better
define my personal goals, and to my daughters, Laurie,
and Rachel, with whom I mourned, grew, and thrived.*
Mary R. Donahue

Acknowledgments

We would like to thank the following people for their assistance with this sixth edition: Lucas Campbell, Nicolette Davicino CFP®, EA, Debra Englander, Rachel Fitzpatrick, Ryan Fleming, CFP®, Elizabeth Fleming, Laurie Harmon, Carl Holubowich CFP®, Virginia McArthur Esquire, Mary Moore CFP®, Christopher Rivers CFP®, Kathy Welton, John Wittelsberger, CFP®.

Special thanks to Josh Kaplan, CFP®, EA, who spent long hours formatting and researching factual and technical data for our book. And to Sumedha Malhotra CFP®, CRPC®, CPWA® who made sure that all the financial planning information was correct.

Table of Contents

Preface

Terror, fear, pain, loneliness, paralysis, anger, numbness, sadness, panic, weakness, helplessness—these are some of the all-too-familiar emotions that crash and swirl around the fragile ego of a woman who has just become a widow.

The loss of your husband is likely to be the most traumatic event of your adult life. You did not choose to be a widow, you don't like being a widow, and you are overwhelmed by the enormity of the issues you are required to resolve as a result of the changes in your personal circumstances.

We first wrote *On Your Own* in 1993 to help widows cope better with the dramatic alteration that occurs in their lives following the loss of their husbands. We updated our book with four subsequent editions in 1995, 2000, 2006 and 2012.

Much has changed in the world since our last revision, so we thought it important to update the book once again. While the information contained in this book is current in 2024, market conditions and tax laws will continue to change, so be sure to talk to your financial and legal advisers before taking any action.

Statistics indicate that most women will be alone at some time, whether by choice or due to divorce or widowhood. To ignore the possibility of bereavement or estrangement and the emotional and financial consequences is to deceive yourself. Not planning for this event does not prevent its occurrence. The reality is that you can reduce the trauma resulting from your loss if you know what to do in your time of crisis.

In this book we view the widow's recovery as a series of building blocks. We start the book with the widow's initial grief response, then move through the recovery process to an ultimate state of emotional and financial well-being. Our book reflects our strong belief that there is a connection between your financial recovery and your psychological recovery.

Not to be overlooked is one's relationship to money. In recent years more research has been done on how one forms one's financial attitudes. There is now evidence that our views about money are formed in childhood and impacted by life events. Psychologists Klontz and Klontz[1] have drawn attention to what they call "financial flashpoints." They define the term as a major experience or event that takes place in childhood that dramatically influences the way we think about money. It may have less to do with a specific incident and more to do with the attempt on the part of the child to understand what is being experienced. They suggest that it is from one's childhood attempt to understand these critical childhood experiences that we develop "money scripts" that determine how we deal with money in the future.

It has been said that grief coupled with lack of financial knowledge is crippling. We believe that the better you as a widow are able to come to terms with your loss emotionally, the better able you will be to address the financial consequences. Similarly, the more you understand about your financial situation, the less anxious you will be, which in turn will contribute to your emotional healing.

As we traveled around the country talking about our book, we were surprised and pleased to find that the book had a broader audience than we had originally envisioned. Women told us *On Your Own* was of interest not only to widows but also to adult women of all ages. It provided an opportunity for many mothers and daughters to discuss an important subject previously ignored. Divorcés too, found that although they were experiencing a different kind of loss, many of the coping devices and financial information provided were helpful to them.

In this latest edition of *On Your Own*, we have updated the content once again, including Web site information as well as current financial

---

1. Klontz, Brad and Klontz, Tad. *Mind Over Money* New York. Random House. 2009.

and psychological trends. Our goal in this latest edition is to provide you with additional information that will enable you to cope better, not only during this critical time but also in the years ahead. We hope our book will help you deal with the enormity of your loss and also guide you along the path to emotional and financial health. We have purposely provided this information in a basic yet comprehensive format. We have presented the material so that you can read our book from cover to cover or select individual topics for specific information as you need it. Our goal is to enable you to be emotionally and financially self-reliant.

In discussing what we thought should be included in this updated version, we reiterated the fact that you cannot put all widows (or widowers, for that matter) in one category. There are young widows and old widows. There are those with dependent children, those with older children, and those without children. Some husbands died after a long illness, and others died suddenly. Some widows have been very dependent on their husbands, others more independent. The marriage might have been happy or only happy when viewed in retrospect.

We also think that the healing process cannot be put into specific time frames. Widows require varying periods of time to heal, depending on a variety of factors, such as the circumstances of the husband's death, the widow's preexisting mental health, her religious orientation, the available emotional support from friends and family, and her financial background and knowledge. Progress is not linear.

It is difficult to recover from the loss of anyone close to you. However, no death has so many psychological and financial implications and leaves the survivor feeling so helpless and alone as the death of a spouse. We recognize that there are unique issues for the widow that attach to a death by suicide or homicide. It is beyond the scope of this book to address these very special circumstances, but we encourage the reader to seek assistance from one of the available resources that deal with these issues.

Our personal experiences contributed to our decision to write this book. Each of us was forced to cope with the major consequences of death in our families. Here are our stories.

Alexandra Armstrong's Story

While I had worked as a financial advisor for many widowed clients over my long career, I was not a widow. However, that changed in March 2023 when I became a widow after 28 years of marriage. I will say that going through the experience personally provided me with additional insights for this latest updated version of our book.

However, my knowledge of widowhood started at an early age when my mother was widowed when she was 48 years old, and I was 8. Dad had been ill for some time and taking care of him had depleted the family's resources. In order to make ends meet, Mother went to work for the first time as a clerk in a dress store two years before he died.

By the time Dad died, there was very little money left, but there was a small life insurance policy. Mother used this money as a down payment on a small house in Georgetown, Washington, D.C. My older sister and brother, who were just starting to work, assumed responsibility for the mortgage. Although I took their generosity for granted at the time, in retrospect I realize how tough that must have been for them on their own limited budgets.

My mother and I lived principally on the income that came from Veterans Administration benefits, Social Security, and her salary. My grandfather had set up a small trust fund that provided some extra income from time to time. The checks from this fund often made it possible for us to get through the end of the month. After a while, Mom noticed that the checks were smaller, and their payment was sporadic. Because she was not knowledgeable about financial matters, she asked Dad's brother to help her investigate what was happening to this important source of income. After he looked into it, he brought her the bad news that she had been the victim of white-collar crime. The person who managed the trust fund for her had "borrowed" the money to cover his own expenses. He intended to pay it back to the fund but was never able to do so. By the time my uncle had taken an inventory of what was in the trust fund, very little money was left.

Although I was young when it happened, I understood the ramifications of this discovery—we didn't have this much-needed income. When I was older, I realized that if Mother had known more about investments, she might have been aware of the problem earlier and might have been able to avert or at least minimize the disaster. This event had a profound impact on my life. I resolved I would learn as much as I could about how money worked so I would have financial control of my own life.

We might not have had much money left after Dad died, but Mom certainly made up for any loss of income by the abundant love and care she gave me when I was growing up. She talked the nuns at the convent school I was attending into giving me a scholarship, because she believed a good education was essential to my future and it seemed clear that I would have to support myself.

In school I discovered that I actually liked and had an aptitude for mathematics. After completing college in 1960, I found a job as a secretary in the research department of a regional New York Stock Exchange firm located in Washington, D.C.

In 1965 I became the personal assistant to a woman partner in the firm, Julia Montgomery Walsh. When I started working for Julia, she was a young widow supporting four sons. It seemed that I was destined to be involved with widows, whatever I did!

In 1966, I passed the test to become a stockbroker and worked with Julia's clients until we started our own firm in 1977. By that time, I had completed the courses to be a CERTIFIED FINANCIAL PLANNER™, a program that taught me about various aspects of financial planning, not just investments. At the time, financial planning was a relatively new concept but one that seemed logical to me. Looking at all aspects of a person's financial situation before giving investment advice made more sense to me than giving investment advice in a vacuum. At the new firm I established the financial planning department.

In 1983 I left that firm and opened an independent financial planning firm in downtown Washington, D.C. Today the firm has more than 20 employees who provide individuals with financial planning and investment advice. At this time, we manage over one billion dollars for our clients. Although our firm has never focused exclusively on single women as clients, many have gravitated to our firm.

In view of my experience with my mother and my clients, helping women learn more about investments has been my mission. As I have told my female clients: Don't confuse a lack of knowledge with a lack of ability to learn. I believe that having this knowledge enables them to better control their financial future. The more women know about finances, the less apt they are to make mistakes. The old adage "Money can't buy happiness" might be true, but I believe that it certainly can make life more comfortable.

Mary Donahue's Story

I was a professional and supposedly enlightened woman when my ostensibly healthy husband, almost 22 years my senior, collapsed and died on January 21, 1980. Until his death, I had never been an active participant in our family's financial decision making, nor did I believe I needed to be.

My childhood and teenage years were relatively uneventful and monetarily trouble free. I attended a private school through eighth grade and a public school through high school in the New York City area. My father, a physician, provided a comfortable lifestyle for us, although we were never indulged. I never gave much thought to money. It was there if I needed something, but it was not limitless. College was a given and not a privilege.

As I reflect on the expansion of women's roles and choices, I often ponder how it was that my traditional dad imbued in me the sense that I could accomplish whatever I chose to accomplish while simultaneously telling me that my professional choices were nursing or teaching. Since he was familiar with the life of a nurse, teaching was it! In addition, I had to have the ability to support myself in the event that something happened to my husband. As it turned out, I had a double major in college—psychology and education—which ultimately led to my private practice of psychology.

Professionally, my young adult years were spent attending graduate school, working first towards a master's degree and subsequently a doctoral degree in psychology. During this time, initially I was employed as an elementary school teacher and then as a school psychologist. This latter position led to a special assignment on a project funded by the National Institute of Mental Health. The project focused on establishing educational programs for seriously disturbed and learning-disabled children utilizing the skills of supervised paraprofessionals. My husband-to-be was one of the project coordinators.

Before our marriage, we had many in-depth conversations about the implications of the disparity in our ages and its potential impact on our intention to have a family. Because we were in allied professions that focused on the well-being of the individual, we were sensitized to this area in our personal lives, in contrast to financial matters. This sensitivity was reflected in our lengthy, probing conversations. Conversely, we spent hardly any time discussing financial matters and did not have a financial philosophy.

My husband's personal background included working from the age of 11 through the Great Depression years to earn money to obtain a higher education, including graduate degrees. There was no family money. Whatever he accrued was the result of his own earning power. Clearly, he could be described as conservative.

As time went on and we had two daughters, we discussed how to divide our available time to maximize their time with both of us. We made a conscious decision to shift our workloads. At this point in our lives, I had begun to develop a private psychology practice. By mutual agreement, my husband took a consulting job that provided him with considerable flexibility in terms of committed time, and I gradually increased my private patient hours from a few hours a week to two-and-a-half days a week. We shared equally in the raising of our daughters. However, again by mutual agreement, he managed matters pertaining to the maintenance of our home and our finances, while I basically organized the children's lives and the internal care of the house—fairly typical and definitely traditional.

The following conversational exchange took place with some degree of regularity and predictability. He would say, "Mary, we really need to find time to review our financial situation, because you need to be more familiar with this area of our lives." I would predictably reply, "Yes, you are absolutely correct" and, equally predictably, never made the time to do so.

Therefore, I was totally unprepared to steer our financial ship following my husband's sudden death. I had no idea where and how to begin to undertake all of the tasks before me and deal with our financial needs as well. My husband had had no life insurance, and there were no provisions for our minor children other than Social Security. So, there I was left without warning: a single parent with total responsibility for my daughters. It appeared that I would have to assume their financial support in full, run our house, and expand my part-time practice if we were to survive financially. I was emotionally in shock and financially overwhelmed! Where to start? Where to turn? I was most familiar with parenting, somewhat familiar with running the house, but not at all familiar with finances.

I had no choice but to start in the area in which I had the least knowledge: finances. There were several reasons. First, at some point my husband and I decided to consult a financial planner to help us look at this area of our life. We had been recommended to Alex Armstrong, met with her, liked her philosophy, and felt she could be of assistance to us. It should not come as any surprise to the reader that the work with Alex was almost exclusively handled by my husband. Second, Alex knew more about my finances than I did. Third, and perhaps of greatest importance, she had the comprehensive financial knowledge I knew I needed. In the process of sorting out where I stood, she was invaluable. This financial planner is now the valued friend with whom I have collaborated in writing this book.

It is my opinion that whether financial news is good or bad, some knowledge is better than no knowledge. I found that my lack of financial information intensified my fears and anxieties and contributed to my remaining in a state of paralysis. This lack of financial information also may intensify a widow's grieving response.

I often remind Alex of the time when, discussing some point with me over which I was equivocating (as usual, trying to determine what George—my husband—would have wanted me to do), she turned to me and in a somewhat stern, frustrated, teacher-to-pupil manner said, "For heaven's sake, Mary, you make decisions every day in your work. What prevents you from making them in this area?" In a sense, at that moment I grew up monetarily. Although I have regressed on occasion, I have for the most part forged ahead, rightly, or wrongly, as a responsible adult, not second-guessing myself or trying to do what I thought my husband or parents would have wanted me to do.

Realizing in retrospect the mistakes I had made in resisting financial knowledge and understanding some of the psychological factors responsible for my resistance, I wanted to join Alex in providing to widows—at a time when they are most vulnerable—some sort of guidance that could integrate the emotional and financial aspects of this painful period.

The Story of four widows— Diane, Susan, Audrey, Elizabeth

This book is based on personal and professional experiences we have had with numerous widows during our careers. From these experiences, we created the stories of four widows. The hypothetical composite profiles that follow were created to illustrate various personality traits, financial situations, financial philosophies, ages, and family circumstances. We hope these composites help you identify factors in your own life that are likely to play a role as you move through the grief process.

We have attempted to present those financial issues that confront most widows. Your personal finances may be different, but your needs are the same. You may identify with the reactions of one or two or possibly all four of these widows. The purpose of the profiles is to make this book not just a textbook or a helpful handbook but one to which a new widow can relate in terms of her own experiences. As you read the ensuing chapters, you will follow the progress of these four widows as they mourn and subsequently rebuild their lives. In the process, you will be rebuilding your own life. We wish you the best on your personal journey to emotional and financial well-being on your own.

Two final points: Since this book is written by women for women, we have used "she" when referring to the various advisors, although we realize some of your advisors may be male, just as your deceased spouse may be male or female.

PART ONE

Picking Up the Pieces

CHAPTER ONE

Reacting to Your Loss

A ccording to the Census Bureau, in 2020 the adult female population in the United States numbered 129,966,000. Of these women, 11,271,000 were widows. In contrast, the same census indicated that the adult male population numbered 122,152,000 and of these men 3,487,000 were widowers. In other words, widows outnumbered widowers by a ratio of three to one.

A woman can become a widow and a man a widower at any age. The 2020 census data indicates the ages at which this life change occurred and the numbers within each age range:

	Widows	Widowers
Under 25	29,000	17,000
25–29	48,000	8,000
30–34	65,000	35,000
35–39	112,000	35,000
40–44	126,000	51,000
45–54	523,000	209,000
55–64	1,519,000	548,000
65–74	2,890,000	893,000
75–84	3,530,000	956,000
85+	2,430,000	735,000

Source: U.S. Census Bureau, *2020 Annual Social & Economic Supplement*

Contemplating these national statistics is sobering. They indicate that any married woman might be forced to become a widow without warning, whether or not she is ready to do so. The individual circum-

On Your Own ~ Part One

stances surrounding the death of your husband, your relationship as a couple, and your individual personality characteristics will have an impact on your response to your loss. Both common denominators and individual factors affect anyone experiencing grief. In this book we will consider the many faces of grief as well as theories with regard to the process of mourning.

For quite some time there was a generally accepted belief that mourning and grief required one to go through prescribed steps in a given sequence in order to heal from loss. Current thinking has recognized that these theories are not applicable to all. It is now widely acknowledged that there are major differences in the mourning experience and process for the widow whose spouse died suddenly and unexpectedly than those of a widow whose spouse died after a lingering illness. Since you may encounter these theories when speaking with others or reading on your own we have included a brief description of them here. The two most common theories are known as the Stages of Grief theory espoused by Elizabeth Kubler Ross and the Task Theory proposed by William Worden.

The Stage Theory

Stage One: Denial and Isolation

Stage Two: Anger

Stage Three: Bargaining

Stage Four: Depression

Stage Five: Acceptance

The Tasks of Mourning Theory

Task One: Acceptance of the loss

Task Two: Addressing the pain of your loss

Task Three: Adjusting to an environment in which your loved one is absent

Task Four: Recognizing that you are in a different place while realizing the role your deceased spouse played in your life.

It is generally accepted that mourning is not a linear exercise to be completed in a stated manner in order for you to move forward. Responding to grief is not the same for everyone. It is very much impacted by the circumstances surrounding the death of a loved one. For instance, was your husband's death the result of an extended challenging illness where he experienced a minimal quality of life or was it the result of a totally unexpected random event over which no one had any control? This type of unexpected death increases the potential for psychological issues such as depression and anxiety.

Some of you may have watched your loved one struggle and deteriorate over time. Sometimes your spouse may have even become unrecognizable related to his former self. This often results in your feeling helpless, powerless and frustrated with your inability to ease his pain.

Most recent theories contend that following death, bonds with the deceased don't need to be severed and that there is a potentially healthy role for maintaining continued bonds but in a different form. Death ends a life but not necessarily a relationship. The deceased may be both present and absent.

Currently one theory about grief over time suggests that it's not that the grief experience lessens as time passes. Rather grief and related emotions will remain the same size, but your on-going life experiences, other thoughts and emotions loom larger and grow over your grief.

It is our contention that you may experience these varied emotions as you move through the grief process. We do not believe that you need to progress through them in consecutive order in order to heal and complete your individual process of mourning. Different emotions may emerge at any time. Sometimes it is hearing a special song that triggers memories for you or the aroma of a special dish you both liked. You may suddenly have an intense response whether or not you thought this incident would impact you in such a powerful way. You never stop loving someone, you just learn to live without their physical presence.

It doesn't make you a failure in the healing process if you experience an emotion from an earlier time in your healing process, after you thought you had made significant progress in moving forward without your loved one. More aptly put, it is the result of the ebb and flow of your life given your unique situation.

The circumstances surrounding the death of your husband plays a key role in your recovery process. For example, if your husband died following a protracted illness it is likely that you experienced what we call a period of "anticipatory mourning". There may even be a sense of relief that the pain your spouse was experiencing is over. This period of pre mourning may have been more stressful than the post death mourning. Do not feel guilty if you feel a sense of relief.

Grief experienced before the death of your spouse may or may not shorten the total mourning process. Your experience is based on the totality of your life to date. There is no right or wrong here.

On the other hand, if the nature of your loss was traumatic, and/or unexpected, you will have a very different experience with which to deal. If you witnessed the violent death of your husband or experienced multiple unexpected losses in a short time frame, the grieving process is more complex, often complicated by lack of closure. Feelings of inadequacy may abound. Don't let prescribed emotions at given stages determine how you should be feeling. Only you can steer your personal course.

In the first year of the COVID 19 pandemic, the suddenness with which people became ill and died led to many feeling lost because of the rapidity with which death followed so quickly after the diagnosis was made. In these types of situations, you first must deal with the trauma you experienced before the work of grieving can actually begin.

Recent studies have identified many types of grief which reflect unique sets of circumstances. They are Ambiguous Grief, Traumatic Grief, and Cumulative Grief to name a few. Each type of grief presents its own symptomatology and unique characteristics that need to be addressed.

A factor in all grief work not to be overlooked is the culture and spiritual life of the grieving woman. It is very Important to know if she is primarily Christian, Jewish, Buddhist or Atheistic. How she deals with loss and grief is greatly influenced by the norms of her cultural identity. It is important to understand this component of grief when looking at the bereavement process. In other words, throw any stated timeline away when it comes to determining how long the grieving process should take in terms of days, weeks, months, or years.

Grieve in the way that is right for you. As Earl Grollman said: "Each person's grief journey is as unique as a fingerprint or a snowflake." Whatever you are feeling, if you are feeling stuck there are skilled grief counselors available to help you assess your situation and provide support to you based on your specific circumstances. These therapists can help you clarify your personal experience and guide you through what you are feeling.

Loneliness is a state of mind experienced by many individuals, both male and female, at different times in their lives. It is particularly acute and prevalent in the lives of widows. The pattern for your life up until this point has been that of being part of a couple. That is no longer the case. Now you are on your own and alone. You may experience feelings of paralyzing sadness and loneliness. In most cases this is not a permanent feeling but one that is in response to your loss. As time goes on you usually return to functioning more as you did before this major event in your life. Something to keep in mind is that while you did not cause your feelings of loneliness you can take actions to pull yourself out of this morass in a way that is comfortable for you. Baby steps eventually will lead to walking.

We would be remiss if we didn't mention that there are support groups available online and in person should you feel that having the opportunity to speak with others in a similar situation would be helpful to your mourning and healing process. Although this group approach has been available for quite some time it was particularly helpful to many during the COVID 19 pandemic.

In this chapter we have focused on relationships that were positive for the couple. If your coupled situation was unhappy, you are undoubtedly having a very different experience. In this case, one of the most common emotions experienced is the loss of the potential for a better life with your partner. This is particularly true if the death was sudden. If such is the case, seek appropriate professional support.

Summary and Conclusion

To summarize, try to remember that you are engaged in a process—a painful process. Many factors impact your recovery.

Death has been described by several philosophers as man's final stage of growth. As a widow, you too are in a growth phase, one not of your own choosing but one that is yours to mold following the healthy process of grieving.

We now introduce you to our four hypothetical widows as they go through the various stages of recovery.

Diane

Suddenly Widowed with Dependent Children

Diane, age 42, looked at her phone. Had she heard right? She had just received a call from Larry, a personal friend and a partner in her husband's law firm, who informed her that in the middle of a partnership meeting her husband had slumped forward in his seat and lost consciousness. When efforts to revive him failed, the rescue squad was called, and he was rushed from his downtown Washington, D.C., office to George Washington University Hospital. Larry said he would pick her up and take her to the hospital.

In a fraction of a second, Diane's world turned black. She felt paralyzed, rooted to where she stood in the familiarity of her cheerful kitchen with her hand on the phone. She didn't know what she had said to Larry. Her three children—Erin (age 15), Jeremy (age 11), and Alice (age 7)—were due home from school in an hour, and Jeremy had soccer practice. How long had she been standing there? The next thing she knew Larry was at the door.

Her next awareness was of being at the hospital in a small room, where a somber doctor stood before her. She really didn't know what he said other than that Mark, her husband of 20 years, had had a massive heart attack and was dead. But she was uncertain about even that. Larry was there beside her, talking in a rational manner to the doctor. Both Larry and the doctor pressed tissues into her hand to stem what she later realized was a flood of tears.

A nurse led her to the room where Mark lay with medical paraphernalia still attached to him. She supposed she should do or say something, but she felt numb, as she dabbed hopelessly at the tears that kept pouring from her eyes. Without warning, Diane's world had changed forever. Somehow, some way, she signed some papers, and then Larry took her home. The children were huddled together in the family room, looking toward her for something. In her current state, she was unable to comprehend what.

Friends and family seemed to materialize out of nowhere and began to take over. In her current state of numbness, Diane let them. Mark had always handled everything. She had felt so protected and cared for by him. Gradually, over the next several days, she comprehended that people expected her to make certain decisions and provide certain information. In her present emotional state, however, she was not capable of making decisions, nor did she have the information she was expected to have.

Before she married Mark, Diane had always been taken care of by her mom and dad. She had never lived alone. After her marriage she had moved from her parents' home to an apartment with Mark. At some point in the days after Mark's death, Diane realized that her dad had resumed his parental role with her. It allowed her to feel somewhat safe yet at the same time somewhat uncomfortable. She got the message that Mark did not have a will. Apparently this was a serious problem. Her dad was particularly critical of Mark for not having attended to this matter. Diane was hurt and angered that her dad could think poorly of him at this moment.

Prior to marrying, Diane had been a paralegal. In fact, she and Mark had met while working for the same law firm, the very one he was working for at the time of his death. Mark had risen to partner status in seven years, and the firm had grown from 10 people when they met to more than 100 currently.

Over the years, with Mark's approval, Diane had spent increasing amounts of money on the household and the children. They lived in an $850,000 home. She learned for the first time that she was responsible for a mortgage of about $500,000. She felt overwhelmed on all levels. She had always been supported by Mark, and now she didn't know where to turn. She was willing to accept help, advice, or kindness from anyone who offered it.

Diane had never been asked to make financial decisions. She had remained in a dependent financial state in her life to date. When she was living with her parents, her father had communicated to her that she did not need to be concerned about money because he would always take care of her. Her mother's total reliance on her father with regard to financial matters reinforced this belief. Mark picked up where her father left off. He encouraged her not to be concerned about money, telling her that he would take care of those issues.

In her initial response to the loss of her husband, Diane was incapable of comprehending the implications of her new state. She felt as if she were in some timeless place surrounded by fog and mist, disconnected from life. Sometimes she was aware of saying something to her mom, dad, the children, or Larry, but she felt detached from the woman who walked through the rooms of her home and responded to questions or comments.

Many people attended the funeral, but Diane wasn't even certain who was responsible for the funeral arrangements. She knew she had been asked a great many questions, but other than selecting the clothes Mark was to be buried in, all the while crying hysterically, she couldn't remember her answers to any of the questions.

Friends and relatives commented on what a beautiful funeral it was and how well-liked Mark had been. Diane restrained herself from beating on them with her fists for their well-meaning but, for her, empty comments. She felt numb and alone—lost in her own disconnected world.

Diane's Profile

Personal Profile When Widowed
- Age: 42
- Occupation: Homemaker (paralegal before marriage)
- Husband: Mark
- His age at time of death: 45

- Cause of death: Heart attack
- His occupation: Attorney (partner in a large firm)
- Years married: 20
- Place of residence: Rockville, Maryland
- Children: Erin (15), Jeremy (11), Alice (7)
- Parents: Father (68), mother (65)
- Siblings: None
- Will: None

Personal and Professional Support People at the Time of Death
- Mark's friend at the firm: Larry
- Larry's wife: Gail
- Estate planning attorney: Mary Sue Ryan
- Stockbroker: Scott Truitt
- Life insurance agent: Jack Blafford

New Personal and Professional Support People
- Erin's friend's widowed mother: Jennifer Greenberg
- Jeremy's friend's divorced mother: Nancy Martin
- Support group friends: Lisa, Robyn, Marcy
- Financial planner: Dorothy Trumbull
- Firm benefits representative: Karen Hutchinson

Susan
Suddenly Widowed with Elderly Mother

Susan, a 50-year-old executive with a nonprofit association based in Seattle, Washington, could not believe she was once again single. She had just about given up the idea of marriage when she met Lance 13 years ago. They had been married for 12 years now and, despite their individual family demands, had been happy. She hasn't been able to process the events that led to his death. It didn't seem possible that it was only two weeks ago that she had been informed of his accident. A teenager had run a red light and plowed into Lance's car. Lance had been taken to the hospital, where doctors had identified internal bleeding as well as several broken bones. Complications stemming from the internal bleeding subsequently led to his death in the early hours of the morning.

Susan was not feeling up to dealing with Lance's two children from his first marriage. They had never really accepted the fact that their father had married her. Adam, age 25, had recently begun to talk with his father about going to graduate school. Leslie, age 21, was a senior in college.

Lance, with his accounting background, by mutual agreement, had managed their finances. This was a big relief for Susan who already had her hands full managing her mother's financial affairs as well as her job. He always told her what he was doing, but she frequently tuned out his lengthy explanations as to why he selected one investment over another. Now she would have to take it over again. However she was confident that she had the ability to address what needed to be done with regard to her present situation as well as manage her financial life in the future. After all, she had handled her personal finances prior to marrying Lance.

In light of their individual financial responsibilities prior to their marriage, Susan and Lance had worked out a premarital agreement that left their respective assets to their dependents—in Lance's case, his children; in Susan's case, her mother—but they had recently amended this agreement. Lance had decided to leave his $500,000 insurance policy in trust for his children. If Lance died, Susan would receive the interest income from this insurance trust until she died, and then the children would receive the principal. Lance's will stipulated his children would receive $25,000 each when he died. The rest of his assets were left to Susan. She anticipated that once Adam and Leslie learned these financial facts, they would be upset and threaten to contest the will.

On this chilly morning, Susan's thoughts turned to the impact of Lance's death on her 80-year-old mother, whom they helped support. A couple of years ago, with the help of a geriatric care manager, she and Lance had selected and moved her mother into a nearby Continuing Care

Retirement Community (CCRC). She had been relatively happy there, but Susan had noticed recently that her short-term memory had started to deteriorate. Certainly, she was glad that she and Lance had decided against bringing her mother to live with them. There was no way she could personally care for her mother given all her new responsibilities.

On learning of Lance's death, Ron, Susan's 55-year-old brother, offered to help in any way possible. Susan had her doubts about how much help he could really be since he had been somewhat estranged from their family in recent years. This was due to his revealing to his family he was gay and his assumption that they would disapprove.

Susan needed to do something to remind herself that Lance was really gone. The last time she spoke to him was just before he left work on the day of his death. They had talked on the phone in the late afternoon, as they usually did, to discuss their plans for dinner and the evening. Lance had volunteered to pick up the milk and bread they needed on his way home from the office. Susan said she would start dinner, and they ended the conversation with their usual "I'll see you in a bit, love you." Little did she know these would be the last words he would say to her. Nothing profound or unusual—just normal and comfortable. Now everything was abnormal, uncomfortable, and unreal.

Lance had wanted to be cremated, so at least Susan didn't have to deal with selecting a coffin. Susan had insisted on making all the memorial service arrangements herself down to the most minute details. This process helped her realize Lance would not be walking through the door at any minute. Susan felt Lance would have been pleased with her plans for his memorial service. "How macabre," she thought.

She kept feeling her reactions were strange, but she was not prepared for such an event. Her husband had been a healthy man—why should she have given any thought to the likelihood of his death? Susan didn't like the lack of control she was experiencing over her thoughts and feelings.

There was much to do in the days ahead, but she wasn't ready to face it. She kept telling herself she needed to focus on one day at a time and get through it. She just hoped and prayed she would find the internal strength to meet the demands about to be made of her. She had no professional advisors of her own. She thought this was something she needed to correct in the ensuing weeks.

Susan's Profile

Personal Profile When Widowed

- Age: 50
- Occupation: Executive, nonprofit association
- Husband: Lance
- His age at time of death: 55
- His cause of death: Car accident
- His occupation: CPA (partner in a large firm)
- Years married: 12
- Place of residence: Seattle, Washington
- Stepchildren: Adam (25), Leslie (21)
- Parents: Mother (80), father (deceased)
- Sibling: Ron (55)
- Will: Yes, plus premarital agreement

Personal and Professional Support People at the Time of Death

- Lance's partner: Harry
- Harry's wife: Emily
- Lance's assistant: Sarah Stone
- Estate Planning Attorney: Tim Longwood
- Stockbroker: Bob O'Brien

New Personal and Professional Support People

- Bank trust officer: John Stepstone
- Assistant trust officer: Ellen Peabody
- Psychologist: Dr. Catherine Coleman

Audrey

Corporate Widow with Adult Children and Grandchildren

Audrey, age 62, had spent the past year, as she had in previous years: trying to meet her husband's needs. John was 66 when he died following a protracted struggle with lung cancer. He had been in and out of the hospital the last year of his life and Audrey had not missed a day being with him before his death. A part of her was relieved that the agony was over; another part looked with apprehension at the tasks ahead.

John had been an executive with a major corporation in St. Louis and had taken early retirement at age 62 because of his poor health. The couple had health insurance through his company. Theirs was a traditional marriage. John had managed their finances, and Audrey had managed their home, particularly the entertaining, at which she was a master. She sometimes wondered how far John would have gone in the company if she hadn't been the excellent hostess she knew she was. As she and her daughter left the hospital on this last day, the doctor commented on what a support Audrey had been to John, and she realized just how draining the last year had been. She was exhausted. She was confident that John Jr., age 40, would arrive shortly to give advice and take over any task requested of him and even some that were not.

Audrey had been married to John for 42 years. Where had the years gone? Theirs wasn't a marriage made in heaven. She had stayed with him because life never seemed that bad, there were children to consider, and you just didn't divorce a man who had always provided for you!

Audrey knew that John had a will. She remembered they had once met with an attorney to review it. Other than that, she knew nothing about their finances. John managed that aspect of their lives and told her what specific items she could and couldn't spend money on. She thought about the day, 22 years ago, when they purchased their home. What a major financial outlay it had seemed at the time! Now it was worth much more. Audrey was glad that they had no mortgage. Her thoughts moved to her daughter, who drove her home on the memorable day of John's death. Joanne, at age 35, had three young children. She and her husband, Keith, never seemed to be able to make ends meet financially.

How different her children were, much like the difference between John and herself. She wasn't looking forward to dealing with John Jr. in the days ahead. She knew he wanted to help, but she resented his patronizing manner. At one time, they had been really close, but since he had become a successful physician, their relationship seemed to be different.

What would she do with her life? She had never worked. There were many unanswered questions that made her somewhat anxious, but at the same time she was experiencing something else—a new sense of being on her own for perhaps the first time in her life. In a way, it was appealing. She didn't think this was what she was supposed to be feeling. This made her feel a little guilty. She thought she would understand it all much better in the days ahead.

One thing that surprised Audrey was her inability to realize that the long ordeal was over. John had actually died. He had been ill for such a long time that the finality of his death seemed somewhat unbelievable. She was having more difficulty accepting his death than she had thought she would. She couldn't get in touch with what she was feeling. Sometimes she thought she felt loss, yet at other times she just felt numb. "How odd," she mused.

Audrey, Joanne, and John Jr worked out the funeral arrangements. Both children were willing to do anything their mother felt unable to do. Audrey didn't find the details of the funeral too taxing. The staff of the funeral home was helpful, which made the process less painful. In addition, the family's minister knew them very well, so discussing the eulogy and service was relatively easy.

Actually, what she found most difficult was talking to their many friends and John's former coworkers, an unfamiliar feeling for Audrey. She was such a social person, yet she did not quite know what to say to these people. On the one hand, she was sorry John had died, but, on the other hand, she was relieved that the agony of his long, drawn-out illness was over. Somehow it didn't feel quite right to express these feelings, even though they were very real to Audrey. She found she left most of the initial conversations with other people to the children.

Audrey selected what she would wear to the funeral without weighing one outfit over another. It was almost as if she had previously made this decision, although she was not conscious of having done so. What an unfamiliar experience, thought Audrey.

Due to John's illness, Audrey had taken over paying the bills, but she knew little about their overall financial situation. When she was growing up, her parents didn't have much money. She remembered them talking about how to make ends meet, but it had little impact on her other than she didn't have as much money to spend on clothes as some of her friends. She was expected to work after school in high school and contribute some to her expenses. Going to college wasn't really an option. However, she never felt deprived. She and John had not talked much about money since there always seemed to be enough to support their somewhat modest lifestyle.

Audrey's Profile

Personal Profile When Widowed

- Age: 62
- Occupation: Homemaker
- Husband: John
- His age at time of death: 66
- His cause of death: Lung cancer
- His occupation: Corporate executive (retired)
- Years married: 42
- Place of residence: St. Louis, Missouri
- Children: John Jr. (40), Joanne (35)
- Grandchildren:
- John Jr.'s children: Casey (14), J.T. (12)
- Joanne's children: Jamie (6), Heidi (4), Noah (2)
- Parents: Deceased
- Will: Yes

Personal and Professional Support People at the Time of Death
- Estate Planning Attorney: Albert Humphrey
- Mr. Humphrey's assistant: Sally
- Accountant: Gary Woo
- Physician: Dr. Peter PaPadisio

New Personal and Professional Support People
- Friends: Lionel Dawson, Janet Pine
- Financial planner: Ken Silver
- Cold-call broker: Walter Postman
- Real estate agent: Georgia Brown

Elizabeth

Older Widow with No Children

Elizabeth and Ben had been married for 55 years. In fact, Elizabeth could barely remember a time when she hadn't been married. Now she was 75, and Ben had just died, at age 83. Eighteen years had gone by since Ben had sold his small business near Boston. His health had been deteriorating over the past several years, and Elizabeth had become frustrated by his memory lapses and confusion. He had always been somewhat of a hypochondriac, but she thought it was his way of guaranteeing him getting her attention. She wondered whether he would still be alive if she had taken his physical complaints more seriously. Yesterday morning she had been unable to wake him. It had been only 24 hours since he had died, yet it felt like so much longer.

At 75, Elizabeth had her own problems. She didn't know how she would manage alone. She had been depressed periodically over the last 15 years and had some heart problems, although "nothing terribly serious," according to her doctor.

Elizabeth and Ben had no children. They had lived a simple life—a few friends, some entertaining, and church suppers. They had paid off the mortgage on their modest home years ago, so they owned it free and clear. Ben had always said he didn't want her to have any financial worries when he "kicked the bucket."

Elizabeth knew Ben had some financial advisors, although she had never met them. She wondered how he came to select them, who they were, and how they would deal with her. She had no knowledge whatsoever of their financial situation. She thought Ben had a will. At some point she remembered his telling her that their investments were worth half a million dollars, but she wasn't sure if she had understood him correctly.

Elizabeth knew she had to make arrangements for Ben's funeral. She had called her older sister, Abigail, as soon as the rescue squad told her they couldn't revive Ben, who had passed away peacefully during the night. She had also called her pastor, who appeared almost immediately after her call.

Pastor Appletorn had been so considerate. He had contacted the funeral home and spoken to the director. He told her which papers she had to sign and why they were necessary. He also insisted on contacting her closest friend, Mabel, and making sure she would be able to spend the night so Elizabeth wouldn't be alone. The pastor promised to return when Abigail arrived to finalize plans for the funeral. Elizabeth was grateful that Mabel had agreed to stay until Abigail arrived. She had always thought Mabel was good at managing things. She would be a big help, and it would be good to have her around

Elizabeth was frightened. She didn't know what she was supposed to feel. She had never been alone. She had always had a role: daughter, sister, and then wife. What was she supposed to do in this new role of widow? Who would take care of her? She had always clung to the thought that Ben would be there to take care of her if anything happened to her, even when she knew he really couldn't do that anymore. Now she could no longer even pretend he would be there. She had been so involved in caring for him that she had never given any thought to the fact that he might die. "Why hadn't I?" she mused. "There must be something wrong with me."

Elizabeth was very nervous. She couldn't eat or sit still or think about anything for more than a few minutes. She cried a lot, but she wasn't sure she knew why she was crying; she was just scared. She felt a little better after Abigail arrived because Abigail had always looked out for her when they were young. She recalled how Abigail used to tease her about being "afraid of her own shadow."

Elizabeth let Abigail take charge of making all the arrangements for Ben's small church funeral. Elizabeth couldn't even decide what to wear. Abigail patiently looked through Elizabeth's closet and selected something dark and conservative. In the evenings, Abigail tried to console Elizabeth, sometimes patting her hand, and encouraging her to relax a bit. Part of Elizabeth felt as if she were lost someplace. It reminded her of the way she had felt following some minor surgery years ago when she was regaining consciousness—there but not there. She hoped she would feel better soon.

Elizabeth was the younger daughter in her family and truly represented what psychologists call "learned helplessness." No one had expected anything of her. Her parents overprotected her and expected her older sister Abigail to assume responsibility for her if they weren't at home. Elizabeth was not expected to make decisions about anything. Ben enjoyed the fact that Elizabeth always went along with what he wanted to do. In fact, this is probably why they had such a happy marriage.

Elizabeth's Profile

Personal Profile When Widowed

- Age: 75
- Occupation: Homemaker
- Husband: Ben
- His age at time of death: 83
- His cause of death: Age-related deteriorating health
- His occupation: Small business owner (retired)
- Years married: 55
- Place of residence: Boston suburb, Massachusetts
- Children: None
- Parents: Deceased
- Siblings: Abigail (77)
- Will: Yes

Personal and Professional Support People at the Time of Death

- Friend: Mabel
- Pastor: Pastor Appletorn
- Estate Planning Attorney: Francis X. Carroll

New Personal and Professional Support People

- Church friends: Sam and Sarah Weatherly
- Friends: Lucy Thornton, Abe Stein
- New attorney: Frederick Grossfeldt
- Trust officer: John Samuels
- Assistant bank manager: Suzy Riley
- Accountant: Deborah Greenfield
- Real estate agent: Jerry Winthrop

CHAPTER TWO

Identifying Your Personal Characteristics and Financial Attitudes

In addition to those emotions experienced by all widows, there are individual differences that are the result of many factors. These may include your individual personality, your personal health, economic factors, your age, the ages of your children (if you have children), the circumstances surrounding the death of your husband, and whether you considered yourself happily married. These factors as well as the role money or finances have played throughout your life will impact how you cope with widowhood. Few of us pay attention to how or where or why we have formed our financial identity, yet it plays an important role in our lives. You are more likely to be aware of your personality traits than your attitude towards money, so we will review them first.

For example, in your current state you are most likely feeling emotionally fragile. If so, is this feeling unfamiliar, or is it compatible with your psychological functioning before your loss? Based on your knowledge of yourself, is this feeling likely to be short-lived or long-standing? Knowing yourself has an effect on how you will proceed.

If you are someone who tends to have very strong emotional reactions to life events but is able to regroup in a relatively short period of time, you may feel comfortable contemplating meeting with a lawyer, an accountant, or a financial advisor within the first month of your loss. If, however, you are someone who has always had a difficult time coping with major emotional upheaval and has needed support from your husband or other family members, the passage of time is not likely to make a major difference in your ability to deal with this aspect of your life by yourself. If so, recognize the need to take someone with you when you meet with these advisors. In fact, whatever your emotional state, it is very important to take someone with you to take notes.

What is critical here is for you to use your knowledge of yourself as a guide to assist you in the process of addressing the emotional and financial challenges you'll face.

It is desirable for each widow to develop an awareness of the personality characteristics that will impact her ability to deal with this new phase in her life. In assessing yourself, take into consideration your basic personality traits and previous as well as present functioning. In addition, you need to review the meaning of money in your life and how you arrived at your beliefs in this area. These individual personality differences and your financial philosophy will affect to a large extent your ability to steer your personal ship to psychological and financial independence.

Perhaps you never gave this much thought and are unfamiliar with the qualities that dominate your decision-making processes. To help you in your self-analysis, we are providing you with three aspects of personality that are common to everyone and to which all widows will be able to relate. These individual factors are significant and will help you understand your reactions as you go through the experience of loss.

Your Personality Characteristics

Are You Primarily a Thinking or a Feeling Person?

Do you respond to your world primarily on an intellectual basis? In other words, before making a decision, do you gather as much information as you are able to obtain, do research, weigh the alternatives, speak with a variety of people, and develop flow charts or whatever else will allow you to make an informed decision? If so, you use primarily thinking or cognitive processes to reach conclusions.

Other individuals are more spontaneous in their decision making. They may wake up in the morning and decide on a given course of action based on such factors as the temperature, the sun, a feeling, or a mood.

The differences between these two types of personalities may be illustrated by the way they would place bets at a track. One person studies the conditions of the track, the odds, and the past performance of the horse, the jockey, and the trainer, while the other places a bet based on the horse's name, the colors of the jockey's shirt, the color of the horse, or something else that evokes a personal response. This is not meant to suggest you never have any emotional responses if you describe yourself as using primarily thought processes, or vice versa.

We have provided you with the extremes of these qualities but recognize that most people do not function in a way that incorporates 100 percent of one approach over the other. All of us have both components within us. What makes us different is the degree to which we use one characteristic or the other.

Are You Primarily Extroverted or Introverted?

It is also important to understand yourself in the areas of extroversion and introversion. For example, if you are a woman who is outgoing, enjoys socializing with others, seeks the company of others, and is frequently described as very friendly, companionable, and active in any number of areas, you would be described as extroverted. If you are extroverted, you are more likely to seek out others for advice, support, information, and even direction. You may look toward social activities as a reason for not addressing what needs to be addressed.

An introverted woman is one who tends to engage in more individual pursuits, such as reading, crafts, music, or any activity you can do by yourself. If you are introverted, you are likely to look within yourself, obtain printed matter, check out the Internet, or consult one trusted friend or spiritual leader in formulating a course of action or direction. Again, few of us fall exclusively in one category or the other. However, on reflection you will be able to identify which behavior pattern you lean toward.

Are You Primarily Dependent or Independent?

Another important characteristic the widow needs to be aware of is whether or not she is a dependent or independent person. Some women have been conditioned or have allowed themselves to believe that it was preferable to leave major decisions to their spouses. They were pleased to be taken care of by their husbands, protected and treated as though there was no need for them to be involved in any decision making outside the home. Perhaps to this widow, being sheltered from such decision making was a statement of her husband's love.

Others, regardless of their involvement with financial decision making, have carved out an area of independent functioning for themselves. Women may involve themselves in all sorts of activities—a profession, a job, volunteer activities, artistic pursuits, various courses of study, and so on. Such women may have wanted to be involved with the financial aspects of their married life but felt it would have been hurtful to the spouse or the marriage to challenge an economic decision or request inclusion when investments were made.

Research indicates that for a married woman, the loss of a spouse is the single most emotionally stressful event in her adult life. For most of these women, the task of managing their finances by themselves follows closely behind this event. This is basically true, regardless of one's personal circumstances at the time of a spouse's death. Even those widows who have paid the monthly household bills during the course of the marriage or in recent years, may find that this familiar task becomes more difficult for the moment.

Understanding which of these personality characteristics have been dominant throughout your life will assist you in determining the most helpful approach to your new personal situation. However, understanding the significance of money in your life will also help you address the critical issues before you.

How You Feel About Money

Perhaps you might have thought less about how you view money than other areas of your life. Whereas you are bombarded by a variety of questionnaires and articles in magazines and on television about how to find and maintain a compatible long-term relationship with the significant other in your life, rarely if ever is there emphasis on the importance of your personal financial views and their impact on the selection of your significant other.

Your attitudes towards money, as well as the development of most of your other traits, go back to childhood. What were your parents' attitudes toward money? What role did money play in your childhood? Along life's journey you internalize financial beliefs. For example, were most of your parents' arguments focused on money issues? Did you as a child dread those times when your parents had financial discussions? Was it your perception that money matters were an area in which your father felt your mother had no place? Did you internalize the belief that women and girls were not competent to have valid opinions or that it wasn't feminine to understand math? Messages with regard to money are incorporated over a lifetime and are a part of your belief system, whether or not you are aware of it. Inaccurate financial beliefs may complicate your life at this time of loss.

Studies indicate that in preschool and elementary school boys and girls tend to exhibit equal achievement in math. Beginning with high school, gender issues surface. Girls do not do as well as boys in math. As a group, they consistently have higher levels of math anxiety and lack confidence in their math skills. Several theories have been proposed by way of explanation, but to date there is no generally accepted hypothesis as to why this is the case.

During childhood, you received financial messages from other sources in addition to your family or school. For instance, you may have attended a particular church that presented a person's financial position in terms of good or evil. In some cases, accumulated money was viewed as a good thing, and in others it might have been associated with the work of the devil. How you respond to these types of money messages is rarely part of your conscious recall.

Another common source of money messages is from the media. In the mid twentieth century, a variety of television series presented stereotypic male-female roles (Leave it to Beaver, I love Lucy). People raised primarily during those years have a very different image of a woman's role with regard to money than women raised later. Younger women have been exposed to television programs where women have a much more dominant role. Thus, we see that a variety of factors as well as society at large contributes to our financial beliefs.

It is still likely that some widows today were raised in an era when male-female roles were clearly defined; namely, the man was the head of the household and the breadwinner, while the woman was the child-care provider and the homemaker. This way of life is no longer typical.

You should not overlook the role money played in your childhood. Was it a given and not often discussed? Was it a means of receiving recognition and approval? Was it attached to the receiving of love? If you did something deserving of reward, was it usually in the form of something monetary? Did you get a coveted doll or a special book or did you receive a dollar award? Whether all of this was formally articulated or merely understood, it should not surprise you to learn that you have a financial history that has resulted in the shaping of your own philosophy about money. It should also not surprise you to learn that many women place a higher value on the quality of their relationships than on obtaining financial success.

Of immediate concern to most widows is the issue of having sufficient funds to survive. Regardless of your financial situation, most widows are worried about making ends meet. There are a few widows at the other end of the spectrum who will enjoy the opportunity to spend money as they want without feeling the need to justify their spending to their spouses. In most cases, however, paying your monthly bills is your primary concern.

This concern is closely related to your embedded feelings about risk. In general, women tend to be more conservative than their male counterparts when it comes to making financial decisions. In the early stages of your widowhood, you may find yourself trying to make decisions in line with what you believe was the decision-making practice of your husband, father, or other significant financial figure in your life.

You have now arrived at a point in your life when it is important for you to review and assess both your individual personality characteristics and your financial perspective. It is time to come to terms with how best to deal with who you are in relation to the decisions you will now have to make.

For example, you may be a woman who is unable to mobilize yourself from your emotional paralysis following your loss. If you are such a woman, you may feel the need to turn to a loved one or friend for assistance. Allow yourself to do whatever you feel is best to help you cope with the issues before you. But do not allow others to make major decisions for you in any area until you feel sufficiently comfortable with decision making and have had an opportunity to meet with an appropriate professional.

You may need to respond to your grief by occupying your time with making lists or itemizing things in order to regain a sense of control over your life. If you are such a woman, is this a pattern with which you are comfortable and familiar? Are concrete tasks helpful to you in meeting your emotional needs?

Recently, psychologists have been focusing on what they call "money disorders." These are conditions that have resulted in people not being able to function appropriately as an adult with regard to money. The three "F's" (fight, flight, and freeze) are terms that they use to describe how individuals have lived their financial lives.

For instance, the widow who is primarily motivated by "fight" tends to blame others for her financial mistakes or even herself for not doing what was necessary to make a good decision. Others with a "flight" reaction might want to sell assets and hold the cash in order to ensure that they have enough money when this action is not warranted based on their individual circumstances. Another common response with widows is the "freeze" reaction. In this case the widow feels so overwhelmed and incapable of action that she takes no action at all, even when it would be desirable to do so.

In your case, what is most important is to understand how you arrived at your views with regard to money and factor that into how you can move forward successfully.

Summary and Conclusion

Only you will be able to determine what is right for you. Whatever your personality characteristics, finding yourself in a position where you are required to take total control of your money might be unfamiliar and uncomfortable. Keep in mind that change is a part of life, and you are not sentenced to maintaining the beliefs or misconceptions of the past. As you gain knowledge, you may find yourself modifying your previous concepts about money in a healthy way. It is now your choice to make decisions with new knowledge or remain where you have been.

Diane

Diane's Personal Characteristics and Financial Attitudes

Diane, our youngest widow, is primarily an extroverted, feeling woman who tends to be more dependent than independent. As you progress through her story, you will note that family issues will motivate Diane to function more independently than at any previous time in her life.

Up until this point in her life, Diane had responded to life events primarily on an intuitive level. She has always been extroverted, likes people, has many friends, and tends to rely on her instincts or feelings when formulating opinions. If she perceived something to be a particular way, she accepted her perception and rarely sought objective information to corroborate her impression. She would often tell Mark her feelings about an individual, an event, or even a movie.

Diane had always been treated as a child with regard to money. In her parents' home, her dad made all the financial decisions for the family. Her mother would ask her father for money for food, clothing, and other household expenses. As Diane matured, it was understood that if she wanted money for a prom dress or a special activity, she would have to ask her father for the money. For the most part, Diane's financial requests were honored. She was never expected to work during high school, and she accepted her father's attitude about money as a given. As previously indicated, she always thought that someone else would make these decisions for her. She had no understanding of finance in general, no less the specifics of her own situation.

It was not surprising then that when Diane married, Mark assumed the role her father had played in her life. Diane never questioned whether this was good or bad; rather, it was the way life was with regard to money. Diane's childlike attitude to money continued into her marriage. Thus, her initial response to Mark's sudden death was to feel helpless and look to someone else to make decisions for her. This immature outlook about money placed an added burden on Diane following his death.

- **Significant personal characteristics:** Extroverted, feeling, dependent
- **Significant financial attitudes:** Childlike, dependent, helpless

Susan

Susan's Personal Characteristics and Financial Attitudes

Susan is relatively independent. She has both extroverted and introverted qualities but leans toward the latter. She has always been an excellent organizer. Sometimes she didn't pay sufficient attention to the feelings and ideas of others in her desire to get a task completed in the most efficient fashion. Effective and relentless in her ability to accomplish a stated goal, she has always been viewed as an excellent executive in her organization. Within her company she is known to have both innovative ideas and the skills to implement them. Her need to get the job done and look at the facts concerning a given issue is one of the qualities with which her stepchildren had always had difficulty. Nothing she had done had endeared her to them.

As far back as she could remember, Susan had been aware of the significance of money. Plainly and simply put, there was never enough of it to make ends meet. The lack of money created constant tension between her parents. She knew her father worked hard, but he never made that much money. He would periodically attempt to get her mother to look seriously with him at their financial problems but to no avail. Susan had always been very conscious of not making unnecessary financial requests of her parents.

At some point in her teenage years, Susan realized that contrary to what she thought was supposed to be the case, her older brother had as little comprehension of money matters as did her mother. It was understood that Susan was the one who could be counted on to be supportive of her father and do without during her growing-up years. As soon as she was old enough to do so, she obtained a part-time job and tried to stretch her money to pay for extras she might want, such as a class trip.

Given her past, Susan had little tolerance for risk. Following her marriage to Lance, she had allowed herself to relax a bit and rely on him to take the lead when it came to money matters. Over the years she had become more knowledgeable and more confident of her ability to make financial decisions. However, she was concerned about whether or not she could maintain the same standard of living she had had with Lance now that she was alone.

When Susan was a child, she felt she was the one who needed to be responsible about money. When she became an adult, her father made it clear that he expected her to take financial responsibility for her mother if he was no longer able to do so. Because of this responsibility, she knew she needed to conserve her resources. Now as a widow, she would return to her previous attitudes about money.

- **Significant personal characteristics:** Mixed features of extroversion/introversion, thinking/feeling, dependence/independence
- **Significant financial attitudes:** Lack of confidence/self-confidence, low risk tolerance, some knowledge

Audrey
Audrey's Personal Characteristics and Financial Attitudes

Audrey has always been outgoing. She has also been realistic about her life. Those who know her think of her as practical and as having a great deal of common sense. Family and friends often look to her for assistance when dealing with personal issues because of her calm, matter-of-fact approach to their problems. She has made it a practice to obtain information about various matters before making a decision; in fact, a part of her analyzes facts without even realizing she is doing so. She possesses the capacity to look at herself realistically, is open to new ideas, and has the ability to change her views.

Audrey had grown up in the Midwest. Her father and mother had traditional family roles. Her father went to work and supported his family on his salary. Her mother stayed at home and was clearly responsible for the nurture and care of the children. Dinner was on the table every night at precisely 6:00 p.m., when her father walked in the door with his newspaper rolled tightly under one arm and a slim briefcase in his other hand.

As with so many things in her life, Audrey had pragmatically accepted whatever was done in her parents' household. She never questioned whether or not it was right or wrong, good or bad; it was just the way life was during her years of growing up. After marrying John, she had followed his lead in financial matters. Audrey had no complaints, although if she had thought about it, there was no real reason why they did the things they did financially as a family. She accepted what life had to offer, including John's financial decisions, and dealt with it. There was always enough money to support a comfortable lifestyle. The corporate life, although sometimes dull, was stable, and she felt financially secure.

In retrospect, Audrey believed she made decisions affecting her life and for the children for primarily pragmatic reasons. This attitude was fostered in childhood and carried over to her married life.

- **Significant personal characteristics:** Mixed features of extroversion/ introversion, thinking/feeling, dependence/independence
- **Significant financial attitudes:** Confidence in her ability to learn, open to learning, questionable risk tolerance, not financially frozen

Elizabeth

Elizabeth's Personal Characteristics and Financial Attitudes

Elizabeth has always been a dependent person in need of a great deal of support. She is usually more content when by herself or in a small group.

Throughout her life she has placed a high priority on loyalty and consideration for the welfare of those closest to her, particularly her husband, Ben. She always worked hard to make their home a comfortable place. Ben appreciated her efforts and was proud of her. The activities she enjoyed the most were her various arts and crafts projects and her involvement in her church's programs. She was particularly pleased with her needlepoint and quilting. Elizabeth always cared deeply about the misfortunes of others, whether it was someone she saw on television, a church member, a personal friend or an acquaintance. She has always related simplistically to her world, relying on her emotions and feelings when assessing a situation or an individual. She has tried to follow the Golden Rule: "Do unto others as you would have them do unto you."

Elizabeth had absolutely no financial knowledge nor did she have any interest in acquiring any. She had internalized from childhood the concept that it was her husband's responsibility to take care of her, just as it had been understood that her father was financially responsible for her when she was young. In reality, Elizabeth was very childlike, expecting to be taken care of by someone.

Growing up, Elizabeth looked to her sister to solve her problems. If she had any question and was uncertain as to whether or not to mention it to her parents, she would consult with her big sister. She had never had a bank account of any sort before her marriage to Ben. Until his health deteriorated, she had never written a check on their joint account without first discussing it with Ben. Being financially knowledgeable was a concept beyond Elizabeth's comprehension. It was plainly and simply something she had never had any interest in, whether as a child, a teenager, or an adult. If Elizabeth were honest with herself, she had to admit that she always enjoyed being taken care of by someone in her life. Somehow being taken care of said to her that she was loved and deserving of care.

- **Significant personal characteristics:** Introverted, emotional, dependent
- **Significant financial attitudes:** Childlike, dependent, vulnerable, resistant to assuming financial responsibility.

CHAPTER THREE

Dealing with Your Emotional Needs

At some point, the finality of your loss becomes real. It might be in a matter of days, weeks, or even a month or more. It is at this moment that you realize your husband is no longer there to protect you or to rely on for emotional or financial support. Acknowledging that your husband is no longer there is a painful awareness, one often accompanied by an emotional response. Remember that during this phase of the mourning process you are likely to experience a variety of strong emotions. In order to move forward you must assess the degree to which your emotional state is affecting your actions and judgments.

Among the factors impacting your passage through this part of the mourning process are your specific personality characteristics and the financial circumstances in which you find yourself. In addition, the nature of your marital relationship plays a role in your responses. The important thing for any widow is to assess her personal reactions and gauge how close they are to her normal emotional responses to stress. Is what you are experiencing now fairly typical of what you are accustomed to experiencing, or do you feel at odds with yourself? You need to make this determination in order to know how to proceed.

Family and Friends

If you are surrounded by family members and close friends when your husband dies, they will undoubtedly make every effort to be there for you in whatever way they can in an effort to be helpful. This may include preparing food, assisting with the funeral arrangements, contacting out-of-town relatives and friends, or doing anything else you may request of them. You are fortunate if you have your loved ones around you during this painful period, but keep in mind that they may not continue to be available to you in this way for any extended time.

In our highly mobile society, at the time of loss you may find yourself in a city in which you have no close family members or friends. Being surrounded by loved ones at a time of personal loss is both emotionally supportive and helpful. For most people it feels easier and safer to express their feelings within their family or to long-standing friends than to others. Some people, however, are more comfortable expressing their emotions to strangers because strangers have no prior knowledge of how you function and therefore they are under no pressure to maintain an image.

Thus, if you are alone or isolated from your family at the time of loss, it is important to find a substitute for what your family would have provided if they were around. Don't feel embarrassed because you are feeling weak and need the support of others. It's normal! Simply allow yourself to act on your realization of this need.

If you are uncomfortable displaying emotion, it may be difficult for you to allow your friends to know you need support. Perhaps you do not know how to ask for help. Sometimes, although willing to help, friends don't know what to do or how to approach you. If your support group consists primarily of friends, allow them to be there for you. Don't think you are imposing yourself on them. Friends, by definition, are there for both the good and bad times. Allowing yourself to depend on existing friends does not preclude the advisability of seeking out new people in your life.

Following loss, many widows find themselves in need of some special assistance beyond that available from family and friends. Those first contacted for additional help or support are usually one's personal physician or spiritual counselor. Keep in mind, however, that the roles of a physician, spiritual advisor, and mental health professional are different and unique.

If you find that your behavior, for what might appear to be an excessive period of time, is uncharacteristic of you and simultaneously you do not feel connected to your life, don't hesitate to seek some professional help. Sometimes it is difficult for you to determine whether what you are experiencing is within the norm or beyond it. If that is the case, it is advisable to seek the services of someone more knowledgeable about these matters in general. It is more harmful to remain miserable and uncertain.

Physician

Your physician is an excellent individual with whom to discuss whether what you are experiencing is normal for the grief process. If your husband died from medical causes, she is aware of what you have recently gone through and is in a good position to help you understand what you are experiencing. A physician can prescribe medications if needed or if advisable make referrals to others who can help. Your physician will also work with you to identify the type of help likely to be most beneficial to you and refer you to the appropriate individual or facility to provide this support.

Spiritual Advisors

Some widows feel unable to move forward without coming to personal terms with the death of their husband. If religion has played a role in your life, either currently or in the past, you may benefit from talking to a spiritual advisors. These advisors have considerable experience counseling people who have suffered a loss and should be consulted if you think their input will in any way be helpful.

In the past, these meetings were in person. Now, as a result of the Covid pandemic, you may be able to meet with these advisors remotely. This approach is often welcomed by widows as they don't have to go to an office and the timing is flexible and mutually convenient.

In addition to the physician and spiritual advisor, there are other professionals available to provide more specialized assistance in the areas of grief and loss.

Widow Support Groups

Some women find more comfort in the companionship of others who have gone through a similar experience in addition to seeking the support of a spiritual advisor or physician. If, for example, before your loss you were essentially a gregarious person who enjoyed the company of others, you might benefit most from a widow support group. Having an opportunity to share your feelings with other widows is often very reassuring.

You may find that your existing friends, although wanting to help, may be unfamiliar with what you are going through. You and your husband probably socialized primarily with other couples. Now, as a widow, you may feel less comfortable with your coupled friends. When they invite you to join them in an activity, you may feel they do so not because they truly enjoy your company but because they feel it is the right thing to do. For example, if they invite you to join them for a dinner, be sure to clarify how you want your portion of the bill to be handled before you go.

Joining a widow support group will provide you with an opportunity to share your feelings with others in similar circumstances. You will hear how other widows have responded to these social situations and how they solved the problem for themselves. Here, too, you will be in a position to develop new social contacts without the awkward aspects of associating with couples. Frequently, these new relationships lead to ongoing friendships.

Widow support groups vary in format from place to place and within areas, but they are basically widow-to-widow, woman-to-woman, or widow-to-widower group situations. Some groups have a professional leader or leaders, while others do not. Some have a defined number of sessions, while others are more open and ongoing. The cost varies, with some basing their fees on a predetermined number of sessions and others allowing one to pay a nominal fee per session attended. Some groups focus on the widow with minor children at home, others on the older widow, and still others on widows in a broad age range. Some groups are designed for the newly widowed, whether male or female. Consider the type of group that will best meet your needs. There are no rights or wrongs! You may have to try out more than one group before you find the right group for your particular situation.

Customarily, the groups are small, providing an opportunity for the widows to get to know one another well. In fact, many women extend these contacts beyond the group, and it is common for strong bonds to develop among the widows. These friendships often long outlast one's active participation in the widow support group. Some women have told us they don't know how they would have made it through the first months of widowhood without the support of the women in their group. No one agency or facility sponsors such groups. For the most part, you can find out about them from a friend, physician, spiritual counselor or online.

Sometimes churches, synagogues or other religious organizations offer groups for the recently bereaved. You might prefer such a group instead of a nonsectarian widow support group. For information regarding such groups, it is best to contact someone at your own church or synagogue or mosque. If they do not have any groups of this nature, they should be able to direct you to a facility that does.

The Internet—Friend or Foe or Both?

The internet is an invaluable source of information. Log on to one of the many Web sites available for the bereaved. It is always a good idea to have your personal professional advisors review the information you receive online; they can help you decide what applies to your particular circumstances.

Among the variety of services the Internet provides is information about groups with whom you are able to discuss your feelings of loss or grief with others who, much like yourself, are attempting to deal with these feelings. However, a word of caution with regard to this complex means of communication: Some people use the Internet to present an image of themselves that is inaccurate and misleading. It provides an opportunity (sometimes to ease the pain of grief) to create a make-believe person, perhaps someone they wish they were, in contrast to the person they are in reality. This may be harmless, but it also provides an opportunity for unscrupulous individuals to abuse your vulnerability at this time for personal gain.

On the other hand, some widows with whom we have spoken report having established both meaningful and significant relationships with other widowed individuals through the Internet. In some cases, this has resulted in deep friendships and even new expansive experiences that otherwise might not have been available to them.

Mental Health Professionals

If you are not inclined to consult your primary care physician or a spiritual advisor about what you are experiencing but feel or fear you are in a dysfunctional state, here are some guidelines to assist you in determining whether or not you could benefit from professional help.

If, for example, you don't understand much of what you are experiencing, feel emotionally out of control a great deal of the time, have rapid and extreme mood swings, are unable to get out of bed at your usual time or find yourself having difficulty organizing and sustaining a thought pattern, you may want to consider consulting a mental health professional or grief counselor. Don't feel embarrassed or think you are crazy if you decide to seek the services of a mental health professional. Like your physician, this professional will help you determine if what you are experiencing falls within the usual range of emotions experienced following a loss or if there are more serious issues that need to be addressed.

Many types of counselors are available to help widows through this difficult period: psychiatrists, psychologists, social workers, and counselors specializing in issues of loss or grief. We present here an overview of the background and training of these specialists to help you understand the differences among them.

Psychiatrists

A psychiatrist is a doctor who has gone to medical school, completed a medical internship, and then completed a psychiatric residency, frequently at a hospital specializing in the care of the mentally ill. She may have obtained additional training in a given treatment technique. Psychiatrists for the most part are the mental health practitioners currently allowed to prescribe medication to alleviate the debilitating feelings associated with depression and other mental or emotional disorders. In a few states, psychologists are also able to prescribe medication after following a specified course of study.

Psychiatrists may also provide psychotherapy on an individual or a group basis. They bill you for their professional time on a fee-per-session basis; the fees for individual sessions are somewhat higher than those for group sessions. Make sure you understand the fee structure and office policies of the individual practitioner you select.

Typically, psychiatrists provide you with an "informed consent" which is a written description of what they will and will not do. Qualified psychiatrists must be licensed in the state in which you live.

If you do not know anyone in a position to provide you with a referral, contact the psychiatric association in your state.

Psychologists

In order to practice as a psychologist, an individual must have completed a four-year college program followed by a four-year or five-year doctoral program designed to prepare her for the practice of psychology. The study of normal and abnormal behavior is required and is a component of any such program. After completing this part of the training, those who decide they want to work with people on a therapeutic level move on to an appropriate internship program in an approved treatment facility. Here, psychotherapy training under supervision is provided. Many undergo additional training in a particular therapeutic approach.

In terms of providing therapy to clients, there is considerable similarity between the treatment provided by a psychiatrist and the treatment provided by a psychologist, although most psychologists are presently unable to prescribe medication for their clients. However, only psychologists are qualified to administer psychological tests.

Psychologists' fees are charged on a per-session basis. Psychologists will clarify the fee structure and office practices either before or at the time of the first session. Like the psychiatrist, they will provide their clients "informed consent" forms which clarify the role of the psychologist and the client. They must be licensed in the state in which you live.

If you do not know anyone in a position to provide you with a referral, contact the psychological association in your state.

Social Workers

Licensed social workers are also required to complete a specific training program. Following the completion of a college course of study, these individuals must proceed to a master's-level and sometimes a doctoral-level program with an emphasis on individual and community services. Social workers also complete an internship in their particular area of interest.

Social workers bill their clients for professional time in the same way that psychiatrists and psychologists do. Their fees are usually somewhat lower than those charged by psychiatrists and psychologists. They too will provide you with written information about their services and must be licensed in the state in which you live.

Professional Counselors

There are other professional counselors who have a master's-level education in a given area, such as grief counseling. They are recognized as certified professional counselors if they have completed the course of study and internship required by the jurisdiction in which they work to practice in a given area of expertise. They are licensed by the state in which they practice. These counselors will charge a fee for their services usually comparable to those charged by social workers.

Physician's Assistants/Nurse Practitioners

There are many similarities between physician's assistants and nurse practitioners but also many differences. Both have extensive training working with patients.

The nurse practitioner's training includes an undergraduate degree followed by a master's degree and/or a doctorate plus one to two years of clinical nursing experience. They are licensed registered nurses and usually specialize in working with a specific patient population. Many states allow nurse practitioners to practice on their own as well as with medical doctors.

Physician's assistants also have an undergraduate degree followed by a master's degree and clinical experience. However, she is not able to practice on her own and does not have to be a registered nurse. She is a generalist rather than focusing on a particular patient population.

If your primary care physician works with either one, these professionals will follow your healing process.

Medical Insurance

Many health insurance policies include some coverage for mental health services provided by licensed psychiatrists, psychologists, and social workers. If you have any questions about your insurance plan, contact your carrier to clarify your coverage. If you are unable to deal with this yourself, ask a family member or close friend to obtain the information for you.

Your mental health provider will assist you in obtaining the appropriate reimbursement for the services rendered. If you have a managed care plan, contact the group for information about obtaining coverage for mental health treatment as well as referrals.

Summary and Conclusion

Regardless of how you have viewed yourself in the past, this may be a time to seek out the services of a professional with experience helping people cope with grief and loss. If not a professional, perhaps you need the support of others who are experiencing what you are experiencing. Regardless of what you are feeling, make an effort to identify what you need and try to locate the appropriate individual, group, or agency for help. Whatever you seek, keep in mind that the choice is yours and the purpose is to help you through the time of maximum stress in your life.

In large measure, your personality type, and the way you have dealt with emotional issues in the past will determine the approach that best meets your needs. Some widows need time alone to work through what they are feeling. Concentrate on what you are experiencing and determine whether or not you need some sort of intervention.

We cannot stress sufficiently the point that there is no right or wrong approach for all widows, this is the time for you to identify what you need and find the necessary assistance to meet that need. In making this decision, consider your basic personality traits and present emotional state. Whatever you do, make yourself and your needs the priority. Even if you feel others need you, keep in mind that your ability to help anyone depends on your ability to help yourself.

Diane

Reactions to Dealing with Her Initial Emotional Needs

Diane had a hard time focusing on anything in the initial stage of grief. She was so disoriented and upset by her husband's sudden death that she could not think clearly. She was using all of her energy just to stop crying. Several weeks after Mark's death, however, she woke up one morning, and after what had now become her familiar feelings of terror and vulnerability had subsided, she thought for the first time about what her children must be going through without their father.

Until this point, Diane had functioned in an almost automatic manner, going through the motions of daily responsibilities, and signing papers that her dad and Larry, Mark's law firm colleague, said needed to be signed. On this particular morning, she thought about the children. She really had not had the emotional strength to address their needs at all. She thought about their reaction to their father's death, even though they never really had much of an opportunity to spend daily time with him, and now had a nonfunctional mother. In a sense, following Mark's sudden death, the children had been forced to manage without either parent. For a moment she contemplated with sadness the fact that the children would never have the opportunity to know their father as she had known him.

Diane needed to move beyond these thoughts and become more functional. What could she do? If only she knew someone who had had a similar experience. She and Mark did not know anyone among their couple friends whose spouse had died. Clearly, their friends would be unable to relate to her present situation. Then she remembered Erin, her older daughter, mentioning that her friend Nicole's dad had been killed in a boating accident a few years ago. She didn't even know Nicole's mother's name. Diane felt somewhat ashamed of herself when she recalled her casual, matter-of-fact response—"Oh, that's too bad"—when Erin told her about Nicole's dad. Now here she was, some years later, in the same situation.

Diane decided to ask Erin for the name of Nicole's mother. She wanted to talk with her and find out how she had dealt with these unbearably painful feelings. When Erin returned from school that day, she gave Diane the name of Nicole's mother, Jennifer Greenberg, and her phone number. Diane wasted no time contacting her and even surprised herself by not being concerned about how her call might appear to Nicole's mom. Jennifer turned out to be very understanding and helpful and spent almost an hour talking to Diane.

For the first time since Mark had disappeared from her life, Diane felt there was someone who understood what she was feeling. Perhaps it was just that she didn't feel quite so alone in the world. Jennifer had many helpful suggestions. She emphasized the importance of two things: exercise and her support group. She told Diane she didn't know how she would have survived without the help of the women in her widow support group. Diane shivered at the mere use of the word "widow". That's what she was, though, a widow, so she had better try to accept it.

A widow support group—Diane had never heard of such a thing. Jennifer explained how such a group worked: The one she went to met once a week for eight weeks and was in the area. Jennifer knew that the coordinator, Lisa, would be able to provide a great deal of support to Diane. Jennifer went on to say she had become very close to two of the women in her group—they had even gone on a vacation together this past summer. She said she was working now but would be available to Diane to provide support and information. Diane thanked her profusely. "What a warm, caring person she is," Diane thought. She called Lisa immediately upon hanging up the phone and left a message on her answering machine. Diane felt calmer, but she wasn't sure why.

Diane and Mark had decided to place the children in private schools, which they believed provided a better educational environment. Would they be able to continue to afford the tuition at these schools? Diane had no idea. With her feeling approach to life, she was able to get in touch with what the children themselves were likely to be feeling. Emotionally, they had been left to fend for themselves. She felt the need to apologize to them for not having been there for them and promised herself that she would be more sensitive to their needs in the future. She resolved to listen to what they were expressing on an emotional level.

Diane wasn't quite sure how she was going to accomplish all that needed to be accomplished. She felt like a child herself because someone had always taken care of her financially. Now, she knew, she was supposed to act like a grown-up, but she didn't really know what that meant. She guessed she would be expected to make decisions about money. A part of her was angry with herself as well as with both Mark and her dad for allowing her to remain financially immature, while another part of her sought ways to remain a child. Her thoughts moved to the helpless glances the children had furtively turned in her direction when they learned of their father's death and how she had been unable to respond to them. She realized she had to be more responsive to them and for their benefit attempt to deal with her financial situation. She needed to pay attention to what she was being told about her economic situation because it would have an impact on all of them. If at all possible, she wanted to keep the children in their present schools, even if it meant making some sacrifices.

Although a logical and pragmatic approach to life was not part of Diane's personality structure, her strong feelings about what she wanted for her children would, in the weeks ahead, help mobilize her. These feelings would also enable her to comprehend what steps she needed to take in order for her to assess her total financial situation and eventually make a decision, which she believed would have a major impact on the development of her children. At this moment, they were the most important consideration in Diane's life.

She resolved to ask her friends how to go about assessing the viability of private schools for the children. Although tempting, on both an emotional and financial level, she knew she didn't want to get into this issue with her dad or Larry as she thought she wasn't ready to hear their advice. Surely her friends would be sympathetic to her point of view in this area.

As indicated in chapter 2, Diane was primarily an extroverted, dependent, feeling woman. Therefore, it is not surprising that she would turn to her friends for assistance when faced with a task with which she had little familiarity. It is common for extroverted individuals to be comfortable seeking the help of others when it's needed. Diane's intuitive characteristics and reliance on her instincts can be seen in her decision not to involve Larry or her father in her review and assessment of the children's school placement.

Susan

Reactions to Dealing with
Her Initial Emotional Needs

Susan had a hard time accepting that Lance was dead. The fact that he had died suddenly was difficult for her to comprehend. This is not surprising because dealing with sudden death, particularly of a healthy person, compounds the mourning process. Habit patterns Susan had used in the past to deal with difficult situations were not working for her, but then she had never had to deal with something so traumatic. She thought she could have handled Lance's death better if he had been older or had had a long-term illness. In fact, he had always been healthy, so his death was totally unexpected.

The only way she could move from her current state of disbelief and shock to some semblance of functioning was by attempting to resume patterns of behavior she had previously found helpful. She had always had a pragmatic approach to life and been attentive to details. In her work, making lists of matters needing her attention and possible ways to approach issues had been productive.

Shortly after the funeral, Susan began to compile a list of tasks related to Lance's death that she needed to be handled and the order in which they needed to be addressed. She found it was helpful to do something that felt familiar and moved her beyond her emotional paralysis. This activity enabled her to feel more in touch with the world and daily events. It was as if her emotional life existed in its own orbit, separate from the requirements of daily life.

While making lists allowed Susan to feel more in touch with life, it also made her realize she was spending her time writing and rewriting her lists, prioritizing, and reprioritizing, yet she was unable to get started on anything. She was becoming frightened. This was not characteristic of her. She had always been able to act on what needed to be done in a timely manner—in fact, it was one of the qualities Lance appreciated most in her. She wondered how long she would be in this state of inactivity, unable to move.

Susan had to do something to come to grips with what was happening to her, but what? She recalled a TV talk show she had once seen that focused on various mental health professionals dealing with different aspects of grieving. At the time she had commented to Lance, "I wonder why anyone would want to spend every day dealing with death." Now she thought this very type of person might be able to help her better understand what was happening to her. Was what she was experiencing normal for women in her circumstances, or was something more serious happening to her?

Susan reflected on the time 15 years ago when she had considered seeing a mental health professional to better understand her feelings about her brother Ron announcing to the family that he was gay. Looking back at their childhood, she wondered why she never suspected this earlier. She knew he never had a girlfriend in high school and always preferred to hang out with his male friends, but Susan never thought much of it. Due to their five year age difference, she and Ron had never been close when they were younger.

She wondered if she still had the name and address of the woman doctor to whom she had been referred by one of her co-workers. At the time, her co-worker had indicated that the doctor was a therapist interested in dealing with women and women's issues. Susan wasn't sure her present situation as a widow was one that would be within this therapist's area of interest or expertise. On the other hand, Susan was a woman, and women's issues were ostensibly one of this therapist's areas of expertise. She guessed this doctor would tell her whether she had the skills to work with her or not. Susan thought she'd feel better if she could talk to someone other than a friend or relative about what was happening to her, someone familiar with what she was experiencing.

Although she hadn't wanted to admit it to herself, Susan had begun to feel symptoms of menopause before Lance's death. She based this conclusion on her realizing she had been feeling hot or cold for no apparent external reason and was more irritable, which was out of character for her. She was also experiencing other signs, including unfamiliar mood swings, increased fatigue, changes in her sleep patterns, and what she was most afraid to acknowledge, memory lapses. She knew she needed to discuss her fears about her total functioning with a professional. Was what she was experiencing her response to Lance's death, menopause, or was it both? Susan knew she could not explore this concern with a man, even though she accepted that there were competent male doctors. How she hated feeling this way!

Since Lance's death, she had had considerable difficulty sleeping through the night. It had been helpful to have her trusty notepad at her bedside to jot down her thoughts and feelings. From reviewing these notes, it was clear to her that she needed some professional help. She thought she still had the doctor's name and phone number in her contact list and saw if she was still in practice. If she couldn't locate this information, Susan thought she would ask another woman in her office for the name of the person she'd taken her daughter to see when her daughter had a miscarriage.

Susan knew she needed to get beyond her present state. There was too much to do, and she didn't have the luxury of remaining immobilized. She acted on these feelings that very day. She located the doctor's name, and, as she stared at the phone number, she realized her palms were sweating. Slowly, she tapped the numbers on her phone and heard the phone ringing. A woman answered, "Dr. Coleman's office."

Susan was pleasantly surprised—this was like calling any other doctor's office. She wondered why she had expected this phone call would be answered differently from phone calls at any other doctor's office. She was taken so off guard the woman had to repeat, "Dr. Coleman's office." Susan asked if Dr. Coleman dealt with grief issues. The woman told her Dr. Coleman was a psychologist familiar with grief counseling but that her practice was not limited to this area. She suggested Susan make an appointment to meet with Dr. Coleman and discuss her specific needs as well as her health insurance coverage. The receptionist gave Susan the office address and a lunchtime appointment for the following Thursday.

Susan was glad she had finally found the strength to see Dr. Coleman. The doctor's office wasn't at all intimidating. It was in an office building not far from where Susan worked. Dr. Coleman was very reassuring and comforting without making Susan feel there was something wrong with her for seeking professional help in dealing with Lance's sudden death. She provided Susan with papers entitled "Practice Guidelines and Informed Consent" which outlined how they would work together. After they reviewed the papers, Susan signed the signature page indicating that she understood how her work with Dr. Coleman would proceed.

She explained to Susan she could help her address what she was experiencing emotionally. She confirmed that Susan's emotional responses were indeed intensified because she had begun to experience normal physical and emotional changes related to menopause.

Dr. Coleman said she had worked with other widows in Susan's situation and appreciated how difficult it was for anyone in such a vulnerable state to begin to deal with all the necessary paperwork and financial issues. They would, therefore, also focus on the demands of daily life. When Dr. Coleman used the word "widow", Susan was taken aback. Her image of a widow was someone her mother's age. She'd have to look at why she had such a negative response to this word. She should probably discuss it with Dr. Coleman, but there was not time for that today because her session was just about over. She thought it would be important to start with these feelings at her next session.

When Susan left Dr. Coleman's office, after having scheduled her next appointment, she felt not quite so alone for the first time since Lance had died. She knew this was an important step for her.

The varied aspects of Susan's personality are seen in her ambivalence about seeing Dr. Coleman. Before making the appointment, she recognized that she needed professional help, but she was reluctant to act on this realization because her private, introverted side resisted this recognition. In a way, she felt that she should be able to handle matters by herself. Her independent, thinking side also resisted, but her dependent side allowed her to accept her present limitations and make an appointment to see Dr. Coleman. Once there, her logical, pragmatic qualities allowed her to take advantage of what Dr. Coleman had to offer her.

Audrey

Reactions to Dealing with
Her Initial Emotional Needs

It was about three weeks after John's death, but to Audrey it felt like the first morning after the funeral. She sat at the scarred, wooden breakfast table and drank her morning coffee by herself while allowing herself to think about her future. She had come to appreciate such private moments during the particularly demanding last months of John's life.

Audrey reflected back on the last days of John's life. She wondered if she had made the right decision when she decided to leave John in the hospital and have hospice help there rather than take him home. She found the hospice people were very helpful to both her and her family. She still felt she had made the right decision.

Audrey, without realizing it, had given a good bit of thought to her life following John's death. She had accepted her future without John as something more than an existence to be endured. Her new status would allow her to explore as yet unidentified avenues she would not have had the courage to investigate while John was alive. She didn't know why that was so, but she was sure that it had been the case. She was determined to take personal charge of her situation and not allow her son to assume the role of primary adviser and financial decision maker, which, knowing him, she felt confident he intended to do.

She had read that some widows have difficulty going through their husband's belongings and deciding what to do with them. She knew she wanted to ask John Jr if he wanted his dad's watch and coin collections. As for Hannah, she would discuss with her what she would like as well. As for herself, she knew she wanted to have a few items which reminded her of significant events in their lives. In her heart, she knew giving away John's belongings would never diminish for her the role he had played in her life.

Audrey had not met with John's attorney in years but knew that he would handle John's will. She decided to make an appointment to see him with Joanne who could help her by taking notes. she thought Joanne was a better choice than John Jr. since while he was well-meaning, he had a tendency to take charge.

Her pragmatic yet thought-oriented approach to life enabled her to think reasonably well in her adjustment to her new circumstances. Perhaps more so than in the situations of our other hypothetical widows, John's lingering illness had gradually accustomed her to her new state. She had read somewhere there was a name for her situation—it was called "anticipatory grief". This meant she had actually started thinking about how her life would change without John long before he died.

Audrey stretched and moved to the sink to place her coffee mug in the dishwasher. In doing so, she caught a glimpse of herself in the large hall mirror and was startled to see how much thinner she appeared. She went upstairs to her colorful yellow-and-blue bedroom and took a good look at herself in the bedroom mirror. She certainly had lost weight. She hadn't even realized it. She wasn't really feeling sick. She was more tired than usual, but she had attributed her fatigue to the toll John's illness had taken on her. What about her weight? It was clear her clothes didn't fit right anymore. She wondered when all this had happened. The green plaid skirt she removed from her closet this morning was at least an inch too big around the waist. Why hadn't she realized this before? It certainly didn't just happen. She couldn't remember when she had last prepared a meal for herself. She usually grabbed some crackers and cheese or other snack with a cup of tea in the evening.

She didn't want to overreact or underreact. Certainly, weight loss was one of the first symptoms of what was subsequently diagnosed as John's lung cancer. She had a positive attitude about life and the future but didn't feel comfortable ignoring health concerns. Better to be safe than sorry. She didn't even need to look up Dr. PaPadisio's phone number; it was engraved in her mind. She called the all-too-familiar number, identified herself to the receptionist, who expressed her sympathy about John's death, and asked for an appointment for an annual physical. As she did so, she recalled she hadn't had a physical since John's cancer had been diagnosed two years ago.

Audrey's childhood had led her to accept much of what life presented without much question. She possessed characteristics of extroversion and introversion, thinking and feeling and dependence and independence. Her balanced personality allowed her to acknowledge as she looked in the mirror that she had indeed lost weight. On a feeling level, she did not want to think about what might have caused her weight loss. However, ignoring weight loss was not acceptable to her because her pragmatic, thinking qualities recognized the need to explore the situation further before jumping to any conclusions.

Elizabeth

Reactions to Dealing with
Her Initial Emotional Needs

Elizabeth, at age 75 with few outside interests or support people, was emotionally very needy. She had really never been on her own before. Her older sister, Abigail, had come from Florida for the funeral. Elizabeth felt safer having Abigail with her but was embarrassed by her dependency on her older sister for support. She wondered if Abigail was more confident and worldly when it came to money matters because she had never married and had been forced to make so many decisions for herself. Elizabeth was dreading Abigail's departure and begged her to extend her stay. Abigail did stay for a few more days than she had planned but finally had to return to her retirement home in Florida. She encouraged Elizabeth to give serious thought to moving to Florida to be closer to her, and Elizabeth promised to consider the idea.

After Abigail left, Elizabeth felt alone. She was terrified, panicked, and didn't know where to turn. Who would take care of her? How would she survive? Her thoughts raced in all directions. She felt lonelier now that Ben had died. She recognized that she had felt lonely and isolated during the last few years of Ben's life, but now she was truly alone and lonely. Being alone felt like a weight bogging her down. She had so many mixed feelings. How would she interact with others now. She had a few friends but had not been able to spend time with them as Ben's health deteriorated. Would they want to spend time with her now.

Her closest friend Mabel had been so kind and had already given so generously of her time. Besides, she didn't know how to go about talking to Mabel about some of these very personal matters. She also felt as though she would be disloyal to Ben if she talked to Mabel about their financial situation. Suddenly, she remembered that her minister, Pastor Appletorn, had made a home visit shortly after Ben's funeral. It had felt good to see his familiar, friendly face. He had encouraged her to come see him at the church. She felt safe with him, too, and in her loneliness determined to accept what she viewed as his ministerial but kind offer to make an appointment to see him. She hoped that he would be able to provide her with some guidance regarding the steps she needed to take in her newly widowed state.

Elizabeth's personality characteristics as well as the way she had lived her life made it difficult for her to cope with her newly widowed state. She was emotional, dependent, and introverted, a combination that did not provide her with good coping skills. She had no financial knowledge and, if the truth were known, she didn't want to deal with financial matters or make decisions about money.

Ben had always said, "There, there, now, no need to worry your pretty little head about money, I will take care of you." Elizabeth had a considerable need to decrease the anxiety and stress of finally having to deal with her finances.

She also knew she would be required to deal with lawyers or other business advisers about Ben's will and estate, but she had no idea how this process began. Did someone contact you, or were you supposed to know you had to contact the lawyer? Perhaps Pastor Appletorn would know someone who could accompany her on this dreaded trip—she felt so stupid about financial matters!

Elizabeth was desperate for support and help. To obtain it, she was willing to risk initiating the contact with her minister. Her timidity would have prevented her from taking such a step in the past, but she did feel comfortable with him, and he was the only person she could think of who might be able to help her with what lay ahead. Her inability to function independently overcame her need to keep to herself. Elizabeth allowed her pattern of turning to others for advice to move her to seek the assistance of someone she viewed as more knowledgeable than herself. She recognized that she did feel comfortable with Pastor Appletorn and that he was the only person she could think of who might be appropriate to talk to and help her with what lay ahead.

She looked at the clock and realized it was too early to call Pastor Appletorn. She suddenly thought about the morning paper. She didn't recall bringing it into the home since Ben had died. She guessed Abigail or Mabel had done that for her. Well, today she would do it herself. She thought she would try to read it while she had her coffee. When she opened the door, she was surprised to see, in addition to the paper, a small, bedraggled, forlorn-looking gray-and-white cat peering up at her. It looked lost and confused. She and Ben had never had pets because he was allergic to both cat and dog hairs. She remembered that some neighbors at the very end of her street had moved away about four days ago. She wondered if the cat had belonged to them.

Elizabeth didn't know what to do. Should she feed the cat and take it in, or should she call the humane society? The cat looked helpless and pathetic, kind of the way she felt and as if it wanted her to do something. She wondered if she and the cat weren't in the same boat—alone and frightened. She didn't think it would hurt to give the cat some milk, although she really didn't know what cats ate or drank. Maybe if she brought it into her home it would provide her with some companionship. She decided to be daring and feed it. She found herself smiling. The cat seemed so pleased to be allowed into the home. It had a really cute face.

PART TWO

Getting Organized

CHAPTER FOUR

Organizing Your Finances

You may have handled all financial matters for your family, or you may not have been involved at all in the financial decision-making aspect of your life when married to your husband. Perhaps you were somewhere in between—you paid the household bills but weren't involved in the investment selection process.

Many people have the misconception that if a woman works outside the home for pay, she is familiar with family finances as well. Often the opposite is true: Working wives are often less involved in finances than nonworking wives because they may feel they have no time to spare after coping with their job, household, children, and husband. Remaining uninvolved in finances works relatively well until a working wife's husband dies and she finds herself with insufficient financial experience and knowledge.

Traditionally money has been considered the male province. However, sometimes men know little about investing. Further—and this is much more dangerous—they may think they know more than they do. This problem is compounded if the husband dies prematurely. He may have thought he had plenty of time to accumulate money for a comfortable retirement, and therefore he may have invested in some riskier ventures than the norm since he thought he had plenty of time to shift to more conservative investments later.

Regardless of how financially knowledgeable you are, the numerous tasks you are currently facing can be overwhelming. How do you start to make order out of chaos? In the next few chapters, we discuss the basics of determining where you are financially. This chapter covers how to organize the information you currently have available. In chapter 5 we discuss the roles of your three key financial advisors: the lawyer, the accountant, and the financial planner. Chapter 6 lists other people and agencies providing additional information you will need to construct an accurate picture of your situation. In chapter 7 you develop a budget, and in chapter 8 you calculate your net worth.

If you are unable to handle any or all these jobs, ask someone to help you—but at least review these chapters so you have an idea of what has to be done. The sooner you understand your financial picture, the sooner you will be able to move forward with your life. The anxiety caused by uncertainty will be removed. Some widows find getting their financial paperwork in order therapeutic, whereas others find it overwhelming, particularly initially.

A word of caution: In this initial stage, as a widow you may feel compelled to take some kind of action—any kind of action—to demonstrate to yourself and others that you are in control of your life. If this is what you feel, resist the impulse. Take no drastic action, such as selling your home, quitting your job, moving in with or closer to your family, buying insurance, loaning money to a family member or friend, or making a significant investment. There is no need to make major decisions immediately. In fact, there are compelling reasons not to make any decisions that are not absolutely necessary at this time. Now is not the time for irrevocable action. Having said this, however, we also advise that you not carry inaction to an extreme. A time will come when action is wise and necessary. Then, if you take no action, you are in fact making a decision not to take responsibility for your financial life, whereas now is the time to determine what your situation is so that you can intelligently plan your financial future.

The following tasks need to be accomplished in the first few months after your husband's death. In our experience the vast majority of widows are overwhelmed by the sheer volume of paperwork that is required to settle the estate. Don't let yourself be paralyzed by this task. You will get through it. Compartmentalize the work and take on one job at a time, and don't get discouraged if each task takes longer than you anticipated.

Organize Your Important Papers

You and your spouse may have kept your important financial records in a filing cabinet, on your computer or even in an old shoe box. If you have records in a safe-deposit box, be aware that in some states a jointly held safe-deposit box is sealed as soon a spouse dies and cannot be opened without a court order.

Regardless of where your important papers are located, you need to have a copy of your husband's will, his and your Social Security cards, your marriage certificate, his military discharge papers (if applicable), his insurance policies, his birth certificate, and birth certificates of your minor children. These papers will be needed to establish claims for Social Security income, life insurance proceeds, and veteran's benefits.

Don't panic if you can't find your husband's will. Most likely you and your husband had worked with a lawyer to put together your wills and other estate planning documents. If so, your lawyer will have the original document.

If you do not have a lawyer and there is no will, then the estate will be settled by the laws of the state in which you live. Contact the probate clerk in your county to find out what action to take. However, we recommend that you use a lawyer to help you settle his estate because it is easy to unintentionally omit something that could cause subsequent problems.

Organize Your Files

Designate a special area devoted specifically to your financial affairs. If you have a file cabinet, fine. Some people prefer to use a portable file which enables them to easily carry multiple documents with them when they meet with their advisors. Do whatever works best for you.

Label the files. If you can't locate a document, make a file folder for it anyway in anticipation of needing it. If you use a file cabinet, one drawer can be devoted to papers you need to settle the estate and another drawer for more current financial papers. In some cases, you will have the same information in each drawer. Eventually, some of these estate files will be combined with your personal files, but while you are settling the estate, these should be kept separate.

We realize this may appear to be an overwhelming amount of paperwork. If you feel unable to cope with all of this, ask a family member or friend for help. Setting up the files offers you an opportunity to socialize with a relative or friend. The most common complaint we hear from widows is the amount of paperwork involved in settling an estate. This is a legitimate complaint, but the paperwork has to be dealt with in order to figure out where you are financially and how best to move forward.

If you are reluctant to ask a friend to help, in most metropolitan areas you can find professionals who will help organize an estate's paperwork. Typically, these "daily money managers" as they are called, will charge an hourly fee depending on the complexity of the work. If the work is ongoing, they may charge a monthly fee. For further information about these professionals, contact the American Association of Daily Money Managers (814-357-9191) or e-mail: info@aadmm.com.

Keep in mind that to settle the estate you will need to provide date of death valuations for assets in your husband's name. The estate files would include statements which show these values. The **estate drawer** typically would include files for the following items. Some of these would apply to all widows, while others depend on your husband's situation.

Legal:
- Your husband's will
- Copies of your husband's death certificate[1]
- Trust agreements for any trusts your husband may have set up or been the beneficiary of
- Birth Certificate
- Marriage Certificate
- Prenuptial or postnuptial agreement
- Naturalization papers (If applicable)
- Divorce agreement (If applicable)

---

1. You may need copies of your husband's death certificate several years hence, so make sure that you request several more copies than you think you need for present use. We suggest you obtain a minimum of 15 death certificates.

- Military Discharge Papers
- Safe-deposit box location and key (or combination)
- Cemetery deed
- Partnership agreements

Tax:
- Last year's tax returns—federal and state

Household:
- Real estate titles and deeds for property owned in his/joint name
- Title insurance for your home(s)

Investments (if applicable)
- Bank and Credit Union Statements in his name and joint names for the month he died
- Stock brokerage statements in his name and joint names
- His retirement asset statements (IRA, 401(k), company pension plan, etc.)
- Mutual fund statements in your husband's name and joint names for month he died.
- Stock option plan statements

Liabilities:
- Mortgage statement reflecting balance due the month he died
- A list of credit cards in his name and joint names
- Credit card statements for the month he died
- Car lease agreements

Insurance:
- Your husband's life insurance policies
- Health insurance policies
- Disability Insurance policy
- Long-term care insurance policy
- Auto Insurance policy

Miscellaneous:
- Social Security/Medicare cards
- List of all usernames and passwords
- Car Registration

Hopefully, most of the information you need for these files is some-place in your home. Your job is to get the files into one central location, so they are easily accessed. Once you no longer need them to settle the estate, some of them will become part of your personal files.

The **personal drawer** would include some or all of the following files:

Legal:
- Your will
- Your living will
- Health and Financial Powers of Attorney
- Trust Agreements
- Birth certificates for each member of the family
- Marriage certificate
- Prenuptial or postnuptial agreements
- Naturalization papers (if applicable)
- Divorce agreement (if applicable)
- Military discharge papers (if applicable)
- Safe-deposit box location and key (or combination)

Tax:
- Your most recent tax returns
- This year's tax records

Household:
- Real Estate titles and deeds for properties owned by you
- Household inventory of valuable items
- Receipts for major improvements to your home

Investments (if applicable):
- Current bank and credit union statements
- Stock brokerage statements

- Retirement asset statements (IRAs, etc.)
- Children's investment account statements
- 529 account statements
- Cemetery deed
- Stock option statements

Liabilities:

- Mortgage statements (put in chronological order)
- Other liabilities (college loans, car loans, personal loans)
- List of credit card numbers and addresses
- Credit card account bills (one for each creditor)
- Car loan or lease agreements
- List of current bills

Insurance:

- Life insurance policies
- Health insurance policies
- Disability insurance (if applicable)
- Long-term-care insurance policy
- Car insurance policy
- Homeowners insurance policy
- Personal liability insurance policy
- Title Insurance (if applicable)

Miscellaneous:

- Warranties and instructions
- Family medical records
- Burial instructions
- Social Security card and recent benefits statement for you and your children
- List of current advisors, addresses, phone numbers and email addresses
- List of all usernames and passwords

Organize and Pay Appropriate Bills

Gather all your bills in one place and then divide them into three groups—your bills, your late husband's bills, and joint bills. You are responsible for paying both your own and joint bills. Your husband's bills should be paid from the estate account which you will set up.

If a bill you receive addressed to your husband is not a familiar one, do not pay it. A stranger (or a friend) may tell you that your husband owed him or her money. If this happens, make sure you have written proof that your husband's debt is legitimate. Have your lawyer check its accuracy before agreeing to pay it. (If you don't have a lawyer, you may need to consult one.) We recommend this precaution because there are unscrupulous people who take advantage of widows by sending them bills demanding payment for items or services they claim the husband ordered.

Itemize the current bills, making clear whose bill it is. If you have a high cash reserve, you may have no trouble paying them all. If your reserve is not high, you will have to decide which bills must be paid and which can be delayed. Mortgage payments, utilities, health and property insurance premiums, and car-related expenses should be paid first. If you don't think you have enough money to pay all your bills, it is best to contact the creditors explaining your situation—that you know you owe them money and plan to pay it, but you will have to pay a lesser amount until you have a better picture of your total financial situation. If you have difficulty doing this, ask someone to help you with this task.

Your husband may have subscribed to magazines which you have no interest in reading. You can call or write to them and ask for a refund of the remaining subscription. This is less about the money but more about getting too much mail.

Record Estate Income and Expenses

We discuss putting together a personal budget in greater detail later, but at this point any income you receive that was due your husband before his death should be kept in an estate account separate from the rest of your money. When you visit your bank, discuss the mechanics of setting up the estate account.

Meanwhile, keep a record of any checks you receive, the date received, the amount of the check, and the payer. Similarly, ask for receipts and keep a record of any expenses you incur while settling the estate since you can be reimbursed for them.

Set Up a Financial Diary and a Monthly Calendar

Most recent widows think they are operating perfectly rationally at the time of a meeting, but a month later they may have no memory of what happened at that meeting. This is why we recommend you take someone with you to your initial meetings with your key professional advisors. This way you will have some kind of record of what has transpired as well as a "to do" list.

There are various ways to do this. You may choose to use a notebook and a month-at-a-glance calendar or a computer record. Whatever you choose, this financial diary will serve as a chronological list of what you have done and when, as well as what you still need to do.

This financial diary will be a helpful reference should you want to recall a conversation you had with one of your advisors or anyone else. On the first page of your financial diary, make a list of projects you want to or must accomplish. Then look at your month-at-a-glance calendar and decide when you are going to do each task.

In your financial diary, keep a daily account of whom you see and what was accomplished. In this book, record all conversations (phone calls or in person) that relate to your financial affairs. When your advisors see that you are keeping records, they know you are serious. A phone call from you that starts, "On June 6th, we agreed that you would do such and such. It is now July 15th. How are things progressing?" puts your advisor on notice that you expect results in a timely fashion.

Most advisors will provide you with a summary of your meetings as well as items in need of attention either in written or email form. Be sure to print out a copy of these emails and create a folder for future reference. If they don't routinely supply this summary, ask them to do so.

A typical to-do list for the first few months might read as follows:

- Get 15 to 20 certified copies of the death certificate
- Make appointments to see my lawyer and accountant (if you don't have either one, see resources at the end of the book)
- Open a bank account in the name of the estate
- Notify all insurance companies involved and file claims
- Report death to Social Security (and Veterans Administration, if applicable) and apply for benefits
- Notify husband's employer(s) to file for benefits (if applicable)
- Transfer jointly held securities to my name
- Notify custodians of IRA, 401(k) and any other retirement plans of my husband's death

Keeping Records of Financial Statements

In addition to keeping current estate records, you should set up a system for keeping your financial statements. For example, make a file for each bank and savings account. Put them in chronological order, putting the most recent statement in front. The purpose of these files is to create a record of all financial transactions that take place during the year. This information will be helpful when you work on your taxes.

Keeping Computer Records

You may want to keep many of these estate and personal records on your computer. For instance, if you have been paying the household bills, you may have been using an income and expense system. which could be adapted to divide income and expense items for your husband's estate and yourself.

On the other hand, if you have not been using your computer for financially related matters, we wouldn't recommend you start now. As helpful as the computer is, setting up a new system to track your finances can be very frustrating, and you don't need to add stress to your life at this point. Six months or more after your husband's death, you may want to explore using one of the appropriate computer software programs which will keep track of your financial life.

In addition to a computer, you need access to a printer/copier. By being able to copy correspondence and records before sending them, you can facilitate your communication with your advisors. Avoid sending original copies of any document unless specifically necessary; send copies instead. If an original document is required, send it via certified mail and ask the recipient to return it to you.

Summary and Conclusion

Although these tasks of organizing your financial records may seem tedious and time consuming, they are essential to determine your current financial situation. In fact, some widows have told us organizing this information has helped them feel better because they thought they were gaining some control of their lives.

Diane

Reactions to Getting Organized

Diane had a very difficult time dealing with the initial requirements of getting organized. She had never been asked to do anything that involved money. The only request Mark had ever made of her in this respect was to write on a piece of paper the checks she wrote, the amount and to whom, and place it on his dresser so he could enter them in their check book and balance the checkbook. When she lived at home, before marrying Mark, her dad just gave her an allowance, and in her early working days she spent her paychecks on whatever she chose. Dad had never asked her to contribute to the household expenses.

The idea of setting up files did not appeal to Diane. Here she was with her world turned upside down, and she was being asked to expend her energy on paperwork! Despite her basic resistance, however, she realized that getting her paperwork in order could help her figure out whether she was able to afford to keep the children in private school, and that was a motivating factor. Also, setting up files would give her something to do with herself other than walking aimlessly around the home, crying, and feeling that her life was over. She realized how difficult it was for her to do anything these days, even something as simple as grocery shopping.

Diane was looking forward to meeting the women in the widow support group that Lisa, the coordinator, had discussed with her. She was pleased the group consisted of women at various stages of dealing with their loss; maybe one of them could relate to what she was feeling. Lisa had said there was at least one woman in the group close to Diane's age. Diane wondered how the other women dealt with all this paperwork. On the other hand, maybe she should call Jennifer Greenberg, the widow whose daughter, Nicole, was still a classmate of Erin's. Obviously, Jennifer had managed to pay Nicole's tuition.

Diane knew she could no longer ignore what had been requested of her: she must set up financial records. Diane vaguely remembered that Mark had told her that their important papers were in his desk. It was difficult for her even to go over to the desk and open the drawers—it brought back so many memories of Mark sitting at the desk working. She wished that she had paid more attention to what he had said about their finances.

She knew Mark had some insurance in addition to what the firm provided. Maybe there was something in his file drawer. Diane pulled the drawer open and found herself crying again as she recognized Mark's neat handwriting on the labels. Not only was there a file for life insurance, but also there were files for car, household, and health insurance. When she pulled out the life insurance file, she found four policies—each from a different company. It appeared that she would receive a total of $200,000 from these policies, but she didn't know what she had to do to receive the benefits.

Diane found another file marked "Estate Planning." Maybe this was where the will was. Unfortunately, it contained only some handwritten notes Mark had made on the subject. She knew that lawyers always joked about the fact that they were the last people to have wills, even though they insisted their clients have them. She wished she understood better the implications of his not having a will.

It was becoming obvious to Diane that she needed someone to help her sort all this out. Perhaps someone in the widow support group could be of help.

Diane's To-Do List
- Call Jennifer regarding tuition options
- Go to widow support group meeting
- Find out about life insurance policies
- Attempt to set up files

Susan

Reactions to Getting Organized

Before marrying Lance, Susan had handled her own financial affairs as well as those of her widowed mother. However, since they had been married, Lance had taken care of the family's finances because he was an accountant and he enjoyed doing it. This had been a relief to Susan because she had her hands full working full-time, taking care of the home, worrying about her mother, and dealing with her stepchildren.

In her initial session with Dr. Coleman, her psychologist, Susan related her anxieties about her inability to act on any of the items she currently had on her many to-do lists in the way she would have in the past. Dr. Coleman had suggested that Susan select the most important item from each list and place it on a single piece of paper. In this way, each sheet of paper would be devoted to the most important item from each list. When she completed acting on that item, she could cross it off and add another. Dr. Coleman suggested that for Susan this approach would be similar to the way she had functioned in the past and would minimize her present sense of being overwhelmed. If this approach didn't work, they would discuss other approaches in their subsequent meetings.

Susan was relieved to find that Dr. Coleman was addressing her practical concerns as well as trying to learn about her background. In their first meeting, she had explained that her therapeutic approach could best be described as eclectic, meaning that she utilized aspects of various schools of psychological thought, rather than only one, in her approach to her clients. Dr. Coleman told Susan she felt it was essential to know something of a client's personal history in order to better understand the basis for what he or she was feeling or why he or she might be reacting in a particular way. However, she stressed that with Susan this would not preclude their focusing on her immediate needs, and she wanted Susan to make her aware of these concerns as they arose.

After her visit with Dr. Coleman, Susan decided her initial task was to set up a work area at home in her spare bedroom. She stopped at an office supply store to buy a small file cabinet and arrange for its delivery. Although she intended to set up computer records herself eventually, she thought she had better start by organizing the papers in the file cabinet. She also picked up a notepad and a calendar because she thought these would help her move ahead in the manner Dr. Coleman had suggested.

Next, Susan made a list of their bills and divided them into those she knew she had to pay—like the mortgage and condo fee—and those which were less urgent. She regretted that these weren't on autopay. Harry had given her Lance's month-end paycheck, but because she wasn't sure what to do with it, she had not cashed it yet.

Susan realized she had a lot of accounts to keep track of and she needed to devise a system that would help her to keep track of all the statements. She had Lance's retirement plan, her 401(k) plan, Lance's stock account, and the new trust account being established for Lance's children. She needed touch base with Harry to help her sort all this out.

Dr. Coleman's approach seemed to be working pretty well. Getting the files in order and making progress on the list of tasks she needed to accomplish made her feel a lot better.

Susan's To-Do List
- Set up and organize files at home
- Discuss with Harry the benefits she was entitled to receive from the firm.
- Cancel subscriptions to Lance's magazines

Audrey

Reactions to Getting Organized

Audrey had spent most of the past year visiting John in the hospital and barely had time to keep their bills paid. She was grateful John had set up a well-organized file system for all their important papers in his big desk in the den. He even had provided a list of their advisors and contact information. She made a note to herself to provide the same information for her children.

Audrey had used his desk to pay the bills, so she had a pretty good idea of what their expenses had been. She decided to start keeping a notebook of her current expenses as well as people she needed to see. She realized that knowing the expenses of the past two years wouldn't be very helpful to her in estimating future expenses; however, it would be a place to start. She had been so wrapped up in taking care of John that she had had no time to spend money on anything except the basic necessities and medical bills. Fortunately, John's health insurance had been wonderful and had covered most of their medical expenses.

Audrey was glad she had decided to have a physical, which had been first on her list of things to do. Dr. PaPadisio's staff had always been helpful and considerate of her as well as attentive to John during the ordeal of his illness. It felt odd to Audrey to be focusing on herself in Dr. PaPadisio's all-too-familiar consultation room—the same room in which he had informed them of John's prognosis. Dr. PaPadisio had her sit down and tell him how she was doing both emotionally and physically. He listened carefully to what she reported and asked questions about her weight loss. He was pleased with her mental attitude and said they'd talk further after he completed his physical examination. Audrey thought Dr. PaPadisio was unusually thorough in his exam and wasn't sure whether he suspected something or was just being careful.

While getting dressed to return to his office, Audrey found that she was quite nervous, dreading what Dr. PaPadisio might say. When she sat down to talk with him, he seemed to sense her anxiety and quickly reassured her. He went on to say that in his initial exam he hadn't found anything that concerned him, but he would wait until he received the results of the blood work and other tests he had ordered before finalizing his medical report. He did tell her, however, that on the basis of what she had told him, and his knowledge of the demands made on her time and energy in the last months of John's illness, he wanted to review her eating and exercise habit patterns with her.

Dr. PaPadisio gently admonished Audrey about the way she was eating and made several specific recommendations. He told her he wanted her to make a practice of eating regularly and offered suggestions about which foods to consider to help her gain weight without increasing her cholesterol level. He suggested she have lunch with a friend or her daughter, Joanne, whenever possible—he thought it would force her to take the time to sit and eat in a more leisurely fashion and concentrate on what she was eating. He advised her to think about making the midday meal her largest meal of the day for the present. He knew from other patients how difficult it is to make the effort to cook only for oneself, but he wanted her to make herself something to eat in the evening, even if it was a microwave meal.

Next, Dr. PaPadisio asked Audrey if she was exercising regularly. She admitted she wasn't. He asked if she still had her German shepherd; she assured him she did, adding that poor Achilles still looked for John and then looked at her as though he were awaiting his return. Saying that made Audrey realize how comforting it was to have had Achilles at home with her all this time. She really had been neglecting him, she thought, by leaving him in the backyard. She or John used to walk him several times a day, but now she couldn't remember when he'd last been walked.

Dr. PaPadisio wanted Audrey to make it a practice of walking the dog at least once a day if the weather was suitable, gradually increasing the length of time she spent walking. He wanted to wait for the lab reports before discussing a more total fitness program with her. He commented that he understood she probably had neglected her own health because of the demands of caring for John and told her he'd have his receptionist contact her to schedule a follow-up visit after he received the lab reports.

When Audrey left Dr. PaPadisio's office, she felt she had taken an important step in caring for herself. During John's illness she really had given up all of the things she enjoyed and felt were important to maintaining her health. She vowed to make an effort to focus on her physical health again, beginning with walking Achilles and eating more nutritiously and regularly.

Audrey decided she was ready to put together an agenda of what to accomplish in the next month. She needed to meet with the lawyer and the banker, check with John's company about his pension, find out about the insurance, and find someone to tell her what to do about his stock. When she drew up the list, it seemed like a lot to do, but she had learned a long time ago that if you tackle a big task one piece at a time, you can get through it all. She was determined to start her new life as soon as possible! The sooner she got started, the sooner she would be able to have an intelligent conversation with her son about where matters stood. She was sure he would want to have a serious financial discussion with her in the near future.

Audrey's To-Do List

- Call Joanne to make a date for lunch
- Eat regularly
- Walk Achilles daily
- Try to gain weight
- See lawyer
- See banker
- Call John's company about his pension
- Call about insurance

Elizabeth

Reactions to Getting Organized

At Ben's request, over the past few years Elizabeth had gradually assumed more responsibility for paying their bills. This was due to the fact that Ben's increasing loss of memory had caused some problems, although she was finding her own memory wasn't what it used to be. If she didn't write down an appointment in a book, she was inclined to forget it, and sometimes she didn't remember everything that was said to her. In fact, it seemed that recently everyone was speaking in lower voices. She was having difficulty hearing what they were saying, and she felt awkward asking them to repeat themselves.

Although their checkbook was in pretty good order, the same could not be said of Ben's papers. The file cabinet she opened appeared to be crammed with old, out-of-date records. Elizabeth wasn't sure what to keep and what to throw out. She needed someone to help her figure out which papers were important and what to do with the rest of the stuff in Ben's file.

Elizabeth did find a file labeled "Safe-Deposit Box," which held an envelope and a key from their local bank; the key was clearly marked "Safe-Deposit Box." Elizabeth had intended to visit their bank anyway to talk with the manager about their accounts. When she went she could also ask about opening the safe-deposit box because she had no recollection of Ben telling her about the contents.

Her close friend, Mabel, had given Elizabeth a notebook, telling her it had been a lifesaver to her in the early months after her own husband's death. Elizabeth stared at the clean, white pages in front of her and felt overwhelmed with all that was ahead of her. What should she put on the pages? How would she ever handle complex financial issues when she had never even balanced the checkbook? Women of her generation were not taught much about money; in fact, it had not been considered ladylike for women to talk about money. Elizabeth was really lost, but she knew she had to start the process so she would have some idea of her total financial situation.

She knew she should make an appointment to see Ben's lawyer, but she really didn't know him very well. She decided to turn once again to Pastor Appletorn. She would ask him if he knew someone who could go with her to the lawyer's office. When Elizabeth met with Pastor Appletorn, he seemed to know what her worries were even before she explained them. He told her he had taken the liberty of speaking to a couple in the congregation about her. Sam Weatherly was a recently retired attorney. Both he and his wife, Sarah, gave a great deal of time to church activities. In fact, he had joined the church's finance committee. If Elizabeth was willing, Pastor Appletorn wanted to ask the Weatherlys to join them for tea. He thought Sam might be able to help Elizabeth deal with her financial questions.

Elizabeth was so grateful she began to cry. Just knowing someone was there was a big comfort. She was sure Ben would not have wanted strangers to know anything about their finances, but she decided to meet this couple and draw her own conclusions. She really wanted help in dealing with Ben's attorney. It felt good to have made even this small decision.

Pastor Appletorn arranged the tea for the following Sunday afternoon. Elizabeth felt guilty because she was looking forward to it. She didn't think she was supposed to look forward to anything at this point in her adjustment to her new state of widowhood. She even thought about what she might wear. She and Ben had practically stopped seeing people during the last year of his life because it was so difficult to predict when Ben would be coherent.

Elizabeth dressed very carefully and was ready considerably earlier than necessary. She wanted to make a good impression and doing anything in a hurry tended to fluster her. She was somewhat amused when she realized that she had asked Mittens (the stray cat she had adopted) which of two outfits he thought she should wear. She had named him Mittens because his white paws reminded her of mittens.

Elizabeth arrived at the rectory punctually at 4:00 p.m. The Weatherlys arrived shortly after she did, and she liked them at once. They made her feel comfortable and talked about many things she could relate to before they began discussing her financial affairs. Sam Weatherly seemed very knowledgeable, and she thought she could trust him, so she gratefully accepted his offer to accompany her when she was ready to meet with Ben's attorney.

Elizabeth's To-Do List

- Visit bank about safe-deposit box and bank accounts
- Make appointment to see Ben's lawyer when convenient for Sam Weatherly
- Try to straighten out Ben's file of financial papers
- Force myself to begin using the notebook Mabel gave me

CHAPTER FIVE

Working with Key Financial Advisors

Settling an estate is not an easy task regardless of the size of the estate. Even if you or your husband never used professional advisors before, this is a time you should seriously consider using their services. We have observed that widows who seek professional help progress more quickly to a state of well-being than those who try to do it all themselves.

Most widows initially rely on advisors their husbands had in place prior to their deaths. After your husband's estate is settled, you may want to find your own advisors, but at this stage it is easiest to work with those people familiar with your situation. However, if you find them unresponsive to your requests, consider replacing them with someone who is more helpful to you. At the end of this chapter, we have included guidelines for selecting advisors.

Well-meaning family members and friends may offer legal or financial advice. Keep in mind they don't know the specifics of your situation, and, as successful as they might be managing their own affairs, their strategies may not be appropriate for you. So, listen to them, but wait until you meet with your own professional advisors before taking action.

As previously stated, we strongly recommend that you bring a family member or friend with you to your initial meetings. This is because you may have emotional difficulty absorbing information from an advisor while you are actively grieving the death of your spouse. This person can help you by asking questions you might not think to ask. Feel free to ask your own questions and write down the answers. There is no such thing as a stupid question—only a lack of knowledge in a particular field—and the advisor should welcome your questions. We realize having another person present when you talk to your attorney might jeopardize the attorney-client privilege, but we think the benefits outweigh those concerns. Check with your attorney as to her preference in this regard.

Reviewing the Will

Your first task is to read and understand the contents of your husband's will. The will names a person to settle the estate, commonly called an **executor,** or **in some states personal representative (PR)**.[1] The first thing you or the PR or the lawyer who is representing you must do is file the original will with the probate court. Many states require you to file the will within a certain period of time after the person's death. Your lawyer can tell you how soon it must be filed, or you can call the probate court and find out for yourself.

If there is no will, the probate court will appoint an *administrator* for the estate, also known as the PR. This may be a person such as yourself, your lawyer, a member of the family, or someone else. If the PR is not experienced in settling estates, she should contact someone who is. Settling estates is not for amateurs even if you think your situation is very simple, and even then the rules and regulations can be confusing.

Here are some questions you need to have answered: Which creditors must be paid and in what time frames? Which expenses are deductible? How much will the PR be paid? Who receives the notices of probate? What reports are required? To whom must they be sent? As a result of ignorance, you could make an incorrect distribution or miss a deadline, both of which could cost you money.

Administration of the Estate

Many people don't understand what the term probate means. It is simply the legal process whereby a court assures itself that a will is valid and appoints as PR the person named to that position in the will. If there is no will, the court authorizes someone to wind up the decedent's affairs,

---

1. Some of the technical and legal terms we refer to in this chapter will vary from one state to another. In the interests of readability, we use generally accepted terminology.

and in most states oversees the distribution of property to creditors and legal beneficiaries.

Not all of your husband's property will have to pass through probate. For instance, property owned in joint tenancy with the right of survivorship will not be probated but will go directly to the survivor. U.S. savings bonds that are co-owned or payable to a beneficiary are not included in the probate estate. Life insurance policies, deferred annuities, IRAs and other retirement plan benefits will be paid to the named beneficiary. Assets held in a living trust also escape the probate process. Other assets that escape probate are ones held in the name of "Transfer on Death" (TOD) or Payable-on-Death (POD) accounts, usually at a bank.

If applicable, the Surrogate's Court (sometimes called the Probate Court) of the county where your spouse resided at death will issue letters of appointment certifying the authority of the personal representative, which you will be required to supply in order to transfer assets. The various banks, brokerage firms, and other entities you contact usually require a recently dated letter of appointment (within the last 60 days). Therefore, you may have to go back to the probate court for more copies later.

As we mentioned in the previous chapter, we recommend you initially request 20 copies of the death certificate. These are usually ordered for you by the funeral director.

The personal representative's responsibilities may include the following:

- Send legally required notices to family and beneficiaries
- Have the value of the property of the estate appraised
- Prepare an inventory of all money and property owned on the date of death and the appraised values of such assets
- Open a bank account in the name of the estate with a tax identification number obtained for the estate
- File periodic reports with the court (if needed in your state) and beneficiaries showing property received and amounts spent or distributed from the estate
- Obtain court permission to sell, lease, or invest property held by the estate (if needed in your state)

- Deal with the creditors (determine validity of claims, reject improper claims, etc.)
- Communicate regularly with the estate beneficiaries
- File any necessary income (personal and fiduciary), estate, or inheritance tax returns. File employee tax forms, business tax forms, etc., as needed
- Account fully for all assets collected and expenditures made from the estate
- Distribute the estate assets

As you can see, this is no easy task and one that is often best delegated to the professionals in the lawyer's office. They know what to do and can do it faster than you can. If you are anxious to reduce the costs of settling the estate, ask if there is anything you can do to help.

The Lawyer's Role

The lawyer's function is to make sure that you are legally protected. Your lawyer should review the terms of the will and the trust (if applicable) with you and explain its implications. Unless your husband's lawyer was named as PR, you are not required to use him or her to settle the estate.

Your First Meeting

The lawyer is usually the first advisor you see. following the death of your spouse. In most cases this would be your husband's estate planning lawyer who drew up his estate planning documents. At this first meeting, ask how long she estimates it will take to settle the estate and when you can expect distributions to begin. If you are the PR, you can determine when these distributions will be made. Request a written estimate of what it will cost to take you through the estate settlement process. Many state bar associations require your lawyer to send you a letter of engagement, which includes this information. The fee is usually an hourly rate, or a percentage of the assets involved and is paid from the estate assets. Many states require court approval of these fees.

Ask whom you should call if you have a question. Most estate planning lawyers have very knowledgeable assistants and paralegals who are more readily available than the lawyer and can answer most questions you might have at lower hourly rates.

You should also establish what records you should keep and what the lawyer will keep. When in doubt, ask—and don't throw anything away. If you are inexperienced in dealing with financial matters, the lawyer can arrange to have a staff member come to your home and sort through the information you have accumulated. Of course, you will be charged for this service, but it will probably be worth the cost to make sure everything is covered. Information improperly discarded may have to be obtained or recreated at great expense.

If your lawyer is unable to provide this service, you might consider using the service of a daily money manager to obtain some help with this task.

Comment

Some widows become overly dependent on their lawyer. Most estate planning lawyers have chosen this area of specialization because they care about people. As much as they would like to drop everything to talk with you every time you call, recognize the fact that they do have other clients who also need their attention.

The Accountant's Role

You and your husband may have used an accountant in the past to prepare your income tax returns. If so, we recommend that you continue to use this same accountant to prepare your income tax return at least for this first, very important year. After the first year, you can assess the work done and the accountant's attitude toward you and responsiveness to your concerns. Then, when life is less stressful, you can decide whether you want to keep working with this accountant with future income tax returns.

There are several tax returns to be prepared starting with your personal federal and state income tax returns. Other returns may include state estate and inheritance tax returns as well as federal estate tax returns. Many lawyers prefer to file your estate tax returns rather than delegating that to your accountant. Make sure your accountant knows who your lawyer is so they can work cooperatively. Also make sure your lawyer and accountant work together to determine who is responsible for preparing which tax returns so there is no needless duplication or misunderstanding.

A federal estate tax return will have to be filed if the value of your husband's gross estate (including both probate and non-probate assets) plus the amount of taxable gifts made by your husband exceeds $13.61 million.[2] The federal estate tax return is due nine months after your husband's death. (Some states have earlier deadlines for filing returns for state estate and inheritance taxes.) If you don't have everything you need, your accountant can request an extension. Even if no estate taxes are due, a return must be filed so that the Internal Revenue Service (IRS) won't come back to you later with a claim. The values on this return also establish a cost basis for assets you may sell in the future. In addition, even if you don't owe a federal estate tax, you may owe an estate tax to your state of residence. State taxation laws vary, so check with your adviser about your state's requirement. Even if your husband's estate assets are less than the current allowance, you might want to file an estate tax return. Your lawyer or accountant can advise you in this regard.

Federal and state income tax returns will have to be filed not only for the year your husband died, but also for the prior year if he died before filing a return for that year. For example, if your husband died in March, you would have to file income tax returns for the year he died and for the previous year (assuming he had not done that before his death).

In the calendar year your husband dies, you are allowed to file a joint personal return as long as you have not remarried by the end of the year. Thereafter, you will file as a single person unless you have dependent

---

2. $13.61 million dollars is the current "federal estate tax exclusion amount" for 2023. The federal estate tax exclusion amount is the dollar amount of a taxable estate on which the federal estate tax is forgiven. Under current law, on January 1, 2026, this number will be cut in half and adjusted for inflation.

children. If you have dependents, then you file as "qualifying widow with dependent children" for the first two years after your husband dies and then as "head of household."

How To Select These Advisors

Each of these key advisors must be knowledgeable, ethical, empathetic, and experienced in working with widows. The following are seven guidelines for selecting these professionals:

1. If you are looking for a particular professional advisor, ask one of your existing professional advisors (accountant, financial advisor, or banker) to recommend someone. Your widowed friends might also suggest someone they have worked with effectively.

2. Check the website for more information about these individuals.

3. Contact the office of two individuals in each profession and ask for an appointment. Explain that you are looking for someone to help you to help with estate planning and you want to meet for an initial consultation before making a decision. Ask what information you should bring to this meeting to make it most productive.

4. When you meet, ask the advisor if he or she will be handling your case personally or delegating it to an assistant or another person in the office. It is not unusual for an advisor to delegate part of the work, which often means that some of the work will be charged at lower rates. What is of importance is that your advisor takes primary responsibility for supervising your situation. If she will not be doing all the work, ask to meet the assistant.

5. Ask what the advisor's hourly rate will be and how much she estimates the total bill will be. The more information you give your advisor in an organized fashion, the fewer hours she will have to spend finding the information and the lower the fee will be. However, you should not necessarily pick the person who gives you the lowest rate. The person who quotes a higher hourly rate may be more efficient or experienced and may take fewer hours to settle the estate.

6. Ask the advisor how they will handle the occasional questions you might have. Although you don't intend to call frequently, you do expect someone knowledgeable to respond to your phone calls in a timely fashion.

Credentials

Each profession has its own credentials. Familiarize yourself with the various professional credentials before selecting your advisors.

Selecting Your Lawyer

Your lawyer should be an estate and trust specialist. Check the *Martindale-Hubbell Law Directory*® online to see if the lawyer you select is described as having had experience working with estates and trusts. If you are unable to obtain personal referrals, contact your local bar association.

For complex situations you may need a more experienced lawyer. If so, there is a professional organization called the American College of Trust and Estate Counsel (ACTEC) composed of lawyers who concentrate on complicated cases. The members must have a minimum of ten years' experience. However, there may not be a member in your town, or you may not need such a high level of expertise. In any case, make sure the lawyer you select has had considerable experience settling estates.

Selecting Your Accountant

The principal credential in the field of accounting is the Certified Public Accountant (CPA). However, some accountants are not CPAs but are Enrolled Agents (EA), who specialize in preparing individual returns and can represent you with the IRS if necessary.

Your primary concern is that the accountant you select is experienced in preparing individual and estate tax returns (rather than corporate returns). If yours is a very simple situation, a tax preparer at a tax service firm might be helpful. However, recognize that the first year you file a tax return after your husband's death everything is more complicated, so be careful in your selection.

Selecting Your Financial Planner

The best-known credential in the financial planning profession is the Certified Financial Planner practitioner (CFP®). To qualify as a CFP® practitioner, the planner must successfully complete a course of study in all aspects of financial planning and pass a comprehensive written exam. In addition, the practitioner must also have at least three years of experience counseling clients on financial planning matters. To find a CFP® practitioner in your area the website is *www.letsmakeaplan.org*. Another useful website is for the National Association of Personal Financial Advisors *www.napfa.org*.

The insurance profession has a designation for financial planners called Chartered Financial Consultants (ChFC®). There is also a group of CPAs who specialize in providing financial planning advice. Their designation is Personal Financial Specialists (PFS®).

Financial planners are compensated in one of three ways: commission-only, fee-only, or fee-based. Commission-only planners charge no fee or a nominal fee and are compensated primarily by the commissions generated by the products you buy through them. Fee-only planners charge an hourly fee or flat fee to provide financial planning advice. If you subsequently invest through them, they usually charge a percentage of assets managed. Fee-based planners also charge hourly rates to provide financial planning advice. If you subsequently invest with them, they may charge you a percentage of the assets managed and/or they may receive commissions on investments you make.

For the initial financial planning services, you require at this stage, we recommend you select a fee-only or fee-based planner who charges an hourly fee, just like your other professional advisors do. Make sure you ask for a written estimate of the fee you will be charged for preparing your financial plan which will help you better understand your current financial situation.

Estate Planning Councils

As you interview these three key advisors, ask if they belong to an Estate Planning Council. Members of this organization come from the legal, accounting, insurance, banking, and financial planning professions. Membership is a good indicator of whether your advisor is interested in working with widows. There are many good advisors who might not belong to this organization, but members will be experienced in this field and have a strong interest in it. Be aware that such councils may not exist in smaller communities.

Summary and Conclusion

These three advisors—your attorney, your accountant, and your financial planner—are your primary helpers in the first stage of dealing with your finances after your husband's death. It is extremely important that these three individuals work together on your behalf. By this time, you should have a sheet in your financial diary that lists the name, address, phone number, and e-mail address of each of these advisors as well as their assistants' names. In the next chapter, we discuss other professionals whom you need to contact to organize your financial affairs.

Diane

Reactions to Meeting with Key Advisors

In her feeling way, Diane knew what she wanted for her children. She anticipated that her family and close friends would try to talk her out of her desire to keep the children in their private schools. They would encourage her instead to be realistic, practical, and financially responsible, which might mean transferring them to public schools.

Upon reflection, Diane realized that Larry and the others at Mark's law firm were doing what they could to be helpful, but they had really only succeeded in confusing her. She decided she needed her own objective advisor—not a family member or friend—to help her reach the right decision about the children's schools. If at all possible, she wanted to keep them in their current schools. Mark had signed contracts with the schools before he died, and the first payments were due soon, so she had better get organized and find a way to figure this out.

She decided to call Jennifer Greenberg and see if she had used someone in this capacity. She was pleased to learn from Jennifer that she had used someone and enthusiastically recommended her financial planner, Dorothy Trumbull. Jennifer explained the role of a financial planner. She encouraged Diane to make an appointment to see Dorothy. Diane was so appreciative of how willing Jennifer was to provide her with helpful information that she asked Jennifer if they could get together sometime for lunch or dinner. She knew Jennifer worked but hoped they could find a way to do so. Jennifer was receptive, which pleased Diane. She realized just how detached she had been before Mark's death from the lives of those who had experienced the loss of a loved one.

Before she lost her nerve or changed her mind, Diane called Dorothy's office and made an appointment to meet with her. She asked what kind of information Dorothy needed to help her make the right decisions. She was tired of hearing from everyone what she should and should not do. In her present state she wasn't up to dealing with this issue with her father, her brother, or even Larry and his wife, Gail, as well meaning as they all were.

Diane was frightened at the thought of meeting Dorothy by herself. This was the first time she had ever initiated anything related to finances. She recognized that she wanted and needed the help of an independent person, but she was afraid of the consequences of revealing her financial ignorance to this expert. She assumed Dorothy would ask her a great many questions she would be unable to answer. Diane wasn't sure she would even understand what this financial planner was talking about. She begged one of her closest friends to accompany her to this initial meeting because she didn't want to involve her family. Diane was greatly relieved when her friend agreed to join her. It hadn't been that long since Mark had died, and she was having a hard time facing the reality of his death.

The meeting turned out to be much less difficult and painful than Diane imagined it would be. Although she didn't have a lot of information, Dorothy didn't laugh at her or tell her she was foolish to even consider continuing her children in their private schools. Dorothy did tell her that she would need more information in order to help her make this decision.

When Dorothy discovered Mark had no will, she had difficulty concealing her dismay. She explained that in Maryland, without a will, one-half of the assets held in Mark's name would go to Diane and the balance to the three children. Diane would be appointed by the court to manage the assets for the children, but one-half of the assets actually belonged to them! Diane now understood why her father had been so upset. Dorothy went on to explain that if most of the assets were jointly held, those assets would go to her and would not be taxed until she died. Diane knew that the home and their checking account were in both of their names, but she wasn't sure what other assets they had or whether they were jointly owned. Obviously, she needed to do some homework.

Dorothy's questions caused Diane to realize that she knew nothing about Mark's life insurance. She remembered that the firm had provided Mark with life insurance coverage. Her dad had told her what she needed to do about the four insurance policies she had found in Mark's files, but, like everything else, she had ignored his instructions, incapable of action. Now that she realized that obtaining the information about the insurance might impact her ability to keep the children in their schools, she was motivated to learn more. It now felt right and necessary to explore this further.

Dorothy discussed the family's health insurance. She told Diane that the firm's insurance under COBRA would cover them for 36 months after Mark's death, but she would have to pay the premiums that were formerly paid by the firm. Diane wondered if she was supposed to have done something about this sooner. She would have to ask Larry, although she was beginning to feel he was tiring of her constant need for his assistance.

Dorothy gave Diane a questionnaire to complete and made an appointment for her to come back and review it all with her. She explained that she would charge Diane an hourly fee for her advice. The more information Diane put together herself, the less Dorothy would charge her. Diane found the questionnaire to be a little intimidating because she was not used to financial matters. However, Dorothy reassured her about her ability to provide her with the information she needed. She checked the items she particularly needed to know to help Diane decide what to do about the children's education. She explained that the most important information she needed was what the family's assets, liabilities, and estimated sources of income were. Knowing that she had a professional advisor who was nonjudgmental about her ignorance or Mark's failure to prepare a will made her feel better.

These thoughts were unfamiliar ones for Diane. Just contemplating gathering all the necessary information was overwhelming. However, her desire to reach a particular goal—keeping the children in private schools—propelled her to overcome her resistance to addressing financial matters. The time had come for her to stop feeling sorry for herself and start doing something for the children. She found herself motivated to move beyond her frozen state of inactivity.

Susan

Reactions to Meeting with Key Advisors

At this point following Lance's sudden death, Susan found managing her daily life almost more than she could handle. However, she knew she had to come to grips with her own financial status, particularly in view of her responsibilities for her mother.

Susan thought she should start by meeting with Harry, Lance's partner, and friend. He was very supportive when she met with him, telling her again how shocked and saddened everyone at the office was about Lance's death. He introduced her to Sarah Stone, Lance's assistant.

Sarah would help her with the estate and income tax returns. In fact, she had already applied for the estate tax identification number. Harry told Susan a return had to be filed for the estate within nine months of Lance's death. Sarah would prepare these returns, and the firm would bear the expense for this work. She also had a list of passwords for his computer which Lance had given her. Susan was grateful for all this help and particularly relieved to receive access to his computer.

Harry told her that Lance had a retirement account which she could leave at the firm to be managed with the other retirement accounts if she wished. In addition, he was aware of the $500,000 insurance trust Lance had created for his children, which would provide Susan with lifetime income. When she died, the remaining principal would go to Lance's children. They discussed the fact that her stepchildren would not be happy that they were not receiving more money now, but she wasn't ready to deal with them yet.

Harry recommended that Susan call the trust department of the bank Lance had named to act as the trustee for the insurance trust and ask for an appointment to go over the details. He volunteered to accompany her to the bank if she would like him to do so. Susan thanked him but said she thought she could handle that meeting by herself, although she recognized she could use some help with the stepchildren. She felt the news about their relatively small immediate inheritance of $25,000 each might be better received from someone other than herself. Also, the fact that the income generated by the children's trust would go to her was sure to be a problem for them. Harry agreed to help. Lance had discussed with him the reasons he had created the trust, and he thought that he could explain it to Lance's children. They might not like the terms of the trust, but he was sure it was a valid document.

He also told Susan that his wife, Emily, wanted to have her over for dinner and would be in touch with her shortly. Susan, usually a social person, hoped she would be able to deal with this kind gesture. Everything seemed to take so much effort these days, and she wasn't sure she was up to making dinner conversation. At the conclusion of her meeting with Harry, she felt somewhat relieved because at least she had put things in motion and was ready for the next round of appointments—with her banker, Lance's stockbroker, and the firm's benefits person.

The following week, Harry and Susan met with Tim Longwood, Lance's attorney. He went over the terms of the will and the trust with them. He assured Susan that there was nothing the stepchildren could do to get additional money. The condo and the cottage were held jointly in her and Lance's names and thus went directly to Susan. The insurance policy proceeds were payable to the trust at the bank. Lance had his pension fund, and Susan was clearly the beneficiary there. The only assets registered in his name exclusively were his stocks.

It did appear that Susan was going to have to sell some of these stocks to raise the $50,000 due to her stepchildren. Tim advised her to do this as soon as possible to reduce family tension. He would be glad to talk with Adam and Leslie about their inheritance if that would be helpful.

Audrey

Reactions to Meeting with Key Advisors

Audrey made an appointment to meet with Mr. Humphrey, the attorney. She anticipated that he would provide the guidance she needed in the near future. Undoubtedly, he would also want her to meet with John's accountant, Mr. Lewis. She was glad that Joanne had agreed to go with her to both meetings. She wanted to make sure she had sufficient information before discussing anything with John Jr.

Actually, she surprised herself. She realized she was enjoying gathering the relevant information and entering it all in her notebook. It allowed her to feel she was not only useful but had the right to begin to make financial decisions for herself. She wondered whether she would have been able to get in touch with these emotions as quickly if John had not been ill for such an extended period of time.

Audrey felt good about her first meeting with Mr. Humphrey. He encouraged her to ask questions and acknowledged that this was a painful and difficult process. He emphasized that he didn't want her to feel foolish about posing any question any number of times. He introduced her to Sally, his assistant, and told her she would be working with him to settle John's estate. Sally was very familiar with the process of settling estates, and if he wasn't available to answer any questions, Sally would be. If for any reason Audrey wanted to speak to him personally, she needed to make that clear to the receptionist or Sally. He would contact her as soon as possible even if he couldn't do so the day she called.

To make sure Audrey was setting up the estate files correctly, Mr. Humphrey recommended that she make an appointment to meet separately with Sally. He was pleased to learn she was already well organized in this area. He also told her how to contact the Social Security Administration to determine what income she would receive in the future.

Mr. Humphrey asked her if she had a financial advisor. She said no but remembered attending a series of retirement lectures sponsored by her husband's corporation. She had been impressed with one of the speakers, a financial planner, and felt she would be comfortable calling him. It turned out that Mr. Humphrey had worked with this planner in the past and encouraged her to do so as he felt she needed someone to help her evaluate her total financial picture.

Audrey left Mr. Humphrey's office feeling better about the future. At least she had a list of instructions to follow and felt Mr. Humphrey would be helpful to her as she moved through the process of settling John's estate. She would ask Joanne to join her when she met with the financial planner.

When she got home, there was a message on her answering machine to call Dr. PaPadisio's office but that it was not an emergency. She appreciated his sensitivity to her built-in anxieties regarding calls from his office. When she returned the call, his pleasant receptionist told her Dr. PaPadisio wanted her to set up a follow-up appointment to go over her lab work and review the progress she was making with her exercise and eating programs. Audrey made an appointment for the following week. She had tried to do better with her eating but really hadn't focused on it. She hadn't yet made any arrangements to meet friends or Joanne for lunch on a regular basis and was hoping Dr. PaPadisio wouldn't ask her about it. The appointment with Dr. PaPadisio would force her to look at this aspect of her life in much the same way she was looking at the financial aspects of her life.

Dr. PaPadisio actually wanted only a consultation with her. He had his nurse weigh her, but, other than that, he just wanted to talk. He shared the lab work results with her, insisting that basically she was in good health but had neglected herself while caring for John. As he had previously indicated, he wanted her to seriously focus on nutrition and exercise. He encouraged her to take a class in nutrition or cooking that focused on cooking for oneself. Other patients had told him about courses they had taken through the local community college. If she wasn't interested in such a class, he would refer her to a nutritionist with whom he had a working relationship. Some of his patients had found this nutritionist both informative and constructive. He said he thought a class might be a better approach for Audrey because she would be with people in a similar situation. This often led to new contacts, which he thought might be enjoyable for her. She promised him she would investigate a class and get back to him about it as he had requested.

Dr. PaPadisio surprised Audrey by next inquiring about her golf game, asking if she was still playing. She hadn't thought about golf in a long time. She and John had been avid golfers, but both had given it up when John became ill. She realized she did miss it. She had played regularly with some women friends on Tuesday and Thursday mornings, and she and John had played a couple's game on the weekends. At this point, she knew, her women friends had replaced her in the foursome, and, even if her game wasn't so rusty, she would be uncomfortable asking them if she could rejoin the group. However, she thought it might be a good idea to schedule some lessons with the golf pro. Although she hadn't given it any consideration before Dr. PaPadisio began asking her about her exercise program, she decided to take up golf again. At least she was able to tell him that she had taken his advice and had begun to take Achilles on a daily walk. She thought she was up to about a mile a day but wasn't sure. He was pleased with that and encouraged her to investigate other fitness activities.

Before Audrey left the office, Dr. PaPadisio asked her to schedule another appointment for the following month. He wanted to check her weight and possibly repeat some of the blood work. He emphasized that a preventive health plan was often the best medicine he could provide.

Elizabeth

Reactions to Meeting with Key Advisors

When Elizabeth received the letter from the law firm with whom Ben dealt asking her to make an appointment with Mr. Carroll as soon as she felt up to it, she panicked. Even his name—Francis Carroll—was unfamiliar. She knew she couldn't face any of this alone. She wished the idea of meeting with Ben's attorney and matters of this type didn't intimidate her so.

Elizabeth didn't agonize for any length of time about whether or not she should call the Weatherlys. She located the phone number and dialed quickly before she allowed herself to have second thoughts. Sam answered the phone, and, after some pleasantries, she read him the letter she had received from Ben's attorney. He reassured her that he had been sincere about his willingness to accompany her when she went for her initial meeting with Ben's attorney. He was somewhat surprised she had no recollection of Ben mentioning Mr. Carroll's name to her but said it would be best to go ahead and schedule an appointment. He gave her some dates when he would be available and asked her to call after she had made the appointment.

Elizabeth scheduled the appointment with the attorney for Wednesday of the same week. Sam and Sarah Weatherly picked her up. All three went to the attorney's office, but Sarah left them to do some shopping while Sam and she had their meeting.

The law firm's reception area was very formal and intimidating to Elizabeth. When Mr. Carroll came out to meet her in the reception area, she was shocked—Mr. Carroll could not have been more than 28 years old! Ben couldn't possibly have worked with this young man! Mr. Carroll introduced himself and quickly explained that Ben's attorney had died about six months earlier and he had been given Ben's file. So that explained her lack of familiarity with the name!

Mr. Carroll perfunctorily expressed regret about her husband's death and started to usher her into his office. Sam slowed him down by introducing himself and stressing that all of this was new to Elizabeth. Sam understood that Mr. Carroll wanted to meet with Elizabeth alone but assured her he would wait until she had finished her meeting and not to worry about how long it took.

Immediately after Elizabeth sat down in his office, Mr. Carroll started chiding her because she had not contacted the Social Security Administration, which reinforced her initial negative feelings towards this brash young lawyer. Sam had provided her with a list of questions to ask Mr. Carroll. As a result, Elizabeth learned for the first time that Ben had left her $1,000,000 in an account that was being managed by an investment advisor.

A million dollars—Elizabeth had no idea that they had that much money! Certainly, their lifestyle was very modest. Ben was always warning her not to spend too much, but maybe that was how he had accumulated $1,000,000. He must have been much better at managing his investments than she had realized. Mr. Carroll seemed to indicate she also would need to meet with the investment advisor.

Elizabeth did not like Mr. Carroll at all. He was patronizing toward her and made her feel stupid. She didn't know how she was going to work with this ill-mannered man. Tears came to her eyes, but she worked at not letting him know how distressed she was. Now that she had met Mr. Carroll, she was especially pleased that such a kind man as Sam had brought her to the meeting. She would speak with him on the way home about whether she was required to work with this lawyer to settle Ben's estate. If she had a choice, she wanted another lawyer.

As soon as Elizabeth was back in the car, she asked Sam if she had to work with that arrogant Mr. Carroll. He told her she didn't. Before he could elaborate on what she could do, Elizabeth asked him if he would take her on as a client. Sam, in his considerate manner, told her he would be more than willing to do so if he were still in practice, but he wouldn't feel comfortable assuming responsibility for her knowing that he no longer kept up with the latest information on estate planning law. The way he said it made Elizabeth feel he was sincere, and she wasn't a burden for whom he didn't want to assume any responsibility. Elizabeth apologized for asking him, but he assured her no apology was necessary.

Sam was quick to offer further help in the selection of a more appropriate lawyer; one with whom he thought Elizabeth would feel comfortable. He even offered to go with her to meet the various advisors she would need to contact to sort out her financial affairs. They agreed to start with the new attorney, whom Sam would contact on her behalf.

When Sam and Sarah Weatherly reached Elizabeth's home, they asked her if she felt up to joining them at their home for lunch after Sunday services that week. She said yes without even thinking. When she was changing her clothes, she wondered if she had agreed too quickly. Ben hadn't been dead that long, and here she was accepting social invitations. Ben would say she was "out gallivanting." She felt guilty, but she was also looking forward to spending some time with this friendly, thoughtful couple. She decided to bake her special angel food cake for the occasion. Mittens seemed to know something good was going on in the kitchen because he followed her every step while she put the ingredients together. He seemed to look at her with approval. She wasn't sure why, but she felt better having him in the home.

Sunday lunch was nice, and to Elizabeth's surprise, when they were ready for dessert, Sam told her he had asked one of the partners in his former law firm, Mr. Grossfeldt, to stop by to informally meet Elizabeth. If she felt comfortable with him, she could make an appointment to see him on a professional basis the following week. While they had coffee and cake, Elizabeth realized how easy Mr. Grossfeldt was to relate to; she knew she could talk to him about her financial affairs.

Sam and Sarah had another pleasant surprise for Elizabeth. They had also invited Pastor Appletorn to stop over for coffee and dessert. She was pleased when he appeared. It made her realize how supportive the pastor and other members of the church had been to her. She decided she would like to donate something to the church. Maybe she could give them Ben's car. It was almost brand new and certainly had not been driven much. She did not feel comfortable driving anymore—it was easier to hire a car service. She would ask Mr. Grossfeldt if gifting the car to the church was a good idea when she met with him in his office.

CHAPTER SIX

Contacting Agencies and Resource People

Now that you have met with your primary advisors, there are other people and agencies you need to notify of your husband's death almost immediately. They will give you a better idea of what your assets are and what sources of income you can expect to receive. These other agencies include your bank and your insurance and mortgage companies. You also need to talk with the Social Security Administration. If applicable, contact the Department of Veterans Affairs and your husband's employer. If you have an account with a stockbroker or an investment advisor, they need to be consulted as well.

Bank

You may be familiar with the people at your bank or not. In any event, you need to speak with someone personally at your bank about your accounts. Explain your situation and ask the banker to help you make any necessary changes to your accounts. If your husband had an account in his name, this should be changed to an account reading "Estate of." If you had a joint account, it will eventually be moved to an account in your name. If you have no account in your own name, you should establish one.

To transfer the bank accounts held in the deceased name, you will need the recently dated Certificates of Administration[1] as proof that you are the personal representative and a certified copy of the death certifi-

---

1. The name of this certificate varies from state to state but it is a document with a court seal showing that the court has named you to settle the decedent's affairs.

cate. As for any outstanding checks on the existing accounts written but not cashed, you can arrange to have these honored or not as you wish. The bank should not automatically make payments out of your husband's account. However, if the bank's personnel didn't know of your husband's death, they will honor any checks presented and continue any automatic payments from his account.

In any event, open a bank account in the name of the estate. To establish this account, you would initially use your spouse's Social Security number and then substitute the estate's tax ID number which is supplied by the Internal Revenue Service. Any income received from assets listed in your spouse's name should be deposited in this account.

All expenses associated with your husband's death and the settling of his estate should be paid from the estate account. These include all expenses related to the funeral as well as medical bills. If you have already made payments from your own funds to cover these expenses, you should keep the receipts and reimburse yourself from the estate account once there are sufficient funds in it to do so. The receipts will be needed if a court accounting is required.

Ask to see a list of all accounts, both individual and joint that you and your husband have at the bank. These may include retirement assets (such as IRA accounts) as well as your checking accounts, savings accounts, and certificates of deposit. You may also have an investment account with your bank.

You may also have a safe-deposit box. The regulations that determine whether you have access to this box vary from state to state. In some states, even if the box is in joint name, you may have to produce some paperwork to gain access to it.

The banker should explain what services the bank offers, just as she would to any new depositor. You may need different services than your husband did. Keep in mind that the banker wants to retain your account. Just as you did with your other advisors, ask for a contact person to call with questions about your account.

You and your husband may have had accounts in more than one bank, which complicates the situation. You should notify each bank of your husband's death. Then follow up your inquiry with a letter instructing the bank to establish a new account. You need to include in your letter a certified death certificate and a Certificate of Administration.

Comment

Bankers are accustomed to helping widows but be cautious about initially making long-term investments at the bank. Certainly, putting money in savings or checking accounts is fine because you can withdraw it at any time. Right now your goal is to gather information about the assets available to you. Don't make any long-term commitments until you have had time to look at your overall picture.

Mortgage Holder

If you had mortgage insurance, the insurance company will pay off the mortgage on your home on notification of your husband's death. If your husband had life insurance, you could use the proceeds to pay off the mortgage, although in most instances this might not be the best use for that money. We recommend you wait until you can ask your financial planner about this decision. In any case, you should advise your mortgage company that you will be the person responsible for making the payments at this point. If you want these payments to be paid automatically from your checking account, make sure that the mortgage company has the bank account number of your new account.

Real Estate Title

As part of settling the estate, it is advisable for you to retitle your joint properties, which involves preparing a new deed and submitting it to the recorder of deeds in your jurisdiction. It is recommended to take this action now to facilitate a sale at a later date. Your lawyer can take care of this for you.

Credit Cards

Many of the credit cards in your husband's name were issued because of his earning ability and credit. If you don't have the same earning power, the credit card companies may be reluctant to provide you with the same lines of credit until you demonstrate your credit worthiness. Some widows solve this by neglecting to notify the credit card companies of their husband's death, but then, if you do this, it will delay your establishing your own credit history. Eventually, you should notify all credit card companies of your husband's death, although there is no urgency to do so.

Most investment firms offer credit cards connected to your investment account. This may be an easy way to start establishing your own credit. One note of caution: don't apply for numerous credit cards. We recommend having two or three credit cards at the most. Having multiple cards increases your exposure to fraud.

Life Insurance Agent

If your husband had an insurance agent, this individual would have information on all the life insurance policies in force and will provide you with the necessary claim forms and instructions to obtain the proceeds of these policies. If your husband bought from various agents over the years, you need to notify each insurance company of his death. The company will require a certified copy of the death certificate and a completed statement of claim.

If you are not sure whether your spouse owned life insurance and you can't find the policy or remember the name of any life insurance agent he might have been working with, look through your spouse's checkbook and canceled checks for payments made to an insurance company. For a fee, the MIB Solution's Policy Locator Service (*www.mib.com*) might be able to help you find his application. Your spouse also may have had a group policy through an employer or former employer or professional or fraternal organizations.

If your husband made the insurance proceeds payable to a trust, then the trustee is the person to complete the claimant's statement and submit the documents to the insurance company.

If you are the beneficiary of life insurance policies, you will be asked how you want to receive the proceeds. You can choose to receive this money in a lump sum, in installments over your lifetime or for a fixed number of years, or in installments of a specified amount until the proceeds run out. This is another decision we recommend you defer until you have been able to look at your total picture. In the meantime, you can leave the money with the insurance company and have the interest on the principal accumulate for you.

The insurance agent may have some suggestions as to how you should invest the money. Once again, at this point, even if the recommendations sound wonderful, don't make an investment you can't change later. Ask the agent to put these recommendations in writing so that you can consider these ideas seriously when you meet with your financial planner. Also, if applicable ask for a review of your own life insurance policies. If your husband was the beneficiary, you will have to change this designation.

Health Insurance

If your husband had been ill, you may be faced with a confusing array of insurance bills. One of your financial advisors can help you sort through the medical bills, review the claims for accuracy, and appeal denied ones. If you use a daily money manager that person will be able to help you with these claims.

If your husband had health insurance through his employer and the firm had at least 20 employees, the so-called COBRA regulations issued by the Department of Labor require his firm to continue to offer insurance coverage to you and your dependents for 36 months. It is likely that while your husband was employed, the firm contributed to or paid for this coverage. If so, your cost for this coverage will be higher than your husband paid. You will pay the group rate for yourself and your dependent children. However, after 36 months, you must find your own insurance, and this can be very expensive.

In some cases, particularly if you are concerned about your health, you might want to go ahead and apply for your own insurance so that you are not in the position of coming to the end of the COBRA protection and find your health will not permit your being insured privately—or at prohibitive rates. If your husband was retired, health insurance may have been one of his retirement benefits.

Long-Term Care Insurance

If your spouse had long-term care insurance, you need to notify the insurance company of his death so they will stop billing you for the premiums. If the premiums were paid quarterly or annually, you should ask the insurance company for a return of unused premiums. If the coverage is joint or "shared" coverage, they need to make the necessary billing changes.

Social Security Administration

If both of you were previously receiving Social Security payments, then you as the survivor may be entitled to receive a higher monthly benefit. At his death you are eligible for 100 percent of his benefits (less if you are between age 62 and your full retirement age). You are not eligible to collect both your benefits and his benefits. To make this change, notify the Social Security office.

The Social Security office will explain this to you in greater detail. The toll-free number for the Social Security Administration is 800-772-1213, and you can call this number weekdays 7:00 a.m. to 7:00 p.m. The Web site is *www.ssa.gov*. However, the line is open 24/7 for certain automated services. These specific services are listed online at the following Web site: *https://www.ssa.gov/agency/contact/phone.html*. Someone from this government organization will be able to answer most of your questions and can refer you to your local office if you want to make an appointment to see a representative. You can apply in person or by phone.

We recommend that you make an appointment to meet with someone at the Social Security Administration office. Claims may be expedited if you go in person to the nearest office to sign a claim for survivor benefits. Social Security employees are very helpful and not intimidating. To file your claim, you will need the following:

- your husband's Social Security number and birth certificate
- your Social Security number and birth certificate
- your husband's death certificate
- your marriage certificate

- the birth certificates and Social Security numbers of your dependent children (if any)
- documentation of your husband's earnings the year he died (if he was still working) as well as the W-2 for the previous year. If your husband was self-employed, there will be no W-2 form available, so bring a copy of last year's tax return instead.

These documents (or certified copies of these documents) will have to be mailed if you apply by phone.

Under present regulations, if you are at least 60 years old, you may claim survivor benefits. However, the amount you receive will be significantly lower than what you would receive if the payments started after you reach your full retirement age (FRA). Currently this FRA is at age 66 to 67, depending on the year in which you were born.

If you are under age 60 and have dependent children who are under the age of 16 or are disabled, you are eligible for a mother's benefit. Your unmarried children will receive benefits if they are under age 18 or up to age 19 if attend secondary school full-time or at any age if they are disabled.

If you are under age 60 and have no dependent children, you are not eligible for any payments, but you should still register your husband's death with the Social Security Administration, so you can apply for the death benefit payment (currently $255). To receive this benefit you need to apply within two years of his death.

You can work while receiving Social Security benefits, and doing so could mean a higher benefit for you in the future. However if you work and have not yet reached your full retirement age, your current Social benefits will be reduced if you earn more than the annual limit. In 2024, the limit is $22,320. (This figure may be increased annually for inflation.) If your earnings exceed the annual limit, your Social Security benefits will be reduced by one dollar for every two dollars your earnings exceed the limit. If you plan to work, you should take this annual earnings limit into consideration. You can read more about Social Security benefits on the Internet *www.ssa.gov.*

Interestingly enough, if your husband was previously married for longer than ten years, his former wife is able to collect from his Social Security benefits as well.

Medicare

The Social Security Administration handles Medicare eligibility and enrollment. You are eligible for Medicare if you are age 65 or older, or if you have received Social Security disability benefits for at least 24 months. Medicare has traditionally had two parts: hospital insurance and medical insurance. Hospital insurance (Part A) helps pay for inpatient hospital care and certain follow-up care. Medical insurance (Part B) pays for physicians' services and some other services not covered by hospital insurance. Medicare offers a third type of coverage (Part D) which provides prescription drug coverage.

In most cases you should opt for Medicare coverage if you are eligible. There is no cost for Part A coverage, but you are charged a monthly premium for Part B, Part C and Part D. In some cases it makes sense to defer enrollment in Part B, Part C and Part D, but it is important to understand the implications of doing so before you take any action.

Veterans Administration

If your husband was a veteran, contact the Department of Veterans Affairs. A toll-free telephone service is available in all states. Most states also provide their own veterans benefits. Both the federal government and the state government will want the same information you furnished the Social Security Administration. If you are eligible for benefits, they will reimburse you for some of the burial and funeral expenses as long as you file a claim within two years after your husband's burial or cremation. You may also be eligible for a pension for yourself or your children. Call 800-698-2411 for VA benefits or visit *www.va.gov*.

Your Husband's Pension Benefits

Whether your husband was still working or was retired when he died, you need to contact the company benefits person at the last place he worked to determine if you should be receiving benefits in the form of pension income, life insurance proceeds, or health insurance coverage.

If you are eligible to receive retirement benefits, you may have to decide how you will receive them from your husband's employer. Usually, you can choose to receive the full amount in either a lump sum or lifetime payments. If you do have a choice, ask for time to consult your financial planner before making this important decision. Most of the time, your money will earn interest until you make the decision.

Your husband may have worked for more than one company and qualified for more than one retirement plan, so it is important to contact all previous employers just in case you might be eligible for retirement benefits from more than one company.

Other Retirement Plans

Your husband may have been self-employed and had a retirement account managed by his financial planner or himself. He also might have had other retirement accounts. If you are uncertain where they are located, last year's tax return can be helpful in obtaining this information.

These accounts are held by a custodian. You need to notify the custodian of your husband's death. The custodian will notify the named beneficiary.

If you are named the beneficiary, these assets can be rolled over into an IRA account in your name. If you are under the age of 59-1/2, you may decide to leave the account in your spouse's name and remain as a beneficiary. That way you will not pay a 10 percent penalty on any withdrawals. You need to consult with your financial planner to help you make the right decision.

What you are trying to establish now is which retirement accounts your husband had and who is the beneficiary of each account. It is a good idea to determine this information as soon as possible even if you don't plan to withdraw any money from these accounts right now. At the same time, if you have any other retirement plans in your own name, you will want to change the beneficiary on these accounts if your husband was the named beneficiary.

Deferred Annuities

A deferred annuity is an investment made with an insurance company where your money earns interest sheltered from current taxation. Your husband may have purchased a deferred annuity through his stockbroker, financial planner, insurance agent, or bank. This investment is usually intended as a supplementary retirement investment because in most cases there are penalties for withdrawing the money before age 59-1/2. When the annuity was purchased, someone was named as beneficiary.

You need to inform the annuity company of your husband's death. The company will require you to send it the death certificate and will notify the beneficiary what options are available. Even if you are not the beneficiary, the proceeds of this annuity are still part of your husband's taxable estate if your husband was the owner of the annuity.

Stockbroker/Financial Planner

Before your husband's death, you or your husband may have worked with a stockbroker. If so, you should inform the stockbroker of your husband's death and ask what paperwork is required to change the name on the account either to an estate account (if it was your husband's account) or to your name (if it was a joint account).

If the assets were in your husband's name alone, then they will go into an estate account and eventually to the heirs once the estate is settled. You or the personal representative can transact business in this account before the estate is settled, but you need the estate tax ID number to do so. The account will be retitled "Estate of John Doe; Mary Doe, Personal Representative."

Ask the stockbroker to value the assets in your husband's account and any joint accounts as of the date of death. The estate valuation for stocks and bonds will be based on the average of the high and low prices on the date of death. If he died on the weekend, you average the high and low prices for Friday and Monday and then average those two prices. For mutual funds, you use the closing price of the date preceding the date of his death.

As we mentioned before, obtaining this information is important because the tax on the estate assets is based on this value or the value of the estate assets six months later. The six months later valuation can be used only when it would reduce the estate tax payable. Further, the value of the assets in the estate used to determine the estate tax bill becomes your cost basis should you sell anything at a later date.

Your husband may have bought limited partnerships or non-traded real estate investment trusts from your stockbroker or financial planner. If so, you need to notify her in writing of your husband's death and ask for an estate valuation as of the date of your husband's death. Request that the units be transferred to the estate name if they were owned by your husband. If the units were in joint name, they can be transferred to your name by the broker or planner, who will advise you as to the information required to affect the transfer. This process varies from company to company, and there may be a charge for the transfer.

Tell the stockbroker you don't want to make any radical moves before you have looked at the total picture. However, if the stockbroker recommends that you sell a particular security sooner rather than later because of negative news about the company, follow that advice. Request that the proceeds be put in an account such as a money market fund which you can easily access if necessary until you finish assessing your financial situation.

Investment Advisors/Money Managers

The terms "investment advisor" and "money manager" are used interchangeably. Investment advisors are paid a fee based on a percentage of money managed. Your husband may have had an investment advisor managing his investments.

You need to notify that investment advisor of your husband's death and ask for an evaluation of his personal investments as of the date of death. In view of your new circumstances, also request written recommendations for any changes in the portfolio that was being managed. Again, this account (if in your husband's name) should be retitled to read "estate of" and should show the new tax ID number for the estate.

Daily Money Managers

As we mentioned previously, Daily Money Managers can help you organize your estate planning paperwork. They can also keep your financial papers in order on an ongoing basis and/or pay your bills. Typically, these daily money managers will charge an hourly fee depending on the complexity of the work. Contact American Association of Daily Money Managers (*Info@aadmm.com*) (814-357-9191)

Bank Trust Officer

Your husband may have been the beneficiary of a trust. The trust document will spell out what is to happen as a result of his death. It is important that you notify the trust officer of your husband's death and ask for a copy of the trust agreement if you are not familiar with its terms.

Your husband may have set up a trust for your benefit and named a bank as trustee. If so, make an appointment to meet with the trust officer so that you can discuss your situation. You will want to know what investment options are available to you, how often you will receive reports, and what the bank's management fees will be. Usually, the bank charges a percentage of the assets to manage the trust and also takes a percentage of the income generated. There is usually a minimum annual fee. Ask for a written schedule of fees for your files.

Often, bank trust officers will invest the trust assets in their own managed funds. You should ask them to give you a written record of how these investments have performed over the past year as well as the past five and ten years. You should have your financial planner review this information for you to assess how well the trust department has managed assets in the past.

Have the trust officer explain how much annual income you might expect to receive from the trust account and how frequently it will be paid. Also ask if the trust document gives you the right to withdraw principal. In most cases, trusts provide the surviving spouse the right to receive the net income (after fees are deducted) earned by the trust as well as the right to access a certain percentage of the principal under certain conditions. Make sure you understand the terms of the trust.

Motor Vehicles

If any of the cars you have were registered solely in your husband's name, you need to notify the local office of your state Department of Motor Vehicles so that the title or registration can be changed. Registration should be in your name when you sell, trade in, or give away the car. If you plan to keep the car and there is an outstanding loan against it, you may choose to keep making payments and delay correcting the registration until you sell the car. These are decisions that should be made with your financial planner.

If your husband's car was leased in his name, you can turn in the car to the car dealership where the car was originally leased. You can terminate the lease, or, if you want to keep the car, the dealership will help you obtain a new lease or let you buy the car outright.

Property and Car Insurance Companies

The insurance on your home, car, and valuables is usually with a different insurance company than the one that provided your husband's life insurance coverage. In addition, you may have your home insurance with a different company than your car insurance. At a future date, you may want to make some changes here, using one company for both types of coverage, but now you need to change the existing policies to delete your husband as an insured party. Presumably, you will need the current level of coverage on your home.

Utility and Telephone Bills

Eventually you will want to change these accounts to your name, but this isn't an urgent matter.

Your Children's Schools

From an emotional as well as a financial point of view, you need to notify the principal or director of your children's schools of your husband's death. If your children attend a private school, you may not be able to afford to keep them there. This is a conversation you need to have with the principal once you know your total situation. After the principal knows your circumstances, then you can have a frank and realistic discussion about your financial options. The principal should also keep you informed of any behavioral or academic changes the children may display after your husband's death.

Following the death of a parent, a child (or children) may display changes in academic achievement and behavior. Some children continue to do well because the school represents the stability that no longer exists at home. Others deteriorate because their emotional upset prevents them from functioning as they have in the past. Some children may no longer be able to maintain their previous level of participation in extracurricular activities. It is important for you to be aware of your children's needs in order to provide them with any assistance in the form of counseling they might need.

Most schools have guidance counselors who meet with children individually or in small groups to deal with issues related to separation and divorce. Some schools provide similar support for children who have experienced the death of a parent.

Clubs, Fraternal Organizations, and Colleges

You should notify all social and business clubs, fraternal organizations, and alumni groups of your husband's death. You may want to remain as a member of the social clubs if eligible. Some offer reduced dues for widows.

Telemarketers

We realize that this last category of people doesn't quite fit in this chapter. However we didn't want to ignore this topic. There are too many stories about widows being victimized by strangers calling them on the phone and trying to sell them something.

If you are receiving unwanted calls from telemarketers, there is action you can take to prevent these calls. The National Do Not Call Registry is managed by the Federal Trade Commission (FTC). You can register up to three personal telephone numbers, including your cell phone. Once you register, telemarketers have 31 days to stop calling you. It does not cost anything, and numbers placed on the registry will remain on it permanently.

You can register online at ***www.donotcall.gov***. If you receive unwanted telemarketer calls more than 31 days after you have registered, you can file a complaint. Note that charities and political organizations are allowed to continue calling you even if you register. If you make a purchase from a company, a representative from that company is also allowed to call you unless you ask the company not to do so.

Summary and Conclusion

By this time, you have set up a work area. You have contacted the people who need to know about your husband's death. Now it is time to organize the information you have gathered so far in order to plan your financial future.

Begin by making a list of people and organizations to notify:

- Banker
- Life insurance agent
- Stockbroker
- Investment advisor/money manager
- Trust officer
- Mortgage holder
- Personnel at children's schools
- Social Security Administration
- Recorder of deeds
- Credit card companies
- Your husband's former employer (If applicable)
- Deferred Annuity company
- State Department of Motor Vehicles
- Property and car insurance companies
- Utility and telephone companies
- Clubs, fraternal organizations, colleges

Now that you have identified your key advisors, make a list of important names and numbers. Put a copy of this list in your file labeled "Professional Contacts" and make sure a responsible person knows where this list is located.

Diane

Reactions to Contacting Agencies
and Resource People

When Diane returned from her initial meeting with her new planner, Dorothy Trumbull, she called Mark's office and asked for the person who handled the firm's insurance plans. She was advised that Karen Hutchinson handled these matters, so she made an appointment to meet with her at the end of the week.

It took a great deal of determination and courage for Diane to cross the threshold of Mark's office. It held so many memories for her. She didn't think she could bear to hear the expressions of condolence and concern from Mark's partners and the murmuring of the secretaries and other support staff to one another, which she was sure identified her as Mark's widow. She was sure they would also be commenting among themselves about her appearance and demeanor.

Diane was relieved that few people she knew were around when she arrived for her meeting with Karen Hutchinson. Karen was ready for her, and, after appropriate but brief condolences, she was all business. She explained that Mark had a life insurance policy with the firm that was worth $800,000. Diane had some options as to how she could receive this money, which the insurance agent handling the firm's account would explain to her. Karen gave Diane the agent's name and phone number. She confirmed that Diane would be able to maintain health insurance for herself and her children through the firm at their group rates for 18 months. Thereafter, she would have to make other arrangements.

In addition, Mark had a retirement account worth about $300,000, which he had managed himself and which was invested in stocks. Karen gave Diane the name and phone number of the stockbroker with whom Mark had worked. Finally, Mark had something called a capital account, which represented his investment in the firm. This account was worth $100,000 and would be available to her in the near future on a tax-free basis.

As Diane sat there and listened to Karen speaking in her dry, matter-of-fact voice, she allowed herself to be encouraged despite her lack of knowledge. By her rough calculations, it appeared that she had $1,200,000 coming to her from the firm. In addition it appeared she would receive $200,000 from Mark's other insurance policies. Surely this would be enough to allow her to keep the children in their present schools. She thanked Karen for her time and the information and prepared to contact both the firm's insurance person, Jack Blafford, and Mark's stockbroker, Scott Truitt.

As she left Mark's office, Diane made a mental note to share her feelings about going into Mark's office at her next widow support group meeting. As she walked toward her car in the parking lot—a familiar route for Diane in the past—she found herself thinking that the woman now crossing the street to the parking lot was not quite the same woman who had been married to Mark, the successful lawyer. Tears welled up in her eyes and rolled slowly down her cheeks. Mark didn't even know the women in the widow support group with whom she now shared her feelings and anxieties. Robyn, the schoolteacher, somewhat older than herself, had discovered that her financial situation was abysmal following her husband's illness and death. However, she was ever ready with a warm smile and words of encouragement for Diane. Marcy, in her late fifties, was eager to do whatever small thing she could to help Diane. Diane had come to rely on these new friends because they understood what she was experiencing. In some ways, she mourned the loss of the old Diane, yet she was finding strengths she never dreamed she had.

In her determination to move ahead in acquiring the financial information necessary to decide about the children's schools, Diane called both the firm's life insurance agent and Mark's stockbroker as soon as she got home. She reached Jack Blafford first and scheduled an appointment with him for the early part of the next week. Then she made an appointment to meet with Scott Truitt for the Friday of the same week.

Diane still had considerable anxiety about going by herself to discuss money matters. But she decided to believe what the women in her support group said about her strengths—they saw her as bright and outgoing. She would "bite the bullet" and try to see the insurance agent by herself. Jack turned out to be a very pleasant, well-dressed man about her age. He explained that she had some choices to make about the insurance money due her. She could receive it as a lump sum and invest it, or she could buy an annuity that would provide her with monthly income for the rest of her life. In fact, he told her that she had several choices as to how to receive the income. Until she decided what she wanted to do with this money, it would be earning interest at the insurance company.

Diane's initial reaction was one of relief. This nice man could handle the insurance for her, and she would not have to worry about managing such a large sum of money herself. She thought investing in the annuity was a good solution, but, to appear more adult, she told him she wanted to think about it for a few days. However, what he had told her made a lot of sense. He was so sympathetic to her situation. After she left, she reminded herself that she had promised Dorothy she wouldn't do anything without at least discussing it with her first. Diane was sure Dorothy would agree with the idea of receiving monthly income from the fixed annuity, but she would run it by her anyway.

Diane felt less secure about dealing with a stockbroker than an insurance agent. She considered asking one of the members of her support group to accompany her on this visit but decided instead to ask the mother of one of Jeremy's friends, Nancy Martin. Nancy was divorced, and Diane knew Nancy was more knowledgeable than she when it came to finances. (Almost anyone would be more knowledgeable than she was, she thought to herself wryly!)

Her appointment with the stockbroker, Scott, to discuss Mark's Keogh plan was not as successful as her meeting with Jack. Scott was a man in his mid-thirties who spoke very rapidly about the investments Mark had made. As nearly as she could determine, Mark had invested in stocks that didn't produce any income. Diane was sure Mark had some reason for doing this but had no idea what it might have been. She did know she needed more information before making any decisions.

As she looked at the list of stocks Scott gave her, the page blurred before her. She had expected to see familiar company names. About 25 different companies were listed, but she had never heard of any of them.

Scott told her this retirement account should be rolled over into an IRA account—whatever that meant—and that she could not start receiving income from this account without paying penalties until she was age 59-1/2. He explained that if she did take money out of this account before that age, then she would be taxed on the income received, and there would be an additional surtax charged on any money she received. (Technical note: If Diane leaves this retirement account in Mark's name, she will not have to pay the 10 percent surtax on her withdrawals, but then she would not be able to name her own beneficiary. There are other exceptions that would allow her to withdraw from her IRA account in her own name before age 59-1/2.)

Diane's spirits sank. If she couldn't access the $300,000 in Mark's retirement account, the $1,400,000 she thought she had available earlier in the week to provide her with income had been reduced to $1,100,000. However, this still seemed like a lot of money.

Based on their meeting she didn't feel that Scott and she could work together effectively. She needed someone who would take the time to explain things to her, and Scott did not seem to be that person. Nancy, who had more experience than she had agreed with her.

Diane took the papers he gave her to complete and decided that she had better see Dorothy sooner rather than later about what action she should take next. As she drove to pick up her children's carpool and drop Nancy off at her office, Diane thought about how much more complicated her life was these days.

Susan

Reactions to Contacting Agencies and Resource People

As promised, Harry's wife, Emily, invited Susan to dinner. She accepted because intellectually she knew she should begin to force herself to socialize with others. Dinner was an emotional struggle for Susan, but she was pleased with herself for having made the effort, and the food was delicious. Susan realized this was the first time since Lance had died that she was aware of what she was eating and how it tasted. During dinner, Susan told Harry and Emily she had set up an appointment with the trust officer at the bank to discuss the $500,000 insurance trust.

Susan asked Harry if he had had a chance to discuss this trust with her two stepchildren—she was very anxious about their reactions. Susan knew that Lance's daughter, Leslie, would be particularly upset because she was entering her senior year of college. The $25,000 in cash left to Leslie would cover most of her college costs for the year. Eventually, Leslie would receive the money from the insurance trust but not until Susan died.

Harry had met with the two stepchildren, and, as Susan had anticipated, they were not pleased with the small amount of money they were to receive in the foreseeable future. They couldn't believe that their father had not left them more! Harry told them that Lance had discussed this with him before making these arrangements. Lance had felt very strongly that it was not good for children to have too much money at an early age. He believed they should make their own way in the world, as he had done. Lance thought that by the time the children received money from the trust they would be mature enough to handle it. Unfortunately, he had not had the chance to tell them this himself and certainly didn't expect to die at this early age.

Susan decided to ask Harry about her mother's situation. Susan was concerned about her mother and felt it was her responsibility to take care of her, even if it meant that she had to personally contribute more to her financial support. It was at times like these that she felt overwhelmed by the tasks ahead of her. She was glad she had Dr. Coleman with whom to discuss these feelings. She wasn't feeling paralyzed and immobile any more, but she did feel reluctant to charge ahead in this unfamiliar territory. She thought she needed to proceed with caution.

Susan hoped that talking to the bank's trust officer would help her understand more about the $500,000 insurance trust Lance had established. She was anxious to know the terms of the trust and what the income from it would be. When she met with Mr. Stepstone, the trust officer, he explained that she would receive income from the trust for life. At her death, her stepchildren would receive whatever principal remained.

Mr. Stepstone said that the trust department would manage the portfolio so that Susan would receive a reasonable amount of income from the money in the trust. He explained that the trust could pay her more income, but that as Trustee he had two responsibilities. The first was to provide her with a reasonable level of income but the second was to preserve and hopefully grow the value of the trust over the years. Susan wasn't sure she wanted the trust to grow—after all, it only meant her stepchildren would inherit more money after she died. Mr. Stepstone explained that in order to increase the annual income, he needed to invest so that the principal would also grow. If he invested the money so that the trust paid a higher income, then the growth potential would be limited. If, on the other hand, the principal increased in value then he expected that the income she would receive would increase over the years.

In his proposed plan, the $500,000 would provide her with some annual income. The management fees for this service would be deducted—50 percent from the income generated by the trust account and 50 percent from the principal.

This approach was reassuring to Susan because she was concerned about meeting her mother's costs in the retirement community, which she knew would increase annually. With the proposed level of income from the trust, it looked as if she could use part of that money to help cover her mother's expenses.

Mr. Stepstone explained that she would receive quarterly statements from the trust department. He would arrange to have the monthly trust income deposited directly into her checking account at the bank. Mr. Stepstone introduced Susan to Ellen Peabody, who would be assigned to manage her account. He told her that he was the head of the trust department and supervised all the accounts, but Ellen would be her personal trust officer and that Susan could call her with any questions she might have.

Next Susan contacted Lance's stockbroker, Bob O'Brien. Following Harry's instructions, she asked Bob to supply her with a current list of Lance's stocks which he told her were worth around $200,000. She also asked him to value the portfolio as of the date of Lance's death. Harry had previously explained to her that because the assets were in Lance's name, these stocks would be valued in the estate as of the date of death or six months later. Harry had told her that the date they chose for valuing the estate assets had to be the same for all estate assets.

During their conversation, Susan asked Bob which stocks he would recommend she sell to raise the $50,000 for her stepchildren. She intended to go over the portfolio in greater detail with him at a later date, but she wanted to make these sales now so she could resolve the situation with them as soon as possible. Bob said he would get back to her with his recommendations as soon as possible.

Susan felt she was making some progress. She had a lot of issues to sort through all at once, and she had to be careful not to neglect her job—after all, she couldn't afford to lose that income. Dr. Coleman had impressed on her that her primary responsibility was to herself, and maintaining her mental health was an important part of that, but she thought Susan was making progress.

Audrey

Reactions to Contacting Agencies and Resource People

John Jr. had asked his mother when she would be ready to sit down with him to review her financial situation, and so far she had been able to postpone this meeting. Fortunately, he hadn't pushed her about it. She realized that he was only trying to help, and she shouldn't be so reluctant to accept his assistance. On the other hand, he was inclined to be somewhat patronizing, and she wanted to sort things out for herself.

Audrey called the Social Security Administration, as Mr. Humphrey, her attorney, had told her to and found that as John's widow she would start receiving $2,000 a month. The person she spoke to told her they would directly deposit the money into her bank account.

Mr. Humphrey told her to call the bank that held their home mortgage. The woman at the bank informed her that the current amount due the bank was $20,000 and that she had eight years left to pay on their 30-year mortgage. She and John had discussed refinancing the mortgage or paying it off, but with John's illness they never got around to making a final decision. She hoped that when she understood her money situation better, she would be in a position to pay it off.

Mr. Humphrey told Audrey that she needed to have the home appraised for the estate valuation. If she decided to sell the home, for tax purposes one-half of the cost of the home would be based on this appraisal and one-half would be based on its original cost plus improvements. Mr. Humphrey also explained that because the home had been their primary residence for two of the past five years and the gain she would realize on the sale of her home did not exceed $500,000, she would owe no capital gains tax. He emphasized that it was important to get an independent appraisal to establish the home's current market value.

It didn't take Audrey long to locate her file with her notes from the retirement lectures given by Mr. Silver, the financial planner. When she called his office and told the receptionist she wanted to meet with him, the receptionist said it might be helpful for Audrey to complete a financial questionnaire before their meeting. Audrey asked if it was mandatory for her to do this before seeing Mr. Silver. The woman assured her that it was not a requirement, but it would make their first meeting more productive. Audrey explained that she had recently been widowed and at this point just wanted to have an initial interview. The receptionist said there would be no problem with that and made an appointment for the following week.

Before Audrey had an opportunity to meet with Mr. Silver, she was contacted by a Mr. Postman, who called her on the phone and said that he worked for a local stock brokerage firm and was sorry to learn of her husband's death. Audrey found this comment a little strange as she had never heard of this man—perhaps he was one of John's friends from Rotary Club. However, as he continued to talk she realized that Mr. Postman did not know her or John; he just read the obituary notices as a way to identify potential clients. She told him firmly but politely that she did not intend to deal with a stranger. She was grateful for the support of the professionals with whom she was working. She was also very pleased with her decision to add what she hoped would be an additional support person by making an appointment to meet with Mr. Silver, the financial planner. She wondered what other widows did who didn't have anyone to trust.

Audrey liked Mr. Silver's initial greeting. His first question was, "How can I help you?" She replied, "I am not quite sure, but I am hoping you can provide me with some advice with regard to my current situation." She explained that her husband had recently died, and she was faced with a number of financial decisions with which she needed help. She told him she had made a list of her questions and would like to go over them with him. He said that that would be a good place to start and complimented her on being so organized at such a difficult time.

Audrey told him about John's pension income and her Social Security income. Audrey mentioned the stock in the company John used to work for as well as the insurance money she had received. She told him of her concerns about Joanne and her anticipation that John Jr. would try to tell her what to do. She wondered if she should sell her home or keep it. Audrey was amazed at all the questions she asked this man whom she had just met, but somehow she really felt at ease with him.

Mr. Silver suggested that she take no immediate action. He told her that in order for him to advise her competently, she needed to fill out the financial questionnaire that would give him a better idea of what her income and expenses might be. At that point, they could determine if she had sufficient income and, ultimately, how best to invest her money. He asked her to fill in as much of the form as she could. If she had trouble, he or his assistant would be glad to help her.

When Mr. Silver asked Audrey how much investment experience she had, she confessed that she had very little. He said that he wanted her to understand what she was doing and assured her that there was no rush to do anything. He recommended that she leave the insurance money with the insurance company, where it would continue to earn interest. Because the company John used to work for was sound financially, he encouraged her to hold that stock for the time being.

Mr. Silver said that with the information she provided he could esti-mate what her taxable income and cash flow would be this year and next. He would also prepare a balance sheet listing her assets and liabilities. In order to do this, he also needed to see their last year's federal and state income tax returns. Audrey gave him the name and phone number of their accountant, Gary Woo. She said she would call Mr. Woo and tell him to send copies of the tax returns to Mr. Silver for his review. Mr. Silver told her that after he reviewed the figures, they could decide together what action to take to ensure that she had an adequate income. To prepare these computations and make recommendations, he would charge her a fee based on the hours needed to prepare her financial plan.

Mr. Silver told Audrey that he would send her a letter of agreement that would outline exactly what services he would provide as well as an estimate of what the final fee would be. This estimate would represent the approximate amount of time he thought it would take to prepare the plan. If the terms in his letter met with her approval, she would sign and return the letter to him, and they could start working on her plan. Audrey liked this approach because it would give her time to discuss the letter of agreement with Mr. Humphrey before she took any final action.

It was just about noon when Audrey left Mr. Silver's office. Dr. PaPadisio's words echoed in her mind, and she thought she should do something about lunch. But what? Should she call Joanne? It was too late to call one of her friends with whom she used to have lunch on a regular basis. She stood on the corner watching people hurry by as the lunch hour began. Rousing herself from her reverie, she decided to call Joanne to ask if she and the younger two children had eaten yet. If not, she thought she'd treat them to a picnic at home. She really hadn't had an opportunity to spend much time with her grandchildren this past year, and it would be fun to see them and have some time to talk to Joanne. Joanne was more than pleased with her mother's suggestion because she was just about to make the children their usual peanut-butter-and-jelly sandwiches for lunch which was their current favorite food. It would be great to have lunch taken care of by her mother. It had been so long since they had done something like that.

Audrey retrieved her car from the parking lot and drove to her favorite delicatessen on her way to Joanne's home. She bought more than they could ever eat and toted the bags to her car in anticipation of surprising the children and her daughter. She felt somewhat lighthearted and allowed herself to enjoy the feeling.

The children were so excited to see her. They jumped up and down and tugged at her skirt. Joanne had to peel them off her legs so she could deposit the bags of food in the kitchen. Little Noah had changed so much since she had really looked at him—he seemed to have jumped from an infant to a toddler. Heidi, at almost four, looked different too. Both of them wanted to drag her off to look at some treasure in their rooms. Joanne allowed "Gran Gran" to be monopolized by the children for a short while before insisting that they all come to the kitchen to eat. The deli sandwiches smelled delicious, and clearly Joanne appreciated the change in daily routine. It turned out to be quite a festive occasion. The children were thrilled with the giant cookies Gran Gran had brought for them.

After lunch, Audrey agreed to read them a story before they lay down for their naps. She told them how much she had missed them and promised to visit again very soon. She thought she would not be there when they awakened from their naps and didn't want them to be disappointed.

Joanne settled the children in their beds for their naps and returned to the kitchen to have tea with her mother. Audrey seemed to be noticing things with new eyes. She had been so preoccupied with John's care, then the funeral, and the sorting out of her financial situation that she had been oblivious to everything else. Joanne looked a little weary, and Audrey felt badly she hadn't noticed earlier. When she asked Joanne if she was all right, her daughter burst into tears and said she was fine, but it was so difficult caring for the three children and simultaneously worrying about how they would manage on Keith's current salary. Also, she had apparently had more of a problem dealing with her father's death than Audrey had realized. They had always been so close.

Audrey put her arms around her daughter and shed some tears of her own. She hadn't thought sufficiently about what Joanne might be going through. As they wiped the tears from their eyes, Audrey shared with Joanne an idea she had just formulated. She told her about Dr. PaPadisio's recommendations about her nutrition. She thought it would be good for them to spend one day a week enjoying lunch and some shopping or whatever. She asked Joanne to find a baby-sitter for the time they would spend together, and Audrey would pay for her. An outing like this would be good for both of them. They really hadn't had time for much mother-daughter togetherness since Joanne had married seven years ago.

Audrey also wanted to have the opportunity to get to know her grandchildren better and proposed to Joanne that she spend half a day a week with the grandchildren. She had always enjoyed participating with her children in their various activities and projects when they were growing up and thought it would be very rewarding to do some of the same things with her grandchildren. If Audrey did this, Joanne could have some time for herself, and Audrey would have an opportunity to do some of the things she had missed doing since her own children were young.

Joanne was touched by her mother's generosity and thought she couldn't allow her mother to do so much for her at this time of stress in her life. Audrey overcame Joanne's reluctance by pointing out that what she was proposing would be beneficial to both of them. This persuaded Joanne to agree. She said she would try to find a sitter so they could get started on their "ladies' day out" as soon as possible. They hugged each other extra hard when Audrey left to return home and walk her dog. While driving home, Audrey considered some of the other things she had been neglecting and determined to make more of an effort to contact some of the women with whom she had formerly been friendly. She knew they had tried to stay in touch, but she just hadn't been ready.

Elizabeth

Reactions to Contacting Agencies and Resource People

Elizabeth wanted to do something for her church because it had meant so much to her to have had Pastor Appletorn's assistance on both a personal and a spiritual level. He had found the time to meet with her and helped her get in touch with her faith. He reminded her of God's plan for all mankind. They talked about how important the church had been to both Ben and herself and that this was a time to lean on both the teachings of the church and members of the congregation. He emphasized that Ben was at peace now. Pastor Appleton had even had one of the members, Lucy Thornton, contact her to spend some time with her and discuss her own personal grief experience since she had lost her husband four years ago. Lucy was so open about her experience. She was able to speak about so many of the feelings Elizabeth had that it made her feel a little less alone. Talking with Lucy made Elizabeth feel somewhat better about facing her situation.

Sam Weatherly accompanied Elizabeth the following Tuesday for her appointment with Mr. Grossfeldt. The atmosphere of the office was leathery but warm. Mr. Grossfeldt explained to her that Ben's account was currently being managed by an investment advisor but in the future she should consider using the services of a bank trust department. He said that banks tend to be conservative, and their approach might be more appropriate at this stage of her life, especially because she had no dependents. He would be glad to introduce her to a trust officer at the bank he had recommended to many of his clients.

Elizabeth told him about her idea of giving Ben's car to the church, and he thought this might be a good idea. He suggested she talk it over with Pastor Appletorn. He might want to sell it and use the proceeds for current church projects. However, before she could do anything, she would have to change the car registration from Ben's name to her name. Elizabeth had a moment of panic—where did Ben keep the registration?

Mr. Grossfeldt also suggested that she consider doing some estate planning of her own. Before they did any of that, however, he thought she should put together the necessary information about her expenses, her income, and her current net worth. In a kindly, nonpatronizing manner he explained to her what each of these terms meant and what she had to do to provide him with the figures. He also made sure she knew where to find the information.

Elizabeth left Mr. Grossfeldt's office greatly relieved and thanked Sam profusely for introducing her to him. She thought that having a bank handle her money might be a good idea—she certainly didn't know anything about investments. She would follow Mr. Grossfeldt's suggestion and meet with the bank trust officer he recommended. Elizabeth needed to get better organized herself before changing advisors. She was most grateful to Sam. What would she have done without his help? Elizabeth told Sam that she thought she could get together the figures Mr. Grossfeldt requested, but that if she had any difficulties, she would like to be able to talk with him. He said in his considerate way that he would be pleased to help her if she needed assistance.

Before going any further, Elizabeth decided to visit her bank and check the contents of the safe-deposit box. Fortunately, before his death, Ben had moved everything into a safe-deposit box in her name, so she had no trouble gaining access to it. Elizabeth found little in the box when she opened it other than a few pieces of Ben's mother's jewelry.

When she was at Mr. Grossfeldt's office, he gave her the federal tax identification number for the estate. Elizabeth gave this number to Ms. Riley, the assistant manager, and she set up an account for Ben's estate into which she should put any checks she received from Ben's estate assets. Ms Riley suggested that she delay closing the joint account for a few months until things settled down. Ms. Riley was very helpful and urged her to call if she had any questions.

Elizabeth was pretty tired by now. She had spent more time with other people than she had in quite some time and had a lot of information to digest. She thought she needed to go home and rest.

As Elizabeth entered the house and was greeted by Mittens, she thought to herself that she felt less like a child related to money matters than at any other time in her life. Normally she would have been in "flight" mode, looking to Abigail or to anyone to make decisions for her. But now she was beginning to feel that perhaps she could begin to make decisions for herself.

CHAPTER SEVEN

Developing a Meaningful Budget

U p until now you have been in the process of accumulating information about your financial situation. Now you are going to use this information to estimate what income you can expect to receive and what you think your expenses will be. Once you have determined what these figures are, then you will be able to know if you have sufficient income on which to live comfortably.

To put together a meaningful budget, you need to do two things. First, you need to list your projected income sources. Then review your checkbook for the past year to determine what your expenses have been. Keep in mind if your husband had been ill for an extended period of time, your recent expenses may not adequately reflect your current or future financial needs. With this information, you should be able to project future income and expense items. We have provided you with sample forms at the end of this chapter to help you to complete this task.

If you discover you need more income than you are currently receiving, in the next chapter we will review your assets and liabilities to determine if any of them could or should be changed to provide you with additional income.

Projected Income Sources

To put together a realistic budget for the future, we suggest that you start a new notebook or create a new computer record, so this information does not get mixed in with the estate settlement issues.

When you contacted Social Security, the Veterans Administration (if applicable), and your husband's former employer(s), you found out how much income you could expect from each source and when payments would start. List these sources and the amount and frequency of the payments in the notebook or computer record.

Under the Income category, list all income you are sure you will receive. If you work, include your employment income. If you are self-employed, list your net income (the gross amount earned less expenses). If you have other sources of income, list them as well. Also list how often the income is paid: monthly (M), quarterly (Q), semiannually (SA), or annually (A).

There may be a time lag before you start receiving the income from your husband's assets. This means for a short period you may have to live on cash reserves. Be careful to keep a record of any cash you receive during this period and its source. With money coming in from various places, you may inadvertently spend principal, which you may need later. If you are concerned about whether or not you will have enough money to pay all your bills, ask your financial advisor what to do. Paying the wrong bills may be a problem later.

Current Expenses

Before estimating what your current expenses are, you need to list your current outstanding bills. As we discussed before, divide them into your bills, your husband's bills, and joint bills. If your husband had outstanding medical and hospital bills, they should be paid from the estate asset account.

Fixed Expenses

In order to project future expenses, first you need to review what your current expenses are. The easiest place to start is with your fixed expenses—those you are committed to pay at regular intervals. Some of them are due monthly; others, such as household and car insurance payments, are due annually, quarterly, or even monthly.

Typical fixed monthly bills include the mortgage or rent, car payments, and utilities. These expenses are fixed because you must pay them each month, but the amount may vary each month. If you want to have predictable monthly payments, contact the utility companies. Ask them to review your past bills and put together a monthly payment schedule for you that will require equal monthly payments. In this way, you can avoid receiving an unanticipated high bill in any month.

You may also need to make quarterly federal and state tax payments, which your accountant will estimate for you. (If you don't have an accountant, you may want to consult with one at this time.) Mark in your notebook and on your monthly calendar when these bills should be paid. Later, when you pay them, enter the amount paid and the date.

Record in your notebook or on your computer an inventory of your fixed expenses.

Discretionary Expenses

Discretionary expenses vary from month to month. These would include groceries, meals eaten out, clothing, dry cleaning, entertainment, vacations, personal care (health club, hairdresser, and drugstore), dues and subscriptions, cleaning people, gifts, and credit card debt, if any. Look at your checkbook to see what these have been in the past, and list them in your notebook. You may want to use one page in your notebook or in your computer for each category. These expenses will probably change in your current situation, but to estimate future expenses, it is helpful to look at past expenses first.

Projected Fixed Expenses

Mortgage Payments and Real Estate Taxes

If you own your own home, when you notify your mortgage company of your husband's death, ask for an explanation of what your current payment includes. Real estate taxes and homeowners' insurance are often included in the payment. Clarify whether your mortgage company is paying the real estate tax or if you are expected to pay it. If the mortgage company is paying, the lender estimates what your real estate taxes will be and incorporates them into your monthly mortgage payments. Once a year the lender looks at the actual real estate taxes you owed versus the estimated amount and makes any necessary adjustments to your payments.

If you are responsible for paying the real estate taxes, they are usually due annually or semiannually. If so, this expense should be included in your budget to avoid the shock of receiving an unexpectedly large tax bill.

You need to know the terms of your mortgage loan. On your monthly statement, or at least annually with your year-end statement, your mortgage company sends you a statement of how much principal you still owe, how many years are left on the mortgage note, and what your current interest rate is.

Interest rates on some mortgage loans change periodically. These are known as adjustable-rate mortgages (ARMs). You need to know if this might happen to you and, if so, when. You might even have an interest-only mortgage where you are paying interest but no principal. If you don't understand the terms of the mortgage (nowadays they are not always easy to figure out), have your accountant or financial planner interpret them for you and explain them to you in writing.

To develop a meaningful budget for the future, you need to know if your mortgage payment might increase or decrease. Many widows panic over the size of these payments. If they have the money available, they may want to pay the mortgage off right away. Usually, this is not a good idea. These payments provide you with tax deductions that you may well need. This is another major decision that should be made only after looking at the total picture. Right now you're trying to determine what bills you must pay on a monthly basis.

Home Equity Loans (HEL)/
Home Equity Line of Credit (HELOC)

A home equity loan (HEL) is a lumpsum payment to the homeowners, at a fixed interest rate, which is repaid over a time of between ten to twenty years. This loan has to be paid off if the home gets sold prior to the payments being completed.

A home equity line of credit (HELOC) is a revolving line of credit which allows homeowners to borrow against their home equity during a set period of time (usually ten years). During the draw period monthly payments are for the interest on the loan only and no principal is repaid. At the end of the draw period, you must start repaying whatever you still owe, typically over twenty years.

Both these home equity loans are usually from a bank other than the one that holds your mortgage and are issued at a higher interest rate compared to your primary mortgage.

If you have a home equity loan, ask the lender to spell out its terms and conditions. If you have a financial planner, ask her to look at the terms of this loan right away; because this loan might be one you want to pay off or change.

Reverse Mortgages

A reverse mortgage is a loan against your primary residence that is available to homeowners age 62 or older who have at least 50 percent equity in their home. With a reverse mortgage, you can convert the equity in your home into money you can access as a lump sum, a monthly payment, or a line of credit. The money you receive is tax free and you do not have to make principal or interest payments as long as you live in your home. The interest you are charged may be fixed or variable (the interest rate can go up or down).

The maximum payout for which you'll qualify depends on your age (the older you are, the more you'll be eligible to borrow), the current interest rate and the appraised value of your home.

One drawback to taking out a reverse mortgage is the upfront fees. These costs can be rolled into the loan but that will reduce the proceeds available to you.

If you had a reverse mortgage when your husband died, you do not have to pay off the loan while you are still living in your home as long as you maintain it in good condition and pay the insurance and your property taxes.

When you die or no longer live in your home, all of the money you borrowed, plus interest, must be repaid. You or your heirs will never owe more than your home's value. If the loan balance is greater than what the home is currently worth, you or your heirs can sell the home for at least

95 percent of the latest appraised value and the mortgage insurance purchased when the reverse mortgage was issued will pay off the balance.

However, if you have to go into a nursing home or if you move but continue to own your home, the lender will require you to pay off the loan after 12 months. This means that unless you have other money available to pay off the loan, you may be forced to sell your home.

Projected Discretionary Expenses

Look at the expenses that seem necessary now but may not be in the future. For instance, it may not be essential to maintain two cars, keep a second home, or remain a member of a club. Again, these are decisions to make after you have gathered all the facts.

Spending money on groceries is not discretionary, but the amount you spend is. Your costs should be lower now because you are feeding one less person. On the other hand, other expenses may increase. For example, if you owned your own home and your husband was an avid gardener, but you don't know the difference between a weed and a plant, you may have to hire someone to help you take care of the garden, which will be an increased expense.

A word of caution: We strongly recommend that you postpone major purchases until you know your total financial picture. The money you spend now on luxuries may be needed later for necessities.

When you estimate your future discretionary expenses, we suggest you put down two budget figures: (column 1) the minimum amount you could live on and (column 2) the amount you would like to spend (including things you can do without if necessary)

Comparing Your Estimated and Actual Expenses

In the first few months following your husband's death, it is important for you to keep a record of how you actually spend your money and then compare it with your estimated expenses. You may be surprised at some of the differences between the two sets of figures. We suggest you make a page in your notebook or on your computer for each expense category and then, as you pay each bill or spend cash, make a record of it. To make this record keeping easier, ask for receipts for everything. Keep records together for each expense category. For example, "Groceries".

Once a month total each expense category and see how close you came to your initial estimate. There is no right or wrong here. Most widows find they have overestimated in some categories and underestimated in others. Initially, your grocery bills may be low because friends bring you food or invite you for dinner or you don't feel like cooking. After a while, this expense will return to something more typical for your new circumstances.

At the end of six months, review your initial estimates, compare them with the actual expenditures and develop a new budget, which should be more accurate. Then check this new budget every six months. After a while, you won't need to keep such close tabs on your expenditures. However, don't lose sight of the fact that it is essential to your future financial security to know how you spend your money.

Cash Flow Statement

Now that you have calculated your income and expenses, you want to total both categories and find out if you have more than enough income (excess income) or insufficient income (excess expense).

This initial estimate of income and expenses will give you a better idea of your current financial situation. However, don't panic if you have a negative cash flow. You are still in the fact-gathering stage.

Conversely, after putting this statement together, you may find that you have sufficient income to cover your current expenses. Although this information is comforting, you must keep your long-term situation in mind. Typically, expenses increase each year. What is sufficient income today may not be ten years from now. Furthermore, there are always unplanned expenses for which you may not have budgeted but that must be covered.

When planning, make sure your income keeps pace with increasing expenses. If the cost-of-living increases at 3 percent annually, you will need 50 percent more after-tax income 14 years from now just to buy the same things you are buying now. In other words, if $50,000 is sufficient annual after-tax income today, you will need $75,000 14 years from now. In addition, periodically taxes (federal and state income, property, and sales) increase, and you need to keep this in mind when developing your budget.

On the next few pages, we have provided you with some sample forms to help you develop your own budget. Not all items apply to everyone.

Sources of Income

	Amount	When Paid (M) (Q) (SA) (A)
Your Salary	$_____	_____
Annual Bonus	$_____	_____
Net Self-Employed Income	$_____	_____
Social Security	$_____	_____
Retirement Pension	$_____	_____
Trust Income	$_____	_____
Stocks	$_____	_____
Bonds	$_____	_____
Mutual funds	$_____	_____
Other _____	$_____	_____
Total	$_____	_____

Inventory of Fixed Expenses

	Amount Due	Date Next Due	When Due (M) (Q) (SA) (A)
Mortgage payment	$_____	_____	_____
Home equity loan	$_____	_____	_____
Homeowner fee	$_____	_____	_____
Rent	$_____	_____	_____
Utilities	$_____	_____	_____
Gas/heating	$_____	_____	_____
Electric	$_____	_____	_____
Water	$_____	_____	_____
Telephone	$_____	_____	_____
Cable	$_____	_____	_____
Internet service	$_____	_____	_____
Loan payments	$_____	_____	_____
Car payments	$_____	_____	_____
Others	$_____	_____	_____
Insurance premiums	$_____	_____	_____
Medical	$_____	_____	_____
Life	$_____	_____	_____
Disability	$_____	_____	_____
Long-term care	$_____	_____	_____
Homeowners	$_____	_____	_____
Car/Boat	$_____	_____	_____
Personal Liability	$_____	_____	_____
Other _____	$_____	_____	_____
Taxes	$_____	_____	_____
Real estate	$_____	_____	_____
Personal property	$_____	_____	_____
Federal	$_____	_____	_____
State	$_____	_____	_____
Other _____	$_____	_____	_____
Total	$_____	_____	_____

Inventory of Discretionary Expenses

	Total Last 12 Months	Monthly Average
Groceries	$	$
Clothing	$	$
Home/yard	$	$
Home improvements	$	$
Car maintenance	$	$
Entertainment	$	$
Dues (club, professional)	$	$
Subscriptions, books	$	$
Vacation trips	$	$
Domestic help	$	$
Household purchases	$	$
Gifts, birthdays	$	$
Laundry/Dry cleaning	$	$
Pharmacy	$	$
Hairdresser, nail care	$	$
Transportation	$	$
Yard maintenance	$	$
Education	$	$
Club Dues	$	$
Unreimbursed medical expenses	$	$
Childcare/activities	$	$
Charity (cash/noncash)	$	$
Tax preparation fee	$	$
Unreimbursed business expenses	$	$
Legal fees	$	$
Accounting fees	$	$
Financial planning fees	$	$
Finance charges (credit cards)	$	$
Parking	$	$
Total	$	$

Cash Flow Statement

Cash Flow Statement as of:_____

For:_____

Estimated Income: $_____

                                              $_____

Estimated Expenses:

  Fixed $_____

  Discretionary $_____

                                    Total $_____

Excess income or Excess expense $_____

Summary and Conclusion

In this chapter, you put together your budget. First you itemized your current outstanding bills and determined which ones to pay and which ones to defer. Then you estimate what your future monthly income will be. Finally, you determined what your monthly expenses have been and what you estimate they will be in the future. These estimates will indicate if you have sufficient income to maintain your current lifestyle or if you have to make some adjustments.

Diane

Reactions to the Budgeting Process

Diane had a difficult time putting together her budget. She had never had to keep track of expenses. She just spent money on items needed for the home and the children, and Mark paid the bills. There always seemed to be enough, so she didn't worry about money. She had taken the children's need for a private school education for granted because she and Mark had decided it was preferable to the education provided by the public schools. For Diane, whether or not the children went to private schools was unrelated to cost—that had always been Mark's department. She was beginning to recognize that it was that way about everything related to money.

A part of Diane wished she could return to her former mode of functioning, but another part of her resented the fact that she had allowed herself to be treated like a child when it came to anything financial. She could still see Mark seated at his desk in the den paying the bills and telling the children, if they interrupted him, he couldn't talk to them right then because he had bills to pay. As disloyal as she felt, Diane realized she was sometimes angry with Mark for leaving her in this mess. At first she couldn't tolerate anyone saying anything the slightest bit negative, about Mark, but now she was finding herself angry with him for the financial mess with which she needed to deal. When she first heard the women in her widow support group talk about the anger they sometimes felt toward their husbands for abandoning them and leaving them to deal with all of life's problems, she couldn't relate to what they were experiencing. She thought they hadn't been fortunate enough to be married to someone like Mark. They told her she'd have similar feelings at some point in the grieving process, but she had rejected what they said as being something they were feeling because of their particular situations.

Here she was, several months later, having the very response she had initially defended herself against with her group. Actually, she didn't know how she would have managed without this group, and particularly

Robyn, these past months. They had become such good friends. Robyn was so understanding. She could talk to her about anything. Jennifer Greenberg had also become a friend. She, too, always made the time to be helpful and available. Diane couldn't believe that now the majority of her social contacts were with people Mark didn't even know. She'd have to think about this further, but right now she had to look at private school education on a dollars-and-cents basis. Everything seemed to be so expensive.

At the urging of Dorothy Trumbull, Diane had gone to the Social Security office to ask what she could expect to receive from Social Security. It was difficult to understand because the amount of money she and the children would receive seemed to keep changing. However, she realized she needed to understand how it worked, so she wrote it down carefully in her notebook.

The bottom line was that Social Security was going to provide her and the children with a monthly income. However, as each child turned 18, the amount they as a family received would decrease. When the youngest, Alice, turned 16, Diane's survivor benefit would end, though she would still receive a benefit on Alice's behalf for two more years. This meant Diane would receive no Social Security benefits as Mark's widow from age 51 until she turned 60, The idea of having no income from Social Security for those nine years was scary, This was all so confusing—what should she do? She couldn't think that far ahead. Even worse, Diane discovered she could lose her portion of the benefits if she worked and earned more than Social Security allowed.

Diane's head began to swim. She really didn't know how she could handle all of this complexity. She knew she had to understand it for the children's sake, so she promised herself that she'd review the information she had obtained to date.

The life insurance agent had told Diane that the $800,000 policy Mark had from the firm could provide her with a lifetime annuity income.

She vaguely remembered signing some papers Mark had given her last year which he said lowered their mortgage payment. Thank goodness for that. if she picked this option, it looked like the family would have to live on the difference between the income she would receive from the annuity payment and the Social Security payments and her mortgage payment

In addition to the cost of the three children's tuitions, there were camp and piano lessons. Maybe she should just pay the tuition for the next year and worry about it later. This was all too much! How would she ever work this all out? Diane wasn't a financial genius, but she didn't think they could live on this amount of monthly income especially with the tuition payments. The only other money she had was the capital account of the firm and the proceeds from Mark's personal insurance policies. She knew she didn't want to touch Mark's retirement account because of the IRS penalties. That was one thing she did understand. Perhaps she didn't have a choice. She made an appointment to see Dorothy right away to find out how she could cover her expenses.

Diane and Mark had put a deposit on a beach home for a couple of weeks for the summer. This would be an opportunity for the family to be together, so that seemed to her to be a necessary expense. She dreaded the thought of going through Christmas without Mark; it was his favorite holiday. They had planned to take the family skiing. She was tempted to do it anyway so they wouldn't be haunted by the memories of Christmases past. Enough! She had to focus on her financial situation.

Dorothy gave Diane a cash-flow statement, which she emphasized was very preliminary. The bad news was that her expenses would exceed her income by a considerable amount. Needless to say, Diane was really upset when she saw this, as she thought the expense estimates she had given Dorothy were very low. They certainly were less than the family had spent when Mark was alive.

Her situation was obviously a lot worse than she thought. Diane tried not to panic. Her biggest expense was private school tuition for the children. Perhaps they would have to go to public school. She might even have to sell their beautiful home and move to a less expensive one. Maybe her father could help out with the expenses, although she certainly didn't want to admit to him that Mark had not provided adequately for her and the family (even though it was beginning to look that way). The fact was that they had no idea he would die so young—had they known they would have bought more insurance! (Editorial comment: The reason many younger couples are underinsured is that they reject the possibility that they may die prematurely!)

Dorothy suggested that Diane review her expense estimates to see if she could reduce them. For instance, if she paid off her credit card debt she would not have to pay the annual high interest rate. Dorothy had some ideas about selecting other investments that might provide more income than the annuity and the money market accounts. She would work on increasing the income side of the cash-flow statement while Diane agreed to work on decreasing her expense estimates.

Dorothy said that she hated to be the bearer of such bad news, but if they both worked hard trying to solve this cash-flow problem, she knew that they would be successful. She also suggested to Diane that in fact she was more fortunate than some widows because she did have money available to her. It was their mutual goal to maximize how it would be used. It was difficult for Diane not to be disheartened as she

left the office, but she resolved to review the budget once again. Although she didn't want to worry them too much, she thought the time had come to discuss the situation with the children.

Susan

Reactions to the Budgeting Process

Susan needed to review their expenses as a couple so she could determine what her new budget would be. At the same time, Susan was worried about supporting her mother since she and Lance had been paying the difference between her mother's monthly income and the cost of her retirement home.

Mr. Stepstone, her bank trust officer, told her that the trust could provide her with sufficient monthly income to help meet her mother's financial needs for the present. Susan was comforted by this information, but she still was concerned about costs for her mom's care rising in the future when and if she needed assisted living care.

In her sessions with Dr. Coleman, Susan was beginning to identify the various ways she dealt with stress and life in general. She had become aware of her tendency to assume full responsibility for things when there was no need to do so. Her mother's financial support was a good case in point. Why had she assumed all of the responsibility for her mother? Her brother, Ron, was single and had no financial obligations other than his own expenses, yet she had never considered discussing with him either the selection of a retirement facility or its cost. She thought it had something to do with the fact that Ron led his own life and was detached from her and their mother.

Here she was charging ahead again and assuming more responsibility than was warranted. Although Ron had never assumed responsibility for their mother on either a financial or personal level, she thought it was time to make him aware of their mother's monetary needs. She decided to ask him to help her financially; his contributing even a small amount would be helpful.

Susan had not been her usual effective self in her job recently, but her boss and co-workers had been very understanding. She found herself working longer hours but accomplishing less. In this area, too, it had been helpful to discuss her feelings with Dr. Coleman. In the past, if she was not working to capacity at all times, she felt guilty. Dr. Coleman was helping her realize that she placed unreasonable demands on herself. Using the analogy of a machine, she reminded Susan that only machines worked at a constant pace, completing the same process without variation. She stressed to Susan that she was not a machine but a human being. There was no need to feel guilty about her decreased functioning on the job. She had suffered a major loss with no warning.

Susan was surprised that Dr. Coleman thought her employer and co-workers would not expect her performance on the job to be quite what it was before Lance's death. She assured her that what she perceived as job inefficiency was not a permanent condition and she would return to her normal functioning as time passed. Susan was beginning to accept the fact that she had always been exceptionally demanding of herself, and she wondered what factors in her life had led her to act this way.

She would have to explore this issue further, but for now she needed to address her financial situation.

When Susan put together her current budget, she had a negative cash flow. Given these figures, it was pretty obvious she could not afford to keep the lake cottage she and Lance had bought. Emotionally, she did not want to sell it because it held so many memories of the happy times she had there with Lance. Perhaps she would also have to sell their condominium, which she really loved. She had become attached to the beautiful view and the space of two bedrooms. It certainly was much more comfortable than the one-bedroom apartment she lived in before marrying Lance.

But facts were facts. It appeared she did not have enough income to support her current lifestyle. Maybe she could find a smaller apartment in the same building, or maybe she should look for a better-paying job—a thought that had not previously crossed her mind. In any case, Susan resolved to keep careful records of how she spent her money.

Thank goodness the Association where she worked paid her insurance premiums (medical, disability, and life). It also matched her contributions to her 401(k) savings plan 25 cents on the dollar for the first $4,000 she contributed. She knew she was allowed to contribute more to her 401(k) than she had been doing. Up to now, she had only contributed the $4,000 that the Association matched since she knew Lance had a good retirement fund. Now it appeared she couldn't even afford to contribute that much.

As for her personal income, Susan thought her salary was pretty secure. She had been at the Association for ten years and had received regular raises.

Audrey

Reactions to the Budgeting Process

Audrey looked at her sources of income, and it seemed as if she had enough to pay her expenses. John's pension would provide her with monthly income for the rest of her life. Since she was only 62 years old, she could also receive 82 percent of his Social Security payment. The Social Security representative told her this payment usually would increase at the beginning of each year in accordance with the cost-of-living adjustment (COLA). (Note that since the cost of living did not increase in 2009, 2010 and 2014, there were no increases in Social Security payments in 2010, 2011 and 2015.)

Audrey reviewed her checkbook for the past year and put together her expenses for Mr. Silver to review. It was obvious to her that they would be higher in the future since she had done little else besides caring for John over the past couple of years. She had not spent much on clothes, they had done no entertaining, she had not had the time or inclination to go to their club, and they had taken no vacations. These were all expenses she expected would increase in the coming year.

Thinking about her lifestyle reminded Audrey of the invitation she had reluctantly accepted to attend a small dinner party given by one of their closest friends. It had felt very different going to a dinner party by herself. She realized not being part of a couple was an adjustment. She didn't really feel terrible—it was just a new role and one to which she would need to become accustomed. Everyone had been very nice, almost too solicitous. As always, Peg had prepared a great dinner. The only really awkward note was the undue attention paid to her by Walter and his wife Jane's very negative response to his behavior. Audrey thought Jane acted as if Audrey was going to take her husband from her! However, Audrey did have to admit that Walter almost made a fool of himself being attentive to her. Their other friends treated her as they had in the past, but she knew she wasn't the same person. She was sure this type of social activity would feel better to her as time went on and she was more comfortable with herself.

Audrey was also pleased with herself for deciding to do volunteer work for the symphony. She was working on the membership committee. One of her close friends, Claudia, had always worked to raise money for the symphony and had encouraged Audrey to volunteer some time to this group. She had enjoyed meeting the women and getting out one day a week to work with them. She became friendly with Heather, another widow with whom she worked. Often they went out to lunch following their work, or she and Claudia would plan to do something.

Audrey was feeling better about the way she was spending her time. Her next step was to call the "Reading Is Fundamental" people. She had seen a small piece about this children's literacy organization on TV and the concept really appealed to her. However, none of her friends or acquaintances did any work with RIF, so she would be going into it cold— on her own. It felt like a big step. She would be trying something totally new. She knew she was almost ready to contact the group.

On the activity side, she was pleased to learn from Mr. Silver that she would have no problem maintaining her country club membership. The dues were not high, and she could easily manage the expense. She had gotten back into playing golf, which she had been forced to give up during John's illness because of time constraints. She had forgotten how much she enjoyed it. The women in her former foursome were pleased to have her back since the woman they had added in her absence had not worked out. They were now talking about taking a golf clinic at some place such as Hilton Head. She liked the idea; it would be great to get away for a while. She hadn't been anywhere in at least a year and a half. She didn't think it would be difficult for her to go on this trip because she had been friendly with these women for most of her adult life. They had raised their children together and shared the joys as well as the trials and tribulations of daily life as wives and mothers. They all knew each other very well and usually had a lot of fun. She remembered a time about two years ago when a group of them had gone off for a golf weekend and spent most of their time laughing.

Because it appeared that she had enough income to live on comfortably, Audrey thought about helping educate Joanne's children. John Jr.

could provide for himself and his family, but Joanne's husband, Keith, didn't make much money, and his prospects for promotion didn't look good. Joanne wanted to send both the younger children to preschool. Earlier, before John had become so ill, Joanne had asked if her parents could help out with the payments for Heidi's preschool. Audrey knew things must have been bad for Joanne to admit she needed assistance. She decided to ask her to be more specific about how much preschool would cost. Audrey wanted to help Joanne, but she also wanted to be fair to John Jr. and his children. She thought she could afford to give them both some money each year without sacrificing her lifestyle but wasn't sure of the best way to go about this. She decided to ask Mr. Silver for his advice.

When Audrey met with Mr. Silver, she gave him her expense figures for the past two years and told him she anticipated spending more in the future on food, clothes, entertainment, and vacations. She also told him she wanted to become more involved in charitable work and give more to charities if she could afford to do so.

Audrey asked Mr. Silver about the best way to help pay for the education of Joanne's preschool-age children. Mr. Silver explained that under current tax law (2024), she could give as much as $18,000 each to John Jr. and Joanne annually. Audrey would not get a tax deduction for giving it, but they would not have to pay taxes on receiving it. If she paid the tuition direct to the school, this payment would be in addition to the $18,000 gift with no adverse tax consequences.

He said he wanted to look at Audrey's estimated income and expenses more closely before giving her a final number, but right now it looked as if she could give Joanne some additional income this year. This amount seemed more appropriate for her budget at this time.

Mr. Silver recommended that if she decided to give this money to Joanne, she discusses it with John, Jr. first. Although he didn't need the money, talking it over with him first could avoid family arguments later. He also suggested that when Audrey spoke to her children about her desire to give annually, she should tell them that she was able to do this now because she had enough income to cover her expenses. However, because the major source of her income was John's pension money and the payments would not increase from current levels, she should explain to them there might come a time in the future when she could not be as generous.

Audrey decided to talk this over with Joanne and John Jr. and made another appointment to meet with Mr. Silver. He wanted to discuss a more realistic budget for her once she provided him with better expense estimates.

Elizabeth

Reactions to the Budgeting Process

It appeared to Elizabeth that her situation was pretty simple. She had two primary sources of income: Social Security and income from Ben's stock portfolio. Ben's portfolio was handled by someone called an investment manager. He told her that Ben's stocks could provide her with monthly income. Ben had never set up a retirement fund at his company, so there was no income from that source.

Mr. Grossfeldt, her new lawyer, gave her a form to complete so he could help her estimate what her expenses might be in the future. In order to complete this form, she went to Ben's scarred roll top wooden desk, she took out their checkbook and she reviewed their past expenses. She knew that her future expenses would be different. While Ben was sick, she had bought no clothes, they rarely went out, and they never entertained—so they spent very little money. She couldn't remember when she had last spent time with the "girls." She had let all her friendships lapse over the past few years because watching out for Ben had taken up all of her time. She had really enjoyed her sewing circle and now realized how much she had missed those get-togethers.

Elizabeth had tried to keep her church activities up but had not been very successful in doing so since Ben didn't like her to be away from him for any longer than an hour, and it was easier to comply than argue. She was beginning to reconnect with the church but didn't know how much time she would spend on church-related activities in the future.

There was no mortgage on the home, so she didn't have that expense. She would need to review how much she had spent on help for the various things that Ben had once done such as taking care of the yard, shoveling snow, etc. A neighborhood boy who had been taking care of their small garden was going off to college in the fall. All in all, it appeared she could afford to continue living in her home, but she wondered if she wanted to do so. She felt as if she were rattling around in all those rooms.

Her older sister, Abigail, enjoyed living in her retirement community in Florida and was urging Elizabeth to visit her. The idea of warm weather after the bitter New England winters appealed to Elizabeth. Ben had refused to visit Abigail, to the point where the effort to convince him to take the trip outweighed the pleasure of visiting with her sister.

In the past few years, because of Ben's deteriorating health, the couple had spent most of their time at home. Although she was basically a homebody, Elizabeth secretly yearned to take a cruise. She wondered if it was foolish of her to consider taking such a trip now at her age. She didn't think she had the courage to take one alone, but maybe she could talk Abigail into joining her. During their marriage, she and Ben never took trips—he always said he couldn't be away from work that long—but she suspected he really didn't like the idea of being someplace unfamiliar.

When Elizabeth added up her projected annual income and compared it to her general living expenses, it appeared she would have more than enough income to cover her expenses. Mr. Grossfeldt had given her the name of an accountant he used, Mrs. Greenfield, to work on her taxes.

Elizabeth contacted Mrs. Greenfield and made an appointment to see her. She surprised herself by not needing to be accompanied by a more knowledgeable individual. When they met, Mrs. Greenfield suggested Elizabeth apply for a credit card, one that would earn her miles on an airline. She recommended that she charge everything she could on this card and then pay it off once a month (thus avoiding interest charges). That way she could keep track of what her expenses actually were as well as get credited with air miles and thus possibly earn a free air ticket to Florida.

Elizabeth had had more meetings and discussions with people related to money matters since Ben died than she had had in her entire life. She appreciated the fact that none of these people made her feel stupid. They all treated her considerately and took the time to explain things to her. She felt she had learned so much these past few months. She was even less afraid to talk about money.

She had even developed a new friendship with another recent widow, Lucy. Since Lucy looked at life and death in a positive way she was a good role model for Elizabeth. For the first time since Ben's death, she started thinking positively about her future.

Abigail had continued to press her about visiting her in Florida. Now that it appeared she could afford to do so, she decided she was ready to travel. Visiting her sister in Florida, maybe even taking a cruise, possibly moving to a warmer climate—all of that sounded pretty good to her. She felt so fortunate that it appeared that financially she had so many options!

CHAPTER EIGHT

Calculating Your Net Worth

When you calculated your expenses and income, you might have discovered (as Diane and Susan did) that there does not seem to be enough income to cover your expenses. The next step is to determine what assets you have that might provide you with sources of income besides Social Security. To do this, you need to figure out your net worth. Calculating your net worth is simply listing what you own and then subtracting from that number the amount you owe.

Assets are defined as anything you own that has commercial or exchange value if you sell it. Thus, when you value personal assets such as jewelry and furniture for the purposes of an asset statement, think in terms of resale value rather than replacement value. (If you are itemizing personal assets for insurance purposes, you would list them at replacement value). When you list your assets, it is a good idea to indicate ownership as well—that is, your assets (P = Personal), your husband's assets (E = Estate), and your joint assets (J = Joint).

In this chapter we describe the kinds of assets and liabilities you might have. At the end of the chapter, we provide you with a sheet where you can list your personal assets and liabilities.

Personal Assets

Your Home

For your residence, you should indicate ownership, approximate market value, original cost, and any major improvements you have made. (If you don't know the cost of improvements, approximate the cost.)

If the home was held jointly, one-half the cost is based on the original cost plus improvements, and one-half is the current value in the estate. Taking advantage of this so-called stepped-up basis for the cost of your home can be helpful in reducing or eliminating any capital gains tax you might incur if and when you decide to sell your home.

If you have a second home that is primarily for personal use and/or if you own time-shares in a vacation home, you need to list similar information for these assets. If the property is primarily a rental property, you would list it under "investment real estate."

Personal Property

Personal property includes your cars, home furnishings, jewelry, furs, antiques, oriental rugs, and art in your home. At a later date, you might decide you don't need as many cars as you now have, but at this point you are just identifying what you currently own. (You may find that your car is worth less than the amount you owe on it.)

If one or more of your cars are leased, you should indicate the terms of the lease, which would appear in your lease agreement. If you are unable to find this agreement, call your leasing agent to obtain a copy of the agreement.

A rough estimate of your personal property will do. Under the category "Other" we are including jewelry, furs, antiques, oriental rugs, or art you may have in your home.

Personal Investments

Cash

Here you would list your checking accounts, savings accounts, money market funds, certificates of deposit, U.S. Treasury bills or notes, and any money due to be paid to you in the next 12 months. This would include the proceeds of any insurance policies payable to you, a trust, or the estate.

A rule of thumb is to keep a cash reserve that equals three to six months' expenses. However, we have found the actual amount of cash reserve you would like to have is an emotional as well as financial decision. Some people are not comfortable unless they have a lot of cash available. Others require smaller amounts. At this point of uncertainty and change in your life, you may prefer to have a larger cash reserve. Once you have a better idea of your expenses, you may choose to decrease the amount of cash reserve you feel you need.

Once you have determined how much you need to have in your cash account in order to feel comfortable, keep this amount in a savings account or invested in a money market account, where it is readily accessible and earning interest. This cash reserve would be available to cover any expected or unexpected large expenses, such as replacing your furnace or a major car repair. Having this cash reserve prevents you from having to liquidate an investment at an undesirable time. Besides, having a cash cushion should give you peace of mind.

Place Held	Owner	Balance	Interest Rate
Checking account	_____	$_____	_____
Savings account	_____	$_____	_____
Money market accounts	_____	$_____	_____
Notes receivable	_____	$_____	_____
Life insurance policies	_____	$_____	_____

Bonds

Here you want to indicate what kinds of bonds you own: U.S. government bonds, tax-free municipal bonds, or corporate bonds. Basically, a bond is an I.O.U. to you from the U.S. government, a municipality, or a corporation. The certificate states to whom you are loaning the money, when you will be repaid, and the rate of interest you will receive from the borrower. The way you can determine to whom you are loaning the money is to look at your statement from a bank or brokerage firm or at the certificate itself.

If the borrower is the U.S. government, then it is a U.S. Treasury bond; if the borrower is a municipality like the city of New York, then it is a municipal bond. On your asset statement you want to list what you own, indicating for each bond the borrower, the amount of the bond, the interest rate it pays, the date it is due, and the ownership.

Notes Receivable

These would include any personal notes due you or your husband. In this category we include money lent by you and/or just your husband to a given individual or company. List the amount owed, by whom, when the note is due, the interest rate being paid, and how often the interest is paid. You might also indicate the likelihood of repayment. For instance, if your husband loaned a friend some money and the friend has failed to repay the money in the past, you may not want to count on this as an asset.

Deferred Annuities

These are investments made with insurance companies. Deferred annuities may be fixed or variable. A fixed annuity pays a set rate of return for a specified period of time. A variable annuity has a variable return depending on the investments held in the annuity.

If you are not receiving current income from a deferred annuity, the income accumulates in a deferred annuity for you on a tax-deferred basis. In other words, you don't pay tax on what your money earns. At the end of each year, the insurance company provides you with a statement of the value of the annuity.

If you are the beneficiary of a deferred annuity your husband bought, you should write the company informing them of your husband's death. Someone from the company will let you know what the current value is and how you can access this money. Right now, all you need to know is the current value of the annuity, the name of the insurance company, and the interest rate the annuity is currently paying.

Stocks

List the name of the companies in which you own stock, the number of shares, cost (if you know it), date purchased (if you have it), and ownership. If you are the owner or the stock was jointly held, the cost and date purchased are relevant; if your husband was the sole owner, these are not relevant because the cost will be determined by the value on the date of death or six months later (depending on the value selected for the estate tax return).

If your husband had stock options with the company where he worked, list these here, with the terms of how and when they should be exercised. This information would be provided to you by his company.

Mutual Funds

Usually you don't have certificates for your mutual fund shares. These are held by the mutual fund company or by the stock brokerage firm. The most recent statement from the mutual fund company will list the number of shares you own, the name of the fund, and the owner of each fund. If you have been reinvesting dividends and capital gains generated by the mutual funds, the cost is difficult to calculate. We will discuss this in greater detail later.

Limited Partnerships and Non-Traded Real Estate Investment Trusts

If you or your spouse owned any limited partnerships or non-traded real estate investment trusts, list the name of each investment. In the first quarter of each year you should receive a tax statement from each company that should list the name and address of the general partner. For limited partnerships, this statement is called a k-1. If you know the date the partnership was originally purchased and the cost, that is helpful but not essential information.

Investment Real Estate

List any real estate investments owned by you or your spouse. Include rental properties as well as undeveloped land. These should be appraised to establish a tax basis. Your most recent tax return along with other data will provide your financial advisor with information needed to help you decide if you want to keep these properties or sell them. However, usually this is not a decision that needs to be made immediately.

Business Interests

Business interests would include your or your husband's ownership in any privately held business. "Privately held" means that the shares are not traded on a public stock exchange such as the New York Stock Exchange (NYSE). A privately held business might have been your husband's business or an investment made in someone else's business. The valuation may be complex, but your professional advisors will help

you with this process. Right now, all you need to know is the approximate value of these business interests and how much cash you may receive from them.

Other

This category would cover anything we haven't previously discussed, such as stamp and coin collections, precious metals, commodities, or other "toys" such as boats or motorcycles. These are often worth less than you may think but should be listed in the asset statement.

Retirement Assets

Retirement Accounts

By now you should know what retirement income you will receive from your husband's previous employment. In addition, he may have other retirement accounts, such as IRA, TIAA/CREF, 401(k), 403(b), and SEP/IRA accounts.

If you are the beneficiary of these accounts, you can put these accounts into a retirement account in your own name. If you choose to receive the cash instead, then any amount you withdraw from a retirement account is taxable to you, and usually there are additional taxes due if you withdraw the money before age 59-1/2. The one exception to this rule is the Roth IRA. Withdrawals from this type of account are not taxable. Taking money out of retirement accounts is a complex decision, so be sure to get professional advice before you do it. If you don't, you may create adverse tax consequences that are costly and irreversible.

Children's Assets

Custodial Accounts

Custodial accounts are set up for the purpose of holding assets for minor children. There are two very similar types of custodial accounts: Uniform Gifts to Minor's Accounts (UGMA) and Uniform Transfers to Minor's Accounts (UTMA). With either type of account, a child is the beneficiary, and an adult custodian is named to oversee the account. Usually the custodian is the parent, but it could be any adult. All of the income paid by the investments in this account is taxed to the child each year.

Assets put into a custodial account are legally owned by the child, and when the child reaches the age of majority (either 18 or 21 depending on state law), the child has the right to spend that money any way he or she wishes. Of course, as the child is growing up, the custodian can spend the money on the child's behalf for things that directly benefit the child, other than food and shelter. This could include things like private schooling, camp, a computer, or a car.

Section 529 Plans (Qualified Tuition Plans)

Section 529 plans are education savings programs. The money in these plans must be used toward education, including any college or university, some trade schools and graduate school. With the changes made to the rules in 2022, the funds from the 529 plan can pay for tuition at any public, private, or religious elementary or secondary school up to $10,000 per year, per beneficiary.

The owner of the account is usually a parent or grandparent, but it could be any adult. Unlike a custodial account, taxes don't have to be paid on the interest and dividends or capital gains as long as the money stays in the 529 account. Section 529 plans differ from custodial accounts in another way: the owner of the account retains ownership of the assets even after the child reaches age 18 or 21. If the money is not needed for the beneficiary's college education, the owner can name another eligible family member as the new beneficiary, per the rules of the plan. Non-qualified withdrawals are subject to income tax, plus a 10 percent federal tax penalty.

We think these savings plans are a good idea for many people, but because of their complexity, we recommend you consult with a financial advisor before investing.

Other Types of Childrens' Accounts

There may be assets in a trust set up for a child, or you may have a joint account with a child named as one of the joint owners. Regardless of the type of account, if you have any accounts that were set up for the benefit of a minor child, you should check out how these work. Each type of account has special tax rules that apply as well as different rules regarding how much money can be put in, how much can be withdrawn, and who actually owns the assets in the account. Each type of account may also have a different impact on the child's ability to qualify for financial aid.

Other Income Sources—Not Your Assets

Charitable Gift Annuities

A charitable gift annuity is a contract between you and a charity. In exchange for your irrevocable gift of cash, securities or other assets, the charity agrees to pay one or two individuals a fixed sum annually each year for life. The older you are at the time of the gift, the higher the income the charity will agree to pay to you. In most cases part of each payments is tax free.

Your husband might have set up one of these charitable gift annuities during his lifetime so that you receive the income as long as you live. When you die, the charity will receive the residual value, so strictly speaking it is not your asset although you receive income from it.

Donor Advised Fund (DAF)

A Donor Advised Fund (DAF) is a charitable vehicle that allows you to give to your favorite charities from a personal fund established through a public charity. By giving appreciated stock to a DAF, you receive an immediate tax benefit and avoid capital gains tax on selling appreciated assets. Once the money is in a DAF, it no longer belongs to you, but you can decide which charities you want to designate at a later date.

Here again, your husband may have established a DAF which still had a balance in it when he died. If it was established jointly with you, then you can decide which charities you want the money in the DAF to receive either now or in the future. If it was solely owned by your husband, then the DAF may be distributed to specific charities or he could have listed someone as the successor to him, meaning that that person would have the ability to recommend grants to charities.

Liabilities

Now that you have a list of your assets and their approximate value, you can begin listing the money you owe other people. These debts are your liabilities.

Mortgages

Once you have estimated the value of your home, condominium, or co-op, it is important to determine how much you owe the mortgage company. Your mortgage company will be glad to provide you with the following information:

Amount of current mortgage $_____

Current interest rate (fixed or adjustable)   _____

Monthly payment (principal and interest) $_____

Years remaining on the mortgage   _____

Amount of second mortgage (if applicable) $_____

Current interest rate (fixed or adjustable   _____

Monthly payment (principal and interest) $_____

Years left on second mortgage   _____

Home Equity Loan (HEL)/
Home Equity Line of Credit (HELOC)

As we previously stated, you may have a home equity loan or line of credit against your home. The specific terms of the loan should be found in the latest statement that the bank will send to your address.

You may be in the "draw period" of the home equity line of credit which may require interest payments only. Alternatively, if you are in the "repayment phase" for both home equity loan or line of credit, then both principal and interest are included in the repayment amount.

Be forewarned, however, now that your husband is deceased, this loan may be reexamined by the bank's loan officer, who may be concerned about your ability to repay it, so it is important you keep paying the minimum amount required each month.

Outstanding Debts

List any debts you owe to anyone: the amount you owe, the interest rate you are paying, how often you make payments, and to whom you make payments. Include the amount you currently owe on your credit cards, on car loans, or to anyone else.

Other Potential Liabilities

Inherent in the concept of debt is the need for repayment. For instance, your husband may have personally guaranteed a loan your son took out to start his business. If your son fails to make payments, your husband's estate may be liable.

Your husband may have signed a pledge to a charity, such as his college's Capital Campaign Fund, but failed to mention this in his will. Depending on local law, the charity may be entitled to be paid.

There are other areas which are less clear. For example, before your husband's death, you both may have agreed to pay for the education of your children or grandchildren. After looking at your total picture, you may find that you can't afford to do this. List any such promises with the idea that you may have to change them.

A Word of Warning Regarding Making New Loans to Family or Friends

Widows are prime targets for people seeking loans. If family or friends believe you have inherited a considerable amount of money, they may ask you to lend them some for various purposes. For example, they may want you to help them finance a "sure-fire" business venture, educate a child, or help them purchase a new home. Although this advice may seem harsh, we would strongly recommend that you make no loans, no matter how worthy the project appears—at least until you have determined your financial situation. If you feel that you must make the loan, we believe you should lend only the amount of money that you never expect to see again and that it is relatively small in relation to your net worth. Always require a written agreement with stated interest rates and repayment terms. That way, if you are not repaid, you can deduct it as a loss on your income tax return.

Summary and Conclusion

Within a few months of your husband's death, you should have put together a comprehensive list of your assets and liabilities. With this information, your financial advisor will prepare a statement of your current financial condition, also called a net worth statement. In the previous chapter, you estimated your income and expenses. Now that you have an idea of your net worth and your budget, you are ready to review all this information with your financial advisor. Your goal is to make sure that you have sufficient income both now and in the future. This may involve changing some of these assets. Finally, you are ready to do some longer-term planning.

Net Worth Statement

Net Worth Statement as of:_____

For:_____

I. Personal Assets

Home Value	$_____	
Second Home(s) Value	$_____	
Automobile(s)	$_____	
	Total	$_____

II. Cash $_____

III. Personal Investments

Bonds	$_____	
Notes Receivable	$_____	
Deferred Annuities	$_____	
Stocks	$_____	
Mutual Funds	$_____	
Limited Partnerships	$_____	
Business Interests	$_____	
Real Estate	$_____	
Other	$_____	
	Total	$_____

IV. Retirement Investments

IRA $_____

IRA Rollover $_____

Roth IRA $_____

SEP/IRA $_____

401(k) $_____

403(b) $_____

TIAA/CREF $_____

Other $_____

                         Total $_____

V. Liabilities

Mortgage Loan on House $_____

Home Equity Loan $_____

Mortgage on Second Home $_____

Automobile Loan(s) $_____

Credit Card Debt $_____

Other Debt $_____

                         Total $_____

Net Worth: (I + II+III+IV- V) $_____

Diane

Reactions to Calculating Her Net Worth

Diane estimated she had about $320,000 in available cash. Dorothy had suggested Diane pay off her credit card debt as soon as possible from this money in view of the high interest rate she was paying on the unpaid balance. She looked at all she owed on her credit card bills for this month with new eyes. How had they gotten so high?

She had not had the home appraised yet, but thought it was worth about $800,000 because the neighbor across the street had recently sold her home for that amount, which was similar to theirs. The value of homes had really increased since they bought theirs ten years ago. The mortgage officer informed her that they had refinanced their home last year; their current mortgage balance was $500,000, and they still had 29 years of mortgage payments. Diane realized that by the time she paid the mortgage off she would be 71 years old! One solution to her negative cash flow might be selling their beautiful home she loved so much. She hoped she could avoid doing that.

Diane knew she needed to make the decision about whether or not to invest the money from the firm's insurance policy on Mark in a fixed annuity pretty soon because she needed to know how much income she could count on to pay her expenses.

The stockbroker, her dad, and Larry all told her she shouldn't touch Mark's retirement account because she would need it for her retirement. At this point, she felt she couldn't worry about retirement. There were too many other immediate needs to worry about. She needed to find money now to educate her children.

It was obvious to Diane that she had better get back together with Dorothy right away to see what she should do. Even to Diane's nonfinancial brain, things looked pretty grim! But she recognized she couldn't just do nothing, which is what she had done in the past.

Susan

Reactions to Calculating Her Net Worth

After reviewing her income and expenses several months into her widowhood, Susan realized that she did have a cash flow problem. It was important that she review her assets more carefully to see if they could produce more income.

Lance and Susan had a savings account with $15,000 in it. Their condominium was worth about $500,000, and the mortgage was $350,000. Their cottage was worth $250,000, and the mortgage was $150,000. They had no credit card debts because Lance paid the bills monthly and really didn't like having any debt. The more Susan looked at the situation, the more obvious it was that the cottage was a luxury she could not afford. She agonized over selling it. It held so many great memories for her. On the other hand, if she had to sell something, she would rather keep the condo. She allowed herself to have a good cry, after which she was ready to call the realtor who had sold it to her and put it up for sale.

Bob O'Brien, Lance's stockbroker, sent Susan the list of Lance's stocks, which were worth $200,000, together with his recommendation of which ones to sell to raise the $50,000 she needed for Lance's children. She met with Bob to finalize these sales and figure out a strategy for the future. Bob explained that the stocks Lance owned paid no income because they were companies which focused on growing in value rather than paying income. She discussed with Bob the advisability of changing these stocks to ones that would produce more income. In view of her relatively young age, he told her he was reluctant to recommend moving too far in this direction; he wanted her portfolio to have the potential to grow in value. He explained that typically most stocks that pay a high level of income don't grow much in value.

Susan had asked Ron about helping with their mother's financial support, but he was not reassuring. He told her that his salary was not high, and he had his own financial problems. At best, he would be able to contribute $200 per month toward their mother's expenses. However, he realized that it wasn't right for Susan to take on all the responsibility. If he could not help much financially, at least he could help personally. He offered to visit Mom weekly in the future and occasionally take her out for lunch or another activity. Susan was grateful he could help with the monthly payments; this meant she could pay less than she was currently paying. Every bit helped!

Susan knew that she could withdraw money from Lance's pension fund if she really needed the money to make ends meet. However, because any income she withdrew would be taxable to her and might involve tax penalties, Susan wanted to avoid doing that. Also, because she didn't have a very large retirement fund of her own, she thought taking money from this fund was really her last resort. This pension plan was invested at Lance's firm. Harry told her she could leave these assets with the firm's pension manager for the time being. Eventually, she would have to make a decision about managing this money, but it was not necessary to do this right now.

Susan knew her own retirement fund at the Association was invested in a fixed-income investment held by an insurance company. It had seemed to be a safe place for her to invest her money, and she had never paid much attention to it. Susan thought to herself it would be a good idea for her to learn more about this account now that she was dealing with larger amounts of money.

Susan was also the income beneficiary of the trust fund Lance had set up for his two children, but she could not list the trust as her asset because she did not own it. For the present, the trust owned the assets. According to the way the trust was written, Susan was entitled to receive the income from the trust for her lifetime even if she remarried. Actually, she also had the right to invade the principal, if necessary. However, her stepchildren were already upset because they felt they'd been cheated out of their inheritance. She didn't want to compound the situation by taking more than the income out of this trust, which ultimately went to them, unless it was absolutely necessary.

On reviewing her situation, Susan seriously considered that she might have to look for a better-paying job. Maybe she should talk to her boss at the Association about raising her salary. Everyone at the Association had been so good to her during these recent painful months that she hated to make a change or ask for more money because she hadn't been functioning in her usual efficient way. However, she had to be realistic about her situation. It was clear she needed more income than she currently had if she was going to keep the condominium.

Susan wanted to discuss these feelings and options in her next session with Dr. Coleman. She realized she was truly benefiting from her sessions with her. She had an entirely different view of psychologists and therapy since she had started her work with Dr. Coleman. She would try to be less judgmental about other things she didn't know about in the future.

Audrey

Reactions to Calculating Her Net Worth

Audrey reviewed her assets. Her home was worth $400,000, and it was really too big for her. It was the home she had lived in most of her married life; now she wanted something newer and easier to take care of than her home with John. On the other hand, she wasn't in any rush to move. She liked the location, particularly because it was close to Joanne. She wanted to help Joanne as much as possible and didn't want to miss the opportunity of seeing her grandchildren grow up.

In addition to the money she had in her and John's joint savings account, Audrey had received some insurance money. She didn't know where to put it, so she added it to her savings account at her local bank. The manager certainly had been nice to her when she made the deposit.

Shortly before John was diagnosed with cancer, they had decided to redo the kitchen and had applied for a home equity loan of $20,000. Fortunately, they hadn't started the work, although they had made all the plans with the contractor. She wondered if she should go ahead with this project. She decided to discuss with Mr. Silver that if she wanted to remodel the kitchen whether she should use the home equity loan or some of the insurance money to finance this expense.

The thought of dealing with all the workers and the mess involved in redoing the kitchen was not appealing to Audrey, especially if she might move sooner rather than later. The idea of spending money on a much-needed vacation was certainly more attractive. The prospect of going to a golf clinic at Hilton Head was becoming increasingly desirable—it would also be a good way to brush up on her skills! She knew Dr. PaPadisio would think it was a good idea. She needed to give more thought to how she wanted to spend her time and money. She was not in a rush but did not want too much time to pass without formulating a plan.

There was also the question of the company stock held in John's name, which was worth about $200,000. It paid her $4,000 per year in income, which wasn't much (2 percent), but John never wanted to sell it because he loved the company so much. Besides, he said, the taxes on the gain would have been prohibitive because his cost for the shares was so low. The lawyer had mentioned something about the fact that because the shares were part of John's estate, the cost basis would be increased to reflect current market values. That meant she could sell these shares without worrying about paying tax on the gain. But she knew John would not have approved! She would have to think about this further in terms of her needs. For now, she would make no decision, but she would discuss it at greater length with Mr. Silver.

By the time Audrey had completed her asset and liability statement, it was time to get ready for her lunch with Joanne. They had begun to meet for lunch regularly on Wednesdays, and both women looked forward to it.

When Audrey had last seen Dr. PaPadisio, he was very pleased with her because she had gained five pounds. She attributed this gain in part to the efforts she had been making to include a lunch out with friends in conjunction with her volunteer work as well as her regularly scheduled lunches with Joanne. Today she was looking forward to discussing the preschool issue with her daughter.

Audrey was also pleased with the results of her conversation with John Jr. He called when he was about to leave for the office a few days ago and asked if he could drop by to see her. He said they hadn't had much time to talk, and he didn't want her to feel neglected by him. She assured him she wasn't feeling neglected and encouraged him to stop by the following week on his way to work. She thought this meeting would provide her with a wonderful opportunity to discuss her financial situation with him.

When John Jr. arrived, he looked somewhat more tired and older than Audrey remembered. She guessed she'd been so preoccupied with John's care and then her financial situation that she hadn't given much thought to how the loss of their father had impacted on her children. She looked at John Jr. as though she hadn't seen him in a long time even though he had been present throughout the planning for the funeral and at the funeral itself. He looked as though he had the weight of the world on his shoulders. Somehow, this older, more vulnerable look made him appear less formidable to her.

She offered him a cup of coffee, and they sat at the kitchen table in the comfortable, well-worn chairs. After telling him about her decision to become involved as a volunteer with the symphony, Audrey told him she was really pleased he had decided to stop over because she had been meaning to talk with him about her financial situation. She could see him imperceptibly stiffen. She immediately went on to say that his father had provided very nicely for her, and she anticipated no financial problems. She laid out the various sheets she had been working on—her assets and liabilities sheet and a summary of her monthly financial needs. She told him about her work with Mr. Humphrey, her lawyer, and with Mr. Silver, her financial planner. She explained that after reviewing her total financial status with these men, she found that she was in a position to give some money to each of her children and wanted to do so on an annual basis.

John Jr. was somewhat taken aback by both her understanding of her financial situation and her generosity. She could tell that he was also relieved that he wouldn't have to help support her. She could see him visibly relax. He was generous with his praise of all she had accomplished, and he seemed to view her with greater respect. She went on to tell him that she had decided on giving each family $6,000 annually. He tried to dissuade her from making that much money available to him in view of the disparity between his income and that of Joanne. She assured him that she had taken all that into consideration but had decided on giving each of her children the same amount. If he wanted the money to go directly to his children, that was all right with her. She told him she would discuss the best way to accomplish this with Mr. Silver. Audrey also asked John Jr. if he would be willing to meet with her and Mr. Silver to review her financial plans for the future. He was most agreeable to doing that and told his mother to make an appointment for them in the next two or three weeks.

Both mother and son realized they had gotten beyond the barrier that had existed between them for such a long time now, although neither one verbally acknowledged it. He invited her over for dinner the next week, and they hugged each other when they parted. Audrey thought she might make more of an effort to see John Jr. than she had done in the recent past. She realized he really wasn't pompous; it was just that he didn't know how to express his concern for her.

She hoped things would go as well with Joanne, with whom she was having lunch. She was running late and called Joanne to take the table she had reserved for them at a new restaurant about which she recently had heard many good things. She was really excited about sharing with Joanne what she had discussed with Mr. Silver. As soon as they ordered, Audrey elaborated on her discussion with Mr. Silver regarding giving her $6,000 this year to help with the children's tuition costs. Audrey could see that Joanne was surprised and somewhat defensive. She apologized to her mother for being a burden and told her she felt like a charity case, which made her very uncomfortable. However, not wanting to hurt her mother's feelings, Joanne went on to tell her how very grateful she was for making the money available. Audrey reassured her and was pleased she could tell her that she had already discussed it with John, Jr. and it was fine with him. Joanne appeared greatly relieved and perked up considerably.

Elizabeth

Reactions to Calculating Her Net Worth

Elizabeth had enough in a savings account to cover her expenses for the first year. Her home was worth about $300,000, and Ben was proud of the fact that they had paid off their mortgage several years ago. She had received a $10,000 check from a small life insurance policy and used that money to pay for the funeral and some outstanding bills. She also had some land in Vermont that Ben had bought years ago with the idea they might someday build a home on it. Somehow they never got around to it.

Elizabeth was having trouble dealing with the stock and bond portfolio she had inherited from Ben. She didn't know what to do with it. Someone was going to have to help her understand it and make some decisions. Should she leave it with the money manager Ben had worked with all these years or take it to a trust department of a bank to be managed, as Mr. Grossfeldt had suggested? She really didn't know enough to make an intelligent decision in this regard. She hated to impose on Sam Weatherly once again to help her, but she didn't know where else to turn. Her friend Mabel told her that municipal bonds were wonderful. They paid income that was federally tax free and were safe. Perhaps she should sell everything and buy them—certainly life would be simpler that way.

Making financial decisions wasn't easy for her, but Elizabeth knew she needed to make some decisions. For example, she had to decide where she wanted to live for the remainder of her life. She had never really given much consideration to major decisions during her marriage. Ben would usually come home and say something like, "I've been thinking it's about time we did such and such, Liz. What do you think?" Her predictable response was, "Whatever you think, dear, is fine with me." She had always thought of herself as somewhat timid. As a child, she had allowed her older sister, Abigail, to make decisions for her and, later, Ben. She had been grateful to them for not expecting anything more of her on this level. Now her new financial advisors expected her to make certain decisions after they provided her with the advantages and disadvantages of each of her options. It was a new and uncomfortable role for her. She would have preferred to do nothing, burying her head in the sand, and allowing others to decide for her. Unfortunately, she knew all too well that it was no longer appropriate to allow others to make her decisions. There was no one to turn to but herself. Even Mittens couldn't help!

Elizabeth was frightened by the thought of living any place other than her home, yet the harsh winters in Boston were beginning to bother her. The idea of moving to Florida was becoming more and more appealing. She enjoyed her church work and her friendship with the Weatherlys, Lucy, and Mabel, but many of her friends had moved away when they retired, and some had died. Actually, if she were truthful with herself, she would have to admit she was often lonely, even though she now had Mittens to keep her company. It would be good to be near her sister.

She realized that in order to make a change of this magnitude, she really needed to visit Abigail. Then she could see where she was living and meet her friends. Her sister had been encouraging her to come for a visit for years and had been insistent in their recent phone conversations. Elizabeth wondered why it was so hard for her to initiate anything. She had dealt with so many new people and money matters since Ben's death. She was becoming annoyed with herself over her ambivalence and lack of action. Mabel had already volunteered to look after Mittens while she was in Florida.

As she mulled over what to do about a visit to Abigail for the umpteenth time one gray morning, Elizabeth became irritated with herself for her own inaction. With a resolve that she wasn't feeling, she picked up the phone and called a travel agent the Weatherlys had recommended to her. She was surprised at how simple it was to arrange a direct flight to Miami. After making the necessary arrangements, she shocked herself by asking the travel agent to send her some information on one-week cruises that left from Ft. Lauderdale or Miami for the Bahamas.

As soon as she hung up, she called Abigail to tell her when she would be arriving. She decided not to mention the cruise until she got there. She wasn't sure how serious she was about it just yet. Somehow it seemed too daring—but maybe not.

CHAPTER NINE

Identifying Today's Financial Attitudes and Realities

The time has come to make sense of all the information you have accumulated. By now you should have a pretty good idea of whether you have enough income to cover your expenses. Whatever your circumstances, your advisors may be able to improve your situation by recommending changes in your investments.

Before making any adjustments, you need to review the attitudes you formed in childhood about money, your risk tolerance, your investment goals, and your investment objectives. In chapter 2 we discussed how your financial attitudes are formed. In this chapter we will review these factors in relation to where you are now.

Financial Conditioning

As indicated in the statistics in chapter 1, the majority of women are widowed after the age of 55. Most women born early in the twentieth century were likely to be affected by beliefs and myths associated with images of the traditional family. Parents had distinct roles: Father was usually head of the household and the decision maker outside the home, and Mother made most of the daily decisions about the home and the children. Women were not supposed to "worry their pretty little heads" about numbers. That was the man's job.

Talking about money was taboo. In general, money was not to be discussed at the dinner table. It was a subject left to the men—father to son. Women were not encouraged to ask questions about finances. It was not considered ladylike for a woman to be competitive. In some families, this view carried over to the area of achievement. For example, if a young girl was better at a subject or a sport than her brothers or her boyfriend, she was encouraged to appear less competent and to make mistakes in order to allow the male to feel better about himself. The message was loud and clear: Women were not supposed to seek knowledge or success for themselves.

This all started to change with the advent of World War II. At that time out of necessity, women started to work outside the home. This was the beginning of the female revolution. After the war, many women found they liked working, for several reasons. They enjoyed the work, they contributed to the family income and their salaries also provided them with some financial independence. Over time, this led to more women graduating from college so that today women outnumber men in college.

However, despite continued change in the workplace and higher education opportunities, attitudes about women working outside the home have not changed as much as you would expect. Today the working wife still is likely to run the household. Due to her responsibilities inside the home and at her place of employment, it is understandable that she often is willing to delegate financial matters to her spouse.

If outdated patterns and ideas were part of your childhood about a woman's role, it is essential that you move past this mindset now that you are on your own. You need to take responsibility and control over your financial life. If you require help, consult a mental health specialist, a financial planner, or both. Without control over your money—and therefore over your life—you are enslaved to those who do understand money.

Your Current Attitude Toward Money

It is a good idea at this point to assess if and how your attitude toward money has changed since you were widowed. Over the past six months to a year, you have gathered a considerable amount of financial information and have been forced to make some financial decisions. Now is a good time to review what you have learned and what areas you have had a difficult time comprehending. Remember: This list is for your eyes alone and to be used only to help you identify where you are with regard to your financial attitude.

In completing your "Who Am I Today Financially?" form, list under "Financial Strengths" those financial tasks you feel competent to handle. Under "Financial Weaknesses," list those tasks you are still having difficulty managing. Under "Financial Needs," indicate those areas where you would like to have more knowledge.

Your Risk Tolerance

Webster's Dictionary defines risk as "the possibility of loss or injury." It has been our experience that the majority of widows (regardless of wealth) say they don't want to take much risk because they are worried about having sufficient income and don't want to lose any of the money they have. After the first year, the widow usually has a better understanding of her situation and is more willing to take some risk. As the years go by and her financial knowledge increases, she may find she is ready to take even more risk. It is like learning to ride a bicycle. At first you are unsteady, but as you become more skilled, you gain self-confidence. The more you ride, the more self-assured you become.

There are different kinds of risk. Most people equate risk taking to gambling. However, all life entails taking chances. You can't even cross the street without some risk! What you can do is try to limit that risk by taking educated risks—in this example, you wait for the light to turn in your favor so you can cross the street safely.

The primary kind of risk you need to be aware of as a widow is the risk of loss of principal. If you don't have much money, you can't afford to lose any principal. Therefore, you should try to limit the amount of risk you take.

It is important to note there are some new widows who spend a lot of money during the first year of widowhood in an attempt to reassure themselves that they are in control of their lives. In some cases, these widows have spent more money than they should have because they didn't grasp the fact that this money wouldn't last forever. In other cases, the widows took more risk than they should have.

How much risk are you willing to take? In chapter 13 we give you some guidelines on how to reduce risk, but right now we are talking about how much risk you can handle emotionally.

Investment Goals

You undoubtedly have certain financial goals you want to achieve with your money. Typical goals include retiring in comfort, educating your children (or grandchildren), reducing income and estate taxes and leaving money to your heirs.

For example, a younger widow like Diane is primarily interested in educating her children; the concept of retirement seems very remote to her. On the other hand, the primary concern of an older widow such as Audrey is likely to be to remain self-sufficient while at the same time being able to help out her children financially.

Write down your financial goals and then prioritize them in order of importance to you.

Your Investment Objectives

After you have determined your risk attitude and listed your investment goals in order of importance, you need to determine how to achieve those goals—in other words what your investment objectives are. Ask yourself what your highest investment priority is. Is it preserving principal, obtaining the highest current income, or having your principal grow? Most of us want to achieve all three objectives in one investment, but it is important to recognize this is not possible. An investment that has more of one advantage—such as safety of principal—will have less of another—such as potential for growth.

You need to decide which investment goal is most important to you and what you have to give up in order to attain it. Basically, it is an issue of trade-offs. For instance, if you want high current income, then the investments you select will have limited potential for growth of principal. If growth of principal is your priority, usually the income you receive from this investment will be low and you will have to take more risk. Even if your stated investment objective is high current income, you will probably select different kinds of investments for you so that there is balance between investments with growth potential and those that provide high current income.

Reviewing Your Financial Statements

At this point, you have determined what your attitude toward money is, your risk tolerance, and your investment goals and objectives. You know your various sources of income and estimated expenses as well as your current assets and liabilities. The next step is to review three statements that will help you plan a secure financial future. These are your taxable income statement, your cash flow statement, and your balance sheet.

Taxable Income Statement

This statement lists your various sources of taxable income and gives you an idea of what your federal and state taxes will be for this year and the next two. At this point, it is still an educated estimate because the estate is not settled, and you are not sure what all your sources of income or actual expenses will be. You might owe estate taxes (federal and state) and estate settlement fees, which will reduce the amount of the assets you inherit. In addition, income tax laws could change at any time. However, this statement will give you an idea of what you will owe in taxes under current law.

The taxable income statement is helpful because your tax status may change over the next few years. For instance, you will file as a "married" taxpayer the year in which your husband died but as a "married," "head of household," or "single" taxpayer the following year. These three categories involve three different tax tables.

The taxable income statement is also useful because it identifies your tax bracket, which will help your advisor determine whether you need to select investments that generate taxable or tax-free income. If you are in a lower tax bracket, you might be better off investing in something that generates taxable income. We find many widows are obsessed with reducing their income taxes, but when we compute what they actually will owe in taxes as a percentage of their total income, they aren't paying that much. Thus they might be better off with more taxable income. If this is true for you, selecting tax-free investments may not be your best choice.

Cash Flow Statement

On this statement will be listed all your estimated sources of income and expenses, including state and federal income taxes. (A few states do not have a state income tax.) The bottom line will show you whether you have more income than expenses or vice versa at the end of each year.

If the bottom-line number is negative, then you need to reexamine your expenses to see if you can reduce them. Your advisor can also look at your investments to see if they can be changed to generate more income without sacrificing too much in the way of future growth potential. For instance, you may be able to increase your income by renting out a room in your home, or you may have to face the fact that your current home is too expensive for you to keep. After looking at your expenses, it may become apparent that you may have to go to work (if you are not already working). If you are currently working, you may have to find a better-paying job or work at more than one job. If you have children, you may have to talk to them about their getting part-time jobs or reducing their expenditures.

The most important thing is to look at your income and expense situation for the long term as well as the present. Remember that your income has to cover your expenses for the rest of your life.

Net Worth Statement

Your Net Worth Statement lists everything you own and everything you owe. The difference between the two numbers is your net worth. In the future, this number should be computed annually to determine whether you are building your net worth or losing ground.

Summary and Conculsion

Now you are more aware of how your attitudes formed in childhood about money have affected you. You have assessed your financial strengths, weaknesses, and needs. You have indicated how much risk you feel comfortable taking with your money. You have prioritized your financial goals and your investment objectives. You have reviewed your taxable income statement so you have a better idea of what your state and federal income tax bill will be as well as your tax bracket. You know whether your current income is sufficient to pay your estimated expenses, and you have a current balance sheet. With this information, your advisor can now help you do some short-term and long-term planning for your future.

Diane

Reactions to Identifying Today's Financial Attitudes and Realities

Diane completed her "Who Am I Today Financially?" form as follows:

Who Am I Today Financially?

Financial Strengths

1. Better understanding of finance
2. Capable of putting together a budget
3. More aware of the interrelationship of financial decisions
4. Have an organized set of files

Financial Weaknesses

1. Hard time adjusting to the reality of my financial situation
2. Have trouble saying no to the children because of lack of money
3. Difficulty comprehending the advantages and disadvantages of different types of investments
4. Want to spend more than I can afford

Financial Needs

1. Need more financial knowledge in order to make better financial decisions
2. Rationale for financial decisions I am making
3. Children to become more financially aware and responsible
4. Discipline myself to review financial situation on a regular basis

Diane told Dorothy when they met that she didn't want to take any risk. Because of this, the security of receiving fixed payments from the insurance company for the rest of her life looked very attractive to her.

Her primary financial goal was to educate her children. She thought she could worry about retirement later—after all, she had 20 years before she was 62, and by that time her youngest child would be 27 years old.

Her investment objective was to have high current income so she could keep her children in private school and not have to sell the home.

Diane's Budget

Diane proudly showed Dorothy the revised budget she and the children had worked out together. After her last visit with Dorothy, she sat down with the children and explained the situation to them. She told them that she thought the family should determine as a unit what to do. She had several ideas as to which expenses could be eliminated from the budget but wanted to hear what the children had to say. To her surprise, the children were enthusiastic about being part of this process.

When they reviewed the budget, they all agreed that they didn't need to belong to the country club. Much as she wanted to go to the beach for two weeks, it was unrealistic. They all agreed to compromise and go for one week. They also agreed to forget the Christmas trip. She needed a housekeeper once a week to help out with the heavy housework, but the older children could certainly pitch in; they could baby-sit when necessary and help with the yard work. Much as she didn't want to, she would have to reduce her charitable contributions—after all, charity begins at home! However, she couldn't eliminate Jeremy's orthodontia—he really needed braces.

Diane thought she could make up the remaining negative cash flow each year by drawing down the cash she had received from Mark's personal insurance policies and the firm's capital account. Dorothy gently told Diane that even though she had lowered her annual expenses somewhat, if she spent the money from these two sources to cover the remaining negative cash flow each year, that money would last only four and a half years. Furthermore, that solution would work only if none of her expenses increased, which appeared highly unlikely. She also pointed out that Diane had to consider college education costs for the children.

College Education Projections

Dorothy told Diane that college expenses had increased annually over the past few years. The good news was the annual costs weren't increasing as much as they had twenty years ago, but they were still going up as you would expect with the overall cost of living. Just looking at the past ten years, costs for public college were increasing on average 2.7 percent and for private college 3.1 percent.

Assuming college costs would continue to increase at these rates, Dorothy projected what it would cost to send Diane's children to college and showed the numbers to her. If these projections were correct, Diane would need the following amounts of money accumulated by each child's freshman year (assuming each child started college at age 18):

	Public*	Private*
Erin (15)	$ 96,835	$222,533
Jeremy (11)	$107,724	$247,557
Alice (7)	$119,838	$275,396

In other words, if Diane was going to send all three to private college, it would cost a mind-boggling figure. If she wanted to put aside sufficient money now to cover this future expense (assuming it earned 7 percent after tax annually), she would need to invest $466,657! Even public college would require her to invest $203,065 now.

	Public*	Private*
Erin (15)	$79,046	$181,653
Jeremy (11)	$67,085	$154,166
Alice (7)	$56,934	$130,838

*These numbers are taken from the 2022 College Board trends in college pricing and represent the national average cost of tuition, fees, room, and board. Public college assumes in-state tuition.

Now Diane was really depressed. She had been so concerned about covering their current education expenses she had not even thought about the cost of their college education. She had vaguely known that college would cost a lot, but Mark made a lot of money, so she had never worried about paying for the children's college education. This was another example of how far she had been removed from their financial situation. The idea of being able to keep the children in private schools throughout high school was becoming less and less feasible. Clearly, this was a case of choosing between long-term and short-term economic goals.

Dorothy's Revised Cash Flow Statement for Diane

Dorothy told Diane that she was not at all comfortable having Diane choose the immediate annuity approach with the life insurance money. While she realized that Diane would find the certainty of receiving a certain monthly amount of income comforting, this monthly payment would be the same amount annually for the rest of her life. This would not work for Diane because her expenses were bound to increase due to inflation. In addition, if she invested in this annuity, she would have no access to this principal in the future. This would be a problem for Diane if she needed additional money to cover expenses, which was highly likely.

As she had promised, Dorothy had worked on Diane's net worth statement. Dorothy told Diane she should also pay off her loan on the van. Diane was grateful that they had paid off Mark's car only a few months ago. If she paid off the van loan, she would be left with only one long-term debt—the mortgage on the home. This would lower her monthly expenses because she wouldn't have to pay the interest on the credit card debt and van loan, which were not tax-deductible items. Dorothy urged her to try to keep her monthly credit card bills current, so she didn't run up any more debt and pay the high interest charges.

Diane asked Dorothy if she should use some of the remaining money to pay off the home mortgage. Dorothy recommended that she not do this right now because the interest rate she was paying was relatively low and the interest payments on the mortgage were tax deductible. Also if she paid off the mortgage she wouldn't have that much left to live on, which wasn't a lot of money given all her future estimated expenses.

Diane had been worrying about how to meet her monthly expenses, so she readily agreed to pay off the loans. Dorothy advised Diane to put aside some of her cash in a money market account. This would be a cash reserve so that Diane would have cash available to pay expenses as they occurred. After six months, they should look at this reserve to see if Diane needed that much. However, initially Dorothy thought it would be a good idea to have a large cash reserve. She emphasized this was a cash reserve to be used for necessary expenses, not for "splurges."

Dorothy recommended investing the remaining money so that it would pay Diane income annually. She reviewed Diane's revised budget but added one additional expense—the premium for a fifteen-year, level-term $1,000,000 life insurance policy. The annual premium would remain the same for fifteen years. She thought this was a necessary expense to provide for Diane's children in case something happened to Diane until Alice, the youngest child, had completed college,. With these adjustments, the annual negative cash flow number had been reduced considerably. They were making progress, but they had to do more.

Diane was confused. Jack Blafford, the insurance agent, seemed so sure when he proposed the annuity to her—it seemed like the solution to all her problems! Dorothy explained to her that Mr. Blafford had not had an opportunity to look at Diane's total situation and review these cash flow projections. Receiving an immediate annuity payment might be a very good solution for some people, but in view of her comparative youth and high expenses, it was not a good choice for her. Diane was right to want the highest possible income, but she also needed to invest where there was a chance for her principal to grow. If her principal grew, then the income could increase and would hopefully keep pace with inflation.

Dorothy indicated that because Diane's Social Security income would decrease as the children grew older, she needed to figure out how to increase her income over the years ahead. She also had to consider how to provide the children with a college education. Her two biggest current expenses kept staring Diane in the face—the children's tuition and the mortgage payments. These two items represented almost half of her expenses.

Dorothy told Diane that because she still had a large negative cash flow, she had to make some choices to reduce her expenses further. One option was selling their home and buying a less expensive one. Another was to consider sending the children to public schools. She pointed out that the public schools in Diane's area had a good reputation and her children might do very well there. She suggested that Diane visit the local schools and talk with the principals about the curriculum and the facilities available to the students.

Although Diane didn't like to hear what Dorothy was telling her, she knew Dorothy was right. Changing her children's schools would be disruptive but so would moving out of their home of many years. Diane decided to call Robyn, who was a teacher in the Montgomery County School System and learn more about the schools in her area. If she was going to change her children's schools, she would like them to start at the new schools in the fall. She also wanted to talk to a real estate agent about what their home was really worth. If they moved to a less expensive home in the Washington, D.C. area, where would they have to go? Maybe they should rent.

Diane realized that going back to work was no longer optional. She really had to do it—but it had been so long since she had worked. What was she qualified to do? She had enjoyed her former career as a paralegal in the estate planning department of Mark's law firm. Perhaps she could take a couple of refresher courses and go back to working at a law firm. But all of this would take time, and it would be a while before she would be earning a salary.

Making all these major decisions was overwhelming. Although Diane had avoided talking with her dad in an effort to be self-sufficient, she thought the time had come to do so. She thanked Dorothy for all her help and said she would be back to her as soon as she gathered more information. There was so much to do! Diane was tempted to give up, but, for the sake of the children, she knew she couldn't.

- **Diane's risk tolerance:** Very low
- **Diane's near-term financial goal:** To cover expenses
- **Diane's long term financial goal:** College education for children
- **Diane's investment objective:** High current income and growth of principal

Susan

Reactions to Identifying Today's Financial Attitudes and Realities

Susan completed her "Who Am I Today Financially?" form as follows:

Who Am I Today Financially?

Financial Strengths

1. Aware of present financial situation
2. Able to assume responsibility for financial decisions
3. Recognize the necessity of looking at the long-term as well as the short-term financial future

Financial Weaknesses

1. Reluctance to focus on career in terms of needed income
2. Not sure why she was struggling with moving forward with financial actions that need to be implemented.
3. Lack of extensive knowledge of different kinds of investments.

Financial Needs

1. More knowledge regarding different types of investments
2. Exploration of personal risk tolerance
3. Assistance from her brother with regard to mother's support

Susan was comfortable taking some risk with her investments. Although she detested gambling, she had come to realize that she had to take a certain amount of risk in order to make money. She probably wasn't as venturesome as Lance had been, but she was willing to take some risk with professional guidance.

Her primary financial goal was to take care of herself. However she was also very concerned about making sure her mother's costs were covered. It appeared that the trust income she would receive would more than meet her mother's current financial needs, but she was worried about her mother needing additional care in the future. Susan's secondary goal was to figure out a way she could stay in their condominium, which she loved so much.

Her investment objective was growth of capital. Although her current income picture did not look that good, she thought she could improve it by rearranging some assets.

Susan knew a widow was not supposed to make momentous decisions, such as selling a primary residence in the first few months of widowhood. It was different when it came to selling their second home. She was fortunate that the real estate agent had been able to sell the lake cottage fairly quickly for her full asking price. Susan wondered if she should have asked more for it, but it was a great relief not to have to worry about meeting the monthly expenses. After paying the realtor's commission, taxes, and the mortgage she would have some cash left which she was glad to see.

At this point, she was eager to replenish her savings account which was at a low level. She was glad that she had eliminated the expense of maintaining the cottage. Although she had reduced her negative cash flow, it still appeared that her expenses this year would exceed her income. She was determined not to touch his retirement account as she anticipated needing it in the future. She decided to keep part of the cottage proceeds in a money market account to cover this shortfall as well as any unexpected expenses. This meant she would still have some of the proceeds from the cottage sale to reinvest.

Susan didn't like to think about it, but she had noticed that her mother's short-term memory was getting worse. She had postponed taking her mother to the doctor to be further evaluated because she had been so preoccupied with her own situation. She decided she should probably make time for that in the near future so she would have a better idea of her mother's overall health, which in turn would have an impact on her housing needs. If her mother needed an environment that provided more care, it would be more expensive. Susan thought she would have to factor these financial implications into her planning. She realized that there was some urgency in doing so, because her mother might have to move to a more expensive facility sooner rather than later. The women in her mother's family historically had lived long lives. Her mother might live to be 95 or 100, and she needed to plan for that possibility.

Susan knew she had to be realistic about her financial future. She knew she couldn't depend on finding a husband to support her. Although she was attractive enough, she was picky. After all, she hadn't found Lance until she was 37 years old, and she didn't think there were many other Lances available. She had been comparatively happy living on her own before, and she imagined she would be again.

As long as she and Lance had been married, money had not been a problem. He earned more than enough to keep them comfortable, so she never considered looking for another job. It was funny how quickly she had become accustomed to living in the comfortable lifestyle that Lance's income made possible. She decided she had better seriously consider the idea of looking for a higher-paying job. On the other hand, she already had experienced a lot of change, and a job shift might be more than she could handle right now. Although the thought of a better-paying job was appealing, she felt a little guilty thinking about leaving her present job, where everyone had been so nice to her.

Right now she had to focus on making an appointment to see her mother's doctor. Next on her list was to review Lance's stock portfolio and invest the money from the cottage sale as well as pension assets.

- **Susan's risk tolerance:** Moderately high
- **Susan's primary financial goal:** To be financially independent and maintain her current lifestyle
- **Susan's investment objective:** Growth of capital

Audrey

*Reactions to Identifying Today's
Financial Attitudes and Realities*

Audrey completed her "Who Am I Today Financially?" form as follows:

Who Am I Today Financially?

Financial Strengths

1. Able to feel comfortable making financial decisions
2. Recognize need to plan ahead

Financial Weaknesses

1. Lacks investment experience.
2. More concerned with my overall financial picture than my monthly budget

Financial Needs

1. Be able to contribute to my grandchildren's education
2. Be in a position to improve my daughter's financial situation
3. Willingness to take some risk

Audrey didn't consider herself much of a risk taker. She had no experience investing, so she didn't want to "gamble" her money. Her investment objective was preservation of principal and current income. Although she had ample income, she liked the idea of investing more for income than growth. She told Mr. Silver she also wanted to preserve her principal.

Her primary financial goal was to be financially independent. Her secondary objective was to help educate her grandchildren.

Audrey had assessed her financial situation with Mr. Silver and felt very comfortable with where things were. Her income situation appeared to be fine. Her expenses were not that high, and her income from John's pension plan was secure. Mr. Silver estimated the amount she needed to reserve each month for tax payments.

They discussed the mortgage situation, and he explained that the interest on a mortgage provided a tax deduction. However, because she and John had owned the home for 22 years, now most of what she paid each year was principal payments, not interest, and thus was no longer tax deductible. Because the tax deduction was low and she could afford to pay off the mortgage, Mr. Silver recommended she do that. With a sigh of relief, Audrey called the bank and asked for the necessary papers.

Mr. Humphrey told Audrey that, as things stood now, John's estate was under $12 million. Since all his assets had been left to her, there would be no federal estate taxes due.

Because the estate would not be taxable, Audrey questioned whether it was worthwhile to have the home appraised. Couldn't she just make an educated guess? Both Mr. Humphrey and Mr. Silver were adamant that she needed to have it appraised. They explained that if she had a professional estate appraisal, the IRS would not be able to question her cost basis when she wanted to sell the home. Because the home had been held in both their names, the cost for half of the home would be based on half of the original cost (plus improvements). The cost for the other half would be based on half of the estate value (the current market value). Audrey knew the original cost was $50,000. She didn't expect to sell the home right away, but she now understood why she needed an appraisal. She would add that to her list of things to do.

John's company stock had always been registered in his name because it was acquired primarily through stock options. Audrey had always been a little annoyed that it was not jointly held. After all, she helped John be the success he was at the company, so she thought her name should be on the stock, too. However, Mr. Silver explained to her that it really was better this way. Because it was part of John's estate, the stock would be valued at the date of his death (or six months later). This estate value would become her cost, and the difference between this price and the price of the stock when it was sold would determine the amount of her taxable gain.

Audrey quickly realized that this was a big benefit. If she wanted to sell this stock, she would pay a relatively small federal capital gains tax. Apart from the sentimental attachment John had for the company stock, he always told her they couldn't afford to sell it because he, as an employee, had purchased it at lower prices; if it were sold at market value, substantial capital gains taxes would be due. Now that she no longer had to worry about paying taxes on the gain, Mr. Silver told her he thought it was unwise to have all her investments in one company. He felt strongly that diversifying her investments was important in order to protect her principal, so he would advise her to sell at least part of her stock in the not-too-distant future. Audrey thought it was a little too soon for her to take the big step of selling John's stock now, but she thought she would be willing to do so eventually. Mr. Silver suggested she consider selling it gradually, and that made sense to her.

Audrey asked Mr. Silver what she should do with the money she had left in the savings account after paying off the mortgage. He suggested she keep part of this money as a cash reserve. This would leave some cash which they could invest at a later date. Until she knew what her expenses were going to be, he suggested she keep this money in a money market account, where it would earn interest. He told her to use her checking account at the bank to pay her monthly bills and have her Social Security and pension checks deposited in that account automatically. She should use her savings account as her investment account and emergency reserve.

Audrey spoke to Mr. Silver about redoing the kitchen, and he agreed with her that it might be a little too soon to tackle such a major renovation. Perhaps six months from now she will be better able to face it.

As for vacations, he encouraged her to consider them. In addition to the possible golf clinic, a widow friend of hers had asked her to consider going to London with her on a theater tour four months from now. Audrey thought that might be a very good idea. Because of John's illness, they had not traveled in a long time, and she would welcome any change of scenery. Besides, it would give her things to look forward to. Maybe she would even buy some new clothes!

- **Audrey's risk tolerance:** Middle of the road
- **Audrey's primary financial goals:** Continue to be financially independent and help to educate Joanne's children
- **Audrey's investment objective:** Preservation of principal

Elizabeth

Reactions to Identifying Today's Financial Attitudes and Realities

Elizabeth completed her "Who Am I Today Financially?" form as follows:

Who Am I Today Financially?

Financial Strengths

1. Recognizing I am capable of make my own financial decisions
2. Understanding my need for professional help
3. Have an understanding of my monthly income and expenses

Financial Weaknesses

1. Still fearful of making independent financial decisions without support
2. Continue to be uncertain about my ability to understand finances
3. No tolerance for risk
4. Prefer to handle as little as possible financially

Financial Needs

1. Financial security
2. To have enough money to spend on myself for items like travel
3. To focus on estate planning and housing issues
4. To review my feelings with regard to risk

Elizabeth was definitely risk averse. Although most people thought business owners such as her husband Ben were risk takers, his had been a pretty traditional business—owning and running a hardware store. Neither she nor Ben liked to take chances.

Her primary financial goal was to have sufficient income to continue living comfortably. After reviewing her budget, she decided that because her home was paid for and her needs were small, she had sufficient income to pay the bills.

193

Her primary investment objective was to preserve principal—that is, to make her money last for the rest of her life. She and Ben had no children, so she didn't have to worry about leaving anyone money. Having taken care of Ben in his declining years, she was well aware of the medical expenses involved in long-term care. She wanted to be financially independent and able to take care of herself.

Next, Elizabeth decided to meet with Mr. Samuels, the trust officer whom Mr. Grossfeldt had recommended to her. Sam Weatherly agreed once again to accompany her. Mr. Samuels had reviewed Ben's portfolio report, which Mr. Grossfeldt had sent him before their meeting. He explained to her that it contained conservative stocks and a few corporate bonds that paid annual income.

Mr. Samuels reviewed the investments Ben owned and told Elizabeth he thought there was no urgent need to make changes to the portfolio because overall the holdings were good quality. He said that if he managed the portfolio, he would recommend she invest in what he called a balanced portfolio, investing about 40 percent in corporate and government bonds and 60 percent in good-quality stocks paying dividends. He indicated that with this mix that after paying the trust fees, her current annual income should increase. Mr. Samuels told her that the management fees would be charged to the account so Elizabeth would not have to pay a separate bill. She was pleased to hear this, as she wanted her financial life to be as uncomplicated as possible.

Mr. Samuels also suggested that she discuss with Mr. Grossfeldt the idea of putting this portfolio into a living revocable trust in her name. If she did this, she could be her own trustee, but the bank could act on her behalf if she wished to travel or became incapacitated. In addition, when she died, the assets would go directly to her heirs without going through the probate process. He said she did not have to make this decision right away, but several of his widowed clients had found it to be a good solution.

Elizabeth left the trust department feeling reassured. It appeared that Mr. Samuels clearly understood that she didn't want to take much risk and that her investment objectives were to preserve her principal as well as provide sufficient income to take care of herself. "Hmm" thought Elizabeth "Look at me, six months ago I didn't even know what an investment objective was. Here I am telling a banker what I want my money to do for me." The fact that Mr. Grossfeldt had recommended Mr. Samuels was comforting to her. She liked the fact that they were used to working together.

After discussing the meeting with Sam Weatherly, Elizabeth decided she would move her investments to the Trust Department. The current portfolio manager may have done a terrific job for Ben, but she didn't know him at all, and she felt much safer working with a bank trust officer. The next step was to transfer the portfolio to Mr. Samuels' bank.

Mr. Grossfeldt told her all that was necessary was to write a letter to the current portfolio manager telling him of her decision. Ben's contract with the manager stipulated that 30 days' written notice was required in order to transfer the account. Mr. Grossfeldt provided her with a letter to send to the manager. In it, she asked for a final bill, a statement of the portfolio value on the date of Ben's death, and a statement of any purchases or sales that had taken place in the account in the calendar year before the date of Ben's death. She should also ask for a separate statement of those sales which took place after his death as well as a statement of any dividends collected, and fees charged during both time periods. Mr. Grossfeldt explained that her accountant would need all these numbers. He also warned her that the portfolio manager might try to talk her out of her decision, because no one likes to lose an account. He urged her to tell him that the decision was final, and if the manager continued to object. Mr. Grossfeldt would be glad to talk to him on her behalf.

Mr. Grossfeldt suggested Elizabeth call Mr. Samuels to tell him of her decision so he could send her the forms she needed to sign and make sure that the transfer occurred. Mr. Grossfeldt made it clear to Elizabeth that this did not have to be an irrevocable decision. If at any time in the future she decided she no longer wanted the bank to manage her money, she could move her assets elsewhere. In addition, he said that he thought setting up this account in a revocable trust was a good idea.

- **Elizabeth's risk tolerance:** Low
- **Elizabeth's primary financial goal:** Maintain financial independence and comfortable lifestyle
- **Elizabeth's investment objective:** Preserve principal

CHAPTER TEN

Identifying Today's Personal Attitudes and Realities

A bout six months to a year following the occurrence of their loss, many widows find themselves looking at where they are personally Again, there are no exact periods when this is likely to take place, and there is nothing amiss if you find it takes more or less time. Some widows, out of economic necessity, are forced to deal with these issues in a much shorter period. Others take longer because they are financially able to do so. The ability to take a new look at where you are in life usually results from the passage of time, a better acceptance of your widowed state, and the courage to face a future without your spouse. Regardless of your financial knowledge at the time of your husband's death and your emotional response to facing financial issues, by this time you have had to address certain realities in your financial situation. Now you are ready to look in a comprehensive way at other issues that affect your life both now and in the future.

Depending on your age, physical and mental health, financial resources, responsibilities, and education, you need to make certain decisions about your future. Such things as life expectancy, financial security, personal goals, dreams, hopes, and fears need to be reevaluated. Whatever your patterns have been in the past, give serious thought to whether or not you wish to maintain these patterns in the future. Surprisingly, on reflection, a number of widows find themselves drawn to activities other than those they previously thought to be of critical importance.

At this juncture in your life, we suggest it is essential for you to assess both your skills and needs. You need to identify for yourself that you might want to do with your life to experience more fulfillment, acknowledging that your husband is no longer there to help you meet your needs or participate in your realizing any objectives you may have set for yourself. Although your life has changed dramatically because you have lost your husband, it has not ended.

In this book, we have not focused on widows who were unhappily married and felt trapped in their marriage for financial, religious, or family reasons. Widows making up this group are those who were physically and/or psychologically abused, those who found themselves in a marriage devoid of emotion, or those whose beliefs about duty to husband and family predominated over any other considerations. This widow's reaction to her loss may be complicated by feelings of relief. She may therefore feel guilty because she is unable to experience the feelings of sorrow she believes she is expected to feel.

If this is your situation, accept where you are and look ahead to what you may realize in the future. You did what you did. The past is now over, and you have the opportunity to focus on yourself and obtain your personal goals. At long last, you can attempt to meet your personal needs. For some widows, just the cessation of the fear, stress, and tension will be sufficient. As you heal, think about your needs and where you are in life. This approach will enable you to move forward. For some, the pace may be rapid, while for others it is interminably slow. The important thing to remember is, despite the pace, you are making progress down your personal path to a new you.

If for any reason at this point in the grief process you are unable to move forward, you may want to seek the services of professionals or groups described in chapter 3, whether or not you did so at an earlier time.

Who Am I Today Personally?

Regardless of your circumstances, you are emerging from what is likely to have been the most painful experience of your life. You have survived, and you are now ready to move forward personally and thrive. To help you identify who and where you are, we have developed the "Who Am I Today Personally?" form.

Who Am I Today Personally?

Personal Strengths

1. _____

2. _____

3. _____

4. _____

Personal Weaknesses

1. _____

2. _____

3. _____

4. _____

Personal Needs

1. _____

2. _____

3. _____

4. _____

In completing your "Who Am I Today Personally?" form, consider as "Personal Strengths" characteristics people admire about you or things that come easily to you. Under "Personal Weaknesses," identify those areas where you have had more difficulty than others you know. We all have strengths and weaknesses. Personality traits should be viewed on a continuum from least to most. Most people have more or less of a certain characteristic, which leads people to say they are outgoing or shy, overly emotional, or stoic, or whatever. It is the combination of these traits in a given individual that results in the image the individual presents to the world.

It is time to clarify your "Personal Needs." Are you a person who requires a great deal of emotional support to feel good about yourself? Do you thrive on social contacts, or do you prefer a quiet life with little intrusion from the outside? Is learning, whether from exposure to cultural events or in an academic environment, important to you? Is travel for recreation or the expansion of horizons important to you? Do you feel best when you are working or volunteering?

What you are attempting to do here is define where you are personally at this time in your life. Once you have identified your strengths, weaknesses, and needs, you are ready to move forward.

Family Issues

If you live in close geographic proximity to your family—whether parents, children, or grandchildren—they may encourage you to spend more time with them. If you enjoy your family, you may be willing to do so. You may also feel closer to your children now and want to be surrounded by their families as often as possible.

If you don't have family nearby, as part of the healing process you should make a concerted effort to participate in social activities.

Elderly Parents

If you have elderly parents in need of your attention, you may now find yourself more focused on their needs. Many of you were unable to do this for a period of time before your husband's death, and perhaps you feel guilty about having neglected them. Elderly parents likewise present financial needs that most children, widowed or not, feel obligated to meet. As the elderly population continues to grow, so do their economic needs. Some elderly parents don't have sufficient financial resources.

This is illustrated in the case of Susan, who is concerned about her mother's situation. She truly feels the need to help her mother and provide her with the best care possible.

Dependent Adult Children

Perhaps the most complex emotional issue on a family level that a widow may confront is that of the dependent adult child. Increasingly, adult children are staying at home longer, marrying later, and seeking their parents' financial support for a variety of reasons. Parents often feel guilty about adult children who are not self-supporting. They may believe having a child who has not found herself or himself by this time in life suggests they have not done a good job of parenting. This tends to increase the likelihood of the widowed mother providing the adult child with money for whatever need is presented to alleviate her guilt. It might be additional education, a business venture, or a place to live.

Consider the family issues presented here and make an effort to evaluate them with respect to what you feel comfortable doing, not what you feel obliged to do. Decide for yourself what you need to do for yourself to best meet your own needs before any other considerations. Do not view this as being selfish. Your primary goal is self-preservation.

Social Contacts

It is quite usual for recent widows to surround themselves with family members and friends if they are available. Initially, seeking comfort from people you know is appropriate and helpful. After six months to a year into your widowhood, however, this approach is too exclusionary. Despite the fact that you may have little or no energy to devote to something or someone unfamiliar, try to do something in your daily life that will bring new people into your world. Determine your comfort level and then work toward some new contacts. You might start with something as simple as a conversation with someone you've met casually or in conjunction with your new responsibilities, such as a member of your congregation whom you don't know, or more formally by contacting a group of widowed persons. Although we have introduced this concept earlier in the book, you may not have been ready to venture beyond your circle of family and friends. Our goal here is to broaden your existing support group. Looking ahead to new activities makes a positive contribution to one's mental health.

Existing Friends and Acquaintances

Widowhood sometimes creates serious shifts in existing friendships. You and your husband may have had a few close couple friends with whom you did most of your socializing and vacationing. Now you may find yourself uncomfortable with these coupled activities and instead choose to share social activities only with the wives during the day. Some widows report they detect a difference in the attitude of their previously close women friends. Sometimes these women, whom they had thought of as close friends, now act as if the widow is a threat to their own marriages and are reluctant to include her in activities that may lead to additional exposure to their husbands. Needless to say, if this occurs, the widow is not eager to continue to socialize with these friends in the way she had in the past.

On the other hand, some widows have friends who go out of their way to encourage them to continue their former social life. If the widow is comfortable with these friends, she needs to deal directly with them about paying her own way. Still other widows had few contacts outside their home and their husband and find themselves at a loss as to how to occupy their time.

Reflect on previous patterns in relation to what you would like for yourself now. You may want to maintain your existing patterns, but you may also want to make some changes. There are many groups one may join to develop new social contacts based on age or interest. Consider joining such a group. This does not mean you are committing to participating with people you don't know that well. Rather, it is exposing yourself to new people while focused on some personal interest or activity. If, for whatever the reason, you find that the group doesn't work for you, do not feel obligated to remain involved. Feel comfortable establishing your personal boundaries from the outset.

Becoming active in a new activity does not preclude maintaining your previous social activities. It is a way of adding to your existing network of friends. Take this opportunity to expand your contacts and knowledge.

New Friends

Perhaps you find yourself sitting in your home or apartment wondering what you are going to do about developing new social contacts. Will you need to find all new friends?

These questions may seem overwhelming at first, but in time they will be answered in what a natural progression for each widow is. Now, as in the past, you will make decisions about your life when you are ready. Decide which areas you feel comfortable exploring first and get started. If you decide to investigate widow support groups, do so. Again, a friend, spiritual leader, physician, or a widowed persons group might be helpful in identifying an appropriate group for you. We have found that the attitudes and needs of the divorced population differ from the attitudes and needs of the widowed population. However, many of these groups feature discussions on various topics dealing with aspects of relationships between men and women following separation and divorce that are applicable to both the widowed and the divorced. You can usually contact a given group and find out about its structure and the topic to be discussed on a given evening. If you are affiliated with a religious group, they may offer group meetings for the widowed or single population.

If a group approach does not appeal to you, think about something you might like to do for personal satisfaction. You might enroll in a class at a local community college, taking anything from flower arranging to Chinese. You might want to join a health club where you can arrange your own routine. Check out classes offered by universities and museums as well as adult education classes sponsored by the library, the public school system, the YWCA/YMCA, your church or synagogue, or senior citizen organizations, just to name a few. Many areas have a variety of singles activities that are advertised in the local newspaper. Some of these may be of interest to you.

Will you or should you think about male social contacts? Will anyone find you attractive again? What if someone asked you out? How would you respond to the introduction or expectation of some physical relationship between yourself and this new person? Could you ever have sex with a man other than your husband?

After the passage of time, widows have turned to online dating sites to meet new male companions. Widows we have spoken to have had varied reactions to this approach. Some found it helpful while others didn't. All were very clear that if you decide to do this, be mindful of what you put on your profile. Be honest, realistic, and clear about what you are looking for in a relationship. Be careful not to initially provide any personal or financial information that would lead to your actual identity. Unfortunately, widows can be targets for scammers seeking your money. Whatever you decide, be cautious!

If you are going to develop a new you, you need to let go of any excessive ties to the past and move into the future. One way to accomplish this goal is to allow yourself to meet new people, acquire new knowledge, and broaden your horizons. Not dwelling on the past and instead adding new dimensions to your life will enable you to find greater satisfaction in the years ahead.

Widowers

Just as not all widows are the same, neither are all widowers. However, be aware of some societal factors that often impact the widowers' mourning process that makes it different from yours. Many men have been raised with the belief that it is unmanly to express emotion. Expressing emotions is frequently thought of as something that is acceptable for girls and women but not for men. It is common for a widower to view expressing emotion as a weakness. A man is supposed to be tough and not express his pain to those around him. If he is an older man, he might think of himself as a rock or a tree upon whom his family can lean.

These distorted views make the healing process more difficult for the widower. He may find himself unable to shed tears. He may not allow himself to seek the solace he so desperately needs. As a result, he may attempt to drown his sorrows in alcohol or other destructive behavior. Basically, he is running away from the emotion that he must express in a healthy way in order to heal and move forward. He may appear insensitive and caught up in pretending that he is strong and able to deal with anything. The death of a wife also reminds a man of his personal vulnerability and mortality. It is not unusual to read stories in the media about a visible public figure behaving in very destructive ways following a loss. Years after the incident, this person may come to terms with what was experienced and attempt to help other men by sharing his personal agony and suggest that these men who are experiencing loss attempt to mourn. They are encouraged not to follow in his footsteps.

Men are conditioned by our society to consider themselves to be in control, even powerful. Nothing challenges this belief system as much as the death of a wife. In place of strength, they feel loneliness and emotional isolation. Perhaps because men often have so much difficulty expressing their emotions, they experience more physical effects as widowers than do widows. They report having a variety of illnesses, most commonly of a cardiac nature. Sometimes they express these concerns to their physician, but equally often they attempt to medicate themselves with over-the-counter drugs and alcohol.

Widowers are also likely to experience mental health problems such as depression. Unfortunately, they are also more resistant to seeking professional help, which, after all, could be interpreted as a sign of weakness.

In general, widowers tend to reattach in a relatively short time after the death of their wives. It is common for a widower to attempt to deal with his grief by seeking female companionship. One widower shared with us that, after his wife died, he experienced no emotion but decided he did not want to face an empty home another night. At that moment he decided to contact a female acquaintance and invite her to dinner. She accepted and within a relatively short period of time he was reattached, committed, and subsequently married. This remarriage took place less than a year after his wife had died. It should not surprise the reader that the relationship did not last. Once again this widower found himself alone, albeit wiser in terms of recognizing the need to deal with his loss.

Other widowers deal with their grief by not allowing themselves to take the time to grieve. These men make every effort to keep themselves frenetically busy by taking on even more work responsibility or spending more time with male friends in various activities such as golf and tennis. In this way they attempt to mask their grief by remaining in constant motion and often fall asleep in a state of total fatigue. This approach rarely works and will most likely lead to other problems.

Sometimes, widowers feel it is not appropriate for their children to see them in a weakened condition. They have bought the myth that they need to be strong for the children. In reality, it would help all family members if they could mourn together, sharing memories, heartaches, and special moments.

Widowers, like widows, experience sexual anxieties. The loss of a wife might make a widower feel impotent because he was unable to prevent his wife's death. This sometimes leads to a need to become sexually active as soon as possible. On the other hand, the widower may have had no sexual experiences with anyone other than his wife in so many years that he is anxious about his ability to perform and please another woman.

There is no one pattern that fits all widowers any more than there is one pattern that fits all widows. Neither widow nor widower is able to replace that which has been lost. Both must accept the need to mourn their loss and move on, gradually allowing themselves to redefine who they are over time. There are different emotions experienced if the death of your spouse follows a drawn-out debilitating illness as contrasted to an unexpected death.

If you as a widow find yourself socializing with a new widower, keep in mind that he is probably experiencing many of the same emotions that you are experiencing but may express them very differently. As always, open communication is recommended.

Exercise

Your physical health is of particular importance at this point in your life. It is crucial both to your recovery and to your future health. Studies show that physical fitness programs are essential to physical and mental well-being. Exercise programs are known to reduce stress and tension, and certainly this has been a time of considerable stress for you.

If you have been involved in an exercise program, make every effort to maintain it in some form. If you have not been involved in an exercise program, try to develop one that is suitable for your age and present physical condition. Your efforts will be rewarded. You will relieve stress and feel better about yourself.

Walking is a great way to begin. In some areas, group walks are sponsored by various agencies or organizations. Many different facilities provide advice on exercise in relation to health. Some are free or charge a minimal fee, such as a hospital or senior citizen group, while health clubs, country clubs, the YMCA, YWCA, and JCC charge a stated fee for participation in their programs and the use of their equipment and facilities. You might consider joining a local health club, where an instructor will show you how to use the equipment. You might also consider taking physical fitness classes on a regular basis, which may be the best way to motivate yourself to maintain a sustained exercise plan.

If in the past you were an avid or even casual player of a particular sport, your health allows you to remain active in that sport, and it still interests you, maintain this activity. You might need to find a new group of people with whom to share your interest. Most municipalities offer group programs in various sports. If you belong to a country club, discuss your situation with the appropriate pro, and he or she will help you find someone to play with at your level.

Groups such as the Sierra Club offer different levels of activities for environmentally oriented hikers and campers. Most areas will have some group focusing on skiing or tennis. Read the papers; ask your friends and relatives about groups in which they have had a successful experience. If you are shy and uncomfortable at the thought of entering some activity on your own, work at overcoming these feelings. These groups are designed to meet your needs, and the members will usually extend a warm welcome to you. You'll find, to your surprise and comfort, others in the group may have had feelings similar to your own.

The most individualized approach is the personal exercise trainer. This person will work with you either in your home, if appropriate, or in a given facility to create an exercise regimen tailored to your needs. Again, information about qualified personal trainers may be obtained online, from newspapers, a health club, or friends.

For women with sufficient funds who are desirous of trying to work on a personal health and exercise program, a trip to a spa is a wonderful way to refocus. For one thing, many people go alone. Being there without a friend or mate is not at all awkward. Some spas have a dining structure designed to promote conversation for those by themselves. Everyone is friendly, and you are able to do as much or as little as you want on the physical side while being pampered. All sorts of beauty and health treatments are available as well as classes in meditation, yoga, stress reduction, and nutrition. The focus is on inner and outer recovery, the very process you need.

Nutrition

Like exercise, nutrition is often overlooked in the early stages of your widowhood and beyond. Now that you are on your own and responsible for just yourself it is easy to neglect eating balanced meals. Some of you may find that you have forgotten to eat for a long block of time and suddenly realize that it is evening and you have not eaten all days. Others of you may snack all day and skip meals. Some may turn to unhealthy patterns such as overeating, increased dependence on alcohol or drugs.

It is important that during this difficult yet transitional time in your life that you are mindful of good nutrition. Your body requires nourishment to cope with all that has to be done and you need to make an effort to provide that nourishment in a healthy and balanced way. Try to find a way to regularize your eating patterns. Don't neglect this aspect of your current life. Make sure that you are providing your body with the nutrients it needs to help you heal.

If you have any concerns about your diet or have lost or gained weight, you might make an appointment to see your primary care physician. She will assess your situation and offer suggestions as how to improve your diet. She might even recommend that you consult with a nutritionist to help you make better food choices to meet your body's needs.

Sex

Many widows with whom we have worked are sensitive and awkward about dating and the thought of a sexual relationship with another man. Sentiments such as "I can't go back to dating the way I did when I was younger," "I feel ridiculous," and "I can't imagine myself in bed with another man" are frequently expressed. Keep in mind that any man whom you might meet at this stage of your life has similar anxieties and feelings—perhaps even more so because his concerns about sexual performance.

It is often advisable to discuss these feelings with a friend or in a group with others who are in a similar situation. You will be able to articulate your fears and questions, and you will recognize that what you are experiencing is probably not unique to you but shared by others. After a while, you will be ready to envision spending time with a man and to think of him as a person with feelings and a lifetime of experiences, just like yourself. If you should meet a man or be introduced to a man you may be interested in, you will begin this relationship by getting to know each other. This process is much the same as when you were younger but now with the addition of maturity and, it is hoped, a better sense of self.

There are no givens! If the relationship progresses, there will come a time when both of you are ready for it to become a sexual one. Many women feel embarrassed and uncomfortable at first because they feel they are betraying their husband or family. It is common to struggle with the issue of loyalty. Do not feel awkward if the only man you ever slept with was your husband. This should not prevent you from seeking a new relationship. The new man in your life will not replace your husband but he may very likely provide you with an equally positive sexual experience.

If you have successfully progressed through the mourning process, you should now be able to get past these normal feelings of discomfort and move forward with your own life in whatever way feels right for you. Some widows have no desire for any new sexual experiences. Others miss sex a great deal and do not know what to do with their feelings.

Sex, in addition to exercise, for example, often provides an emotional release for the tension that a widow experiences in her new state. The lessening of tension and stress is something most widows need.

We are all sexual beings, and self-satisfaction is also an option. Some young widows—and some not so young—find themselves seeking sexual encounters early on in their widowhood just to affirm their femininity and sexuality. Others have no interest in pursuing this approach. Once again, there are no real guidelines here. Do what is right for you. For many widows, more important than the need for sex is the need for the warmth, closeness, tenderness, and affection previously provided within the marital relationship. Some women feel a greater loss on this level than they do on the sexual one. The familiar pat on the head, occasional peck on the cheek, or hug when needed—all that is gone. The absence of these shared intimacies creates a major void. Some widows would be most grateful to have this need met without any sexual component.

For some women, socializing with other widows or friends is satisfactory. They feel no strong desire for another man in their life. They feel too old or are uncomfortable trying out new experiences that expose them to new people. If such is your case and you are content with your decision, go ahead with it. If your decision is based on feelings of inadequacy or uncertainty and you are aware of that, seek group or professional help to move forward (see chapter 3).

Summary and Conclusion

After you have dealt with the feelings and issues associated with initial loss, you will find yourself at a point where you need to review your own present and future. It is time to think about yourself in a new light, to explore new horizons. Perhaps being in a position to maintain your existing activities and contacts is sufficient. Perhaps you are still uncertain as to what you would like to do in the future. Whatever you are experiencing, it is essential to allow yourself to think about your own needs, desires, and aspirations in a new light. It is time to make the most of what has been for you such a painful experience. As with childbirth, out of pain can come a rewarding new beginning.

Diane

Reactions to Identifying Today's
Personal Attitudes and Realities

Diane completed her "Who Am I Today Personally?" form as follows:

Who Am I Today Personally?

Personal Strengths

1. Outgoing
2. Better organized
3. Better able to address and solve problems
4. Becoming more self-confident

Personal Weaknesses

1. Seek excessive approval for personal decisions
2. Underestimate my intelligence
3. Tend to spoil children (to compensate for loss of father)
4. Preoccupied by children's needs

Personal Needs

1. Affection
2. Approval from others
3. Friends
4. Financial security

As she reviewed her responses, Diane realized how much she had personally changed since Mark's death. She had learned so much. Now, for the first time in her life, she was responsible for herself and—even scarier—her children.

She reflected on her general acceptance of what anyone she viewed as an authority in the financial area told her shortly after Mark died. She remembered how willing she was to accept the advice of Jack Bradford, the insurance agent, regarding putting all her money into an annuity. What if she had gone ahead and done that? She now knew that would not have been a good decision for her. It was now difficult for Diane to relate to the woman she was when she was married to Mark. Why was it that she had never questioned him about anything?

In her widow support group, Diane had identified that she had resisted growing up and Mark had assumed the role of her father, especially in the financial area, probably because he thought it was expected of him. Perhaps she had married Mark because he allowed her to maintain her childhood views with regard to money—namely it was the man's responsibility. After all, her dad had always paid her bills. In her musings, she thought that she would be a much different marital partner today than when she was married to Mark. She also wondered, when she allowed herself to, whether Mark would have loved the person she was today. They had obviously done so well together because they fulfilled each other's needs at the time they met. Did he enjoy having her so dependent on him? She'd never know the answer to that question.

Diane and Robyn had become such close friends that Diane had no trouble turning to her to discuss her dilemma about the children's education. Robyn told her about the various programs the public schools offered to children depending on their needs. Diane was surprised to learn that they made an effort to identify children who were particularly bright as well as those with learning difficulties. There were specialized enrichment programs in what were designated as magnet schools; there were schools in which the children were instructed in English as well as one of several foreign languages; there were various honors classes, advanced placement classes, and so on. Schools had school counselors and some even had support groups for children living in a single-parent home.

Diane had no idea the public school system provided its students with so many different options. Robyn encouraged her to make appointments to meet with the principals of the schools the children would attend if they went to public school. She assured Diane these professionals would be very cordial and wouldn't mind discussing their particular school with her. Diane followed Robyn's advice and was very pleased with the outcome of her meetings with the principals. If she had to go this route, she would now be comfortable with the quality of the instructional programs that would be available to the children.

Dorothy Trumbull had been very definite with Diane about her financial options: She would have to either sell her home and buy a less expensive one or move the children from their private schools to public schools. She might even have to do both. In addition, she would have to go back to work. Diane knew she had resisted dealing with this issue long enough. She knew she needed to discuss this with the children the way she had earlier discussed the budget. Before doing so, however, she decided to talk with her dad. She had avoided getting him involved in her financial problems, but she knew how much he loved and cared about the children. She could no longer worry about what he thought of Mark. She had to resolve this matter now.

She called her dad and asked him if he would meet her for lunch at a local restaurant because she wanted to go over some things with him. Diane had always talked to her parents in the home in which she had grown up, and she wanted this to be different. She was making progress toward the comfort level she hoped she'd eventually achieve when it came to money matters, and she didn't want to regress to her former dependency.

After they had ordered their lunch, Diane brought out the most recent financial statements she had developed with Dorothy. They clearly indicated her assets and liabilities as well as a negative cash flow. Diane told her dad about her visits to the schools. She had reconciled herself to the idea of putting the children in the local public schools but wanted his input as to the advisability of selling the home. She really felt the stability provided by staying in the home was exceedingly valuable for the children.

After Diane had laid all of this out for her father, she sat back somewhat nervously to hear his response. For a few seconds, which seemed much longer, her dad said nothing. She looked up at him expectantly and was shocked to see a tear in his eye. What had she said or done to sadden or upset him? She couldn't think of anything.

At this point, her dad reached across the table and took her hand. "Diane," he said, "I can't believe how much you've changed since Mark died. You'll always be my little girl, but now you are an adult woman, and I am so proud of how much you've grown. I don't know this financial planning woman you've been seeing, but she has certainly given you good advice. I basically agree with the direction in which you are moving and think you should stay in your current home. But I am really concerned about Erin. She'll be going into her junior year next year, and I would hate to see her have to adjust to a new school during a year that's so critical to college preparation. I know I don't need to tell you this, but Erin will always have a special place in my heart because she was my first grandchild. In any case, I'd like you to allow me to take up the financial responsibility for her tuition for the next two years. I'm sure your mother will agree."

Diane smiled to herself, thinking her mother would go along with anything her father suggested, just the way she would have with Mark. She wasn't sure how she felt about this offer. Was it fair to Alice and Jeremy? How would they feel about their sister having the opportunity to remain in her school while they had to go to a public school? On the other hand, she had the same concerns about Erin her dad had expressed. Before she could reply and thank Dad for his generous offer, he went on to say he wanted to do something for the other two children, but it would have to be at a later date. Perhaps he could pay for one year of college tuition for each of them. Diane thanked him profusely but said she would have to discuss it with the children.

Seeing his quizzical look, she explained that they functioned differently as a family now and discussed as a unit decisions that involved all of them. Diane realized this was the first time she had eaten a meal with her dad by herself since she graduated from high school. She felt good about it. She recognized from the way he looked at her that he had a new respect for her. She didn't have a problem with his paying for the lunch; it was just the way it was. He hugged her extra hard when they parted in the restaurant parking lot.

That very evening Diane resolved to discuss with the children the financial realities that prevented them from continuing in their present schools. She had expected a big fuss and lots of tears. She was pleasantly surprised. The children all said, given the choice, they would rather stay in their home than attend their present schools. However, Erin did not feel it was fair for her to continue at her school if Jeremy and Alice had to go to public school. Jeremy told her she was being ridiculous. He could accept what his grandfather proposed and was willing to risk that his grandfather would be willing and able to help him when he entered college. Alice said she was scared, but if Jeremy could deal with public school, she guessed she could too. She wanted to know if she could still see her present school friends. They had a good discussion about the schools. In the end, everyone agreed that Erin should finish her last two years in her present school.

Diane was so proud of her children. She was pleased with their family meetings. When Mark was alive, all of them seemed to function individually, although she never looked at it that way at the time. They had all matured. It was hard for Diane to acknowledge that they worked better as a family unit now than they ever had in the past. She thought it was a healthy change. Erin asked if she could call her grandfather to thank him and tell him that they had talked it over and she was going to accept his generous offer. Diane thought that was a nice idea.

Diane felt relieved when the discussion about schools was over. She had been preoccupied with the question of the private schools since she had "come to" following Mark's sudden death. She was now ready to pay attention to her own needs. She decided to investigate whether the University of Maryland had a program that would allow her to update her paralegal skills. If they didn't offer one, they might know of a course that was offered by another school in the area. She had seen ads on TV for online universities. Perhaps that would work for her. She wondered how she would feel about working again. It would all be so different now.

Diane called Robyn because she wanted her to be the first to know she had resolved the school issue. She had never had a friend like her before, yet they might never have met and become friends if it weren't for the widow support group. Robyn was so pleased to learn of Diane's decision.

Robyn told Diane she would not accept any more excuses from her about not going to the health club. Robyn knew Diane had played tennis when Mark was alive but that she had not been ready to do anything on a physical level since his death. Robyn had often told her how working out at the health club had enabled her to survive after her husband's death. She would no longer accept no as an answer because of this or that—she was going to take Diane as her guest this coming weekend!

Diane laughed and said, "Okay, you win. I'll go with you and see what I think. I'm so out of shape I would be embarrassed to be seen in shorts and a T-shirt!" Robyn told her, no matter what, she would look better in those clothes than some of the others did, and she had really benefited from her exercise program. She assured Diane the other people would make her feel welcome and comfortable. As always, Diane felt good about her conversation with Robyn.

Next, Diane called Dorothy to update her on where she was with regard to the schools and the home. She had checked with Montgomery College, a community college near her. They did have a paralegal studies program that she could take which would enable her to update her paralegal skills. The counselor there had been very helpful about what courses she would need to take to qualify for a job. She and Dorothy agreed that this was a necessary investment in her future. Then Diane somewhat reluctantly told Dorothy that she really wanted to join the health club. The club had this promotional offer and she wanted to take advantage of it. She realized it was an extravagance, but she thought it was necessary for her mental and physical health. Could she afford it?

Dorothy reviewed Diane's budget once again. Needless to say, eliminating the tuition costs had helped a lot. She had to add the expense of a semester for the paralegal course, the membership fee for the health club and the cost of a new computer Diane would need to help her complete her course work and keep better track of any number of other things. The result was that Diane still had a negative cash flow in her projected annual budget. This discouraged Diane, but Dorothy reassured her that this figure was much better than the previous negative cash flow.

The reason she had advised Diane to set aside the large cash reserve was so she would be in a position to cover this negative cash flow. Next year, assuming she was able to get a job as a paralegal, she should be able to cover expenses and replenish her cash reserve. However, it was obvious to Diane she would need to continue to try to reduce their expenses. Time for another family meeting!

Susan

Reactions to Identifying Today's Personal Attitudes and Realities

Susan completed her "Who Am I Today Personally?" form as follows:

Who Am I Today Personally?

Personal Strengths

1. More self-confident on a personal and professional level
2. Willing to reach out to her brother for help with her mother

Personal Weaknesses

1. Tends to withdraw into herself and avoid socialization
2. Reluctant to delegate responsibility
3. Difficulty to recognizing her self-worth professionally

Personal Needs

1. Learn to advocate for herself
2. Regular fitness program
3. Need to be perceived as a good daughter

In contemplating her responses to the "Who Am I Today Personally?" form, Susan realized that Lance's death and her work with Dr. Coleman had impacted the way she saw herself. She now saw herself in her personal life as someone capable of being proactive, whereas before she would have described herself as reactive—in other words, waiting for something to happen and then responding. Today, she was more likely to analyze a situation, giving thought to possible actions she might initiate to resolve the matter as opposed to waiting for she knew not what. Her increased understanding of her financial situation had made her aware of her need to earn more money. Her sessions with Dr. Coleman had increased her sense of self-worth. They had discussed her functioning at her job. She now realized she was underpaid for the work she was doing in her present job. The Association had given her regular salary increases; however, if she was honest with herself, she had to acknowledge that her pay was not commensurate with her job responsibilities. She also realized she was capable of assuming greater responsibility than her current job entailed.

Susan knew she would be attending the American Society of Association Executives (ASAE) convention in two weeks. She found herself actually looking forward to having the opportunity to talk with her peers about the current job market. As she boarded the plane for the convention, she surprised herself with the realization that she was no longer afraid to think about the future without Lance. The time away from home and the demands of daily life would allow her to reflect on her options in a more leisurely fashion. She noted, as she seemed to do with most events that had occurred following Lance's death, that this was the first flight she had taken since Lance died. Before she knew it, she had landed, transported herself to the hotel, and checked into her room.

After getting settled in her room, she went downstairs to register for the convention. Susan found herself in a short line in front of a man about her age who began to chat with her while they waited. He asked which association she represented and identified both the city in which he lived and the association with which he was affiliated. The line moved very slowly. Apparently, one of the registrants in front of them had lost his badge. It took some time for the registration personnel to locate the information and replace the badge, delaying the registration process for those in line behind him.

Susan and the man, who had now identified himself as Andrew Neily, commiserated about the interminable pace at which their line was proceeding. By the time Susan reached the head of their line, Andrew had asked her to have a drink with him later on that day. Both of them were attending the convention without coworkers. Susan found herself hesitating. She had never considered the possibility of having this type of social contact at the convention. She had been exclusively focused on her career and business concerns. Her lack of response caused Andrew to inquire if something was wrong. She assured him no, and without further thought accepted the invitation.

When she returned to her room, she panicked. What had she done? What would this outwardly friendly guy think of her? How could she socialize with a man other than Lance? She wanted to escape but realized Andrew had caught her so off guard she had neglected to find out which hotel he was staying at, so she could not call him to cancel. Oh, well, she guessed one drink couldn't hurt. As the time to meet Andrew approached, Susan found herself thinking about what she would wear. She felt almost girlish yet simultaneously was ashamed and guilty about her feelings. She put on what she thought was a professional-looking dress, softened somewhat by a scarf. "Well," she thought, "If I'm going to do this, I'm going to put my best foot forward."

Andrew was waiting for her in front of the bar—she was relieved she wouldn't have to wait for him. They found a table and placed their order. Susan was unprepared for how easy it was to talk to Andrew. She told him about Lance, and he told her he had recently separated from his wife and was having a difficult time dealing with it. Drinks led to dinner in the hotel. Andrew insisted on paying for the drinks but was amenable to each paying separately for dinner. The evening seemed to fly by, and Susan realized how much she had missed talking to a man about anything other than Lance's estate, varied financial matters, her mother, or her work. She wondered to herself if she would ever find another man with whom she could have a relationship. This was the most pleasant evening she'd had since Lance died. Until now, she had taken for granted that there would not be another man in her life. She experienced a twinge of guilt when she returned to her room and made a note to herself to discuss these feelings with Dr. Coleman. As she prepared for bed, she returned to her earlier thoughts about taking advantage of this convention to get a better sense of what was going on regarding career and salary advancement opportunities in the association world.

Over the next several days, she reestablished some former contacts and made some new ones. She was busy and had little opportunity for socializing other than on a work-related basis. On the evening of the banquet she found herself chatting with Andrew again. They exchanged business cards and agreed to keep in touch, although Susan doubted there would be much opportunity for them to meet again since she lived in Seattle, and he lived in Chicago. Perhaps it was just as well. Susan knew that Andrew would have liked to pursue a relationship with her. Although he had made her realize she was not dead as a woman, she was not yet ready for a relationship with a man. She was glad she had met Andrew but was also grateful for the geographic distance between them.

Susan was very pleased with what she learned about job opportunities. One of the people she met had talked to her about a job that would be opening up soon for an executive director with an association based in Seattle. The salary would be considerably higher than her current salary. Susan thought this possibility sounded interesting—at this point she was about ready to take on a job with greater responsibility. However, before making a final decision, she knew she would discuss her options with Dr. Coleman. Her inclination was to move ahead to something new, but she wondered if Dr. Coleman would think she should first investigate a raise with her present association. Even if she was able to get the raise, she wasn't sure she wanted to maintain her present role. Going to a new association would enable her to move beyond her life with Lance and open doors to viewing her financial attitudes in a different light. The prospective job would be a greater challenge, and she felt ready for it.

On the plane back to Seattle, Susan allowed herself to contemplate where she was in her life in a somewhat new way. Since Lance's death, she had devoted more time to her mother than ever before. Dr. Coleman had suggested to her that she was becoming preoccupied with her mother's situation in order to delay facing more painful personal issues. She knew just how important Susan's mother was to her but emphasized that she could not be all things to her mother. Dr. Coleman did not feel it was healthy for her to assume the role she had in the past to the exclusion of her brother. She was pleased that Susan had spoken to him, and he had agreed to take on a more active role with her mother. His help would be particularly valuable if she pursued this new job.

As the plane brought her back to Seattle, Susan recognized that her psychological need to order her life was causing her to review just about every aspect of her life. Having dinner with a man had caused her to think about her physical and emotional well-being. She and Lance had been fairly active people, but she realized she hadn't done anything physical since his death. She wondered if she could bear to go bicycling. This was an activity from which she and Lance had derived much pleasure. She knew her memories of their rides together would be too painful if she attempted to ride on any of the bicycle paths they had taken. Once, Lance had investigated a cycling club because they had given some thought to taking a bicycle tour through France. Without warning, tears came to her eyes as she thought about the trip they would never take. However, she thought she might be able to get back into her bicycling if she had the opportunity to do it with others. This was another area she needed to investigate sooner rather than later; she even thought she had seen the information on Lance's desk.

Thinking about the bicycle trips she and Lance had taken reminded her of the one they attempted with his children. She had not seen or even heard from Leslie and Adam in quite some time. She guessed they would no longer play a role in one another's lives; perhaps they would send each other perfunctory Christmas cards. In some ways, Susan wished things were different with them because they were a part of Lance. Both she and the children had shared a special relationship with him. Unfortunately, Susan knew all too well that wishing didn't accomplish anything. Instead of ruminating about something that would never be, she should pay more attention to something she did have control over—mainly her friends and her job. Dr. Coleman had been stressing to Susan the need for her to reestablish relationships with some of her former friends and to investigate some new contacts. Attending the convention had moved her to the point where she was ready to deal with people. It felt good to talk to people and share common interests. She hadn't been ready before, but now she was, and she planned to do something about her social life on her return.

Dr. Coleman would be pleased with her response to the convention and her willingness to give serious thought to a new job. Her work with

Dr. Coleman had resulted in Susan's seeing herself in a new light. She had contacted Dr. Coleman to help her deal with the aftermath of Lance's death, but in the process, she had begun to look at herself in ways she never had before. She hated to admit it to herself, but her work with Dr. Coleman had been very valuable and gone far beyond the issues surrounding Lance's death.

Audrey

Reactions to Identifying Today's
Personal Attitudes and Realities

Audrey completed her "Who Am I Today Personally?" form as follows:

Who Am I Today Personally?

Personal Strengths

1. Willingness to assume personal responsibility

2. Socially conscious

3. Desire to learn

4. Enthusiastic about the opportunity for new experiences

Personal Weaknesses

1. Tendency to become overly committed

2. Tendency to neglect my health

Personal Needs

1. To be my own person

2. To be more actively involved with my family

3. To contribute to society

4. To continue to seek new experiences and widen my horizons

Going to the golf clinic at Hilton Head with her friends had been just what the doctor ordered. The golf pros had improved her game considerably, but, even more important, she enjoyed being away with her friends. They were upbeat and teased her about finding a man. Several of her friends were insisting that she consider some sort of online dating. Two of them had other friends who had had very positive experiences finding appropriate companions this way. They even came up with elaborate schemes to attract one man they saw in the clubhouse. They thought he was just right for her.

In fact, they were all surprised when, having inquired about her marital status and learning that she was a widow, he approached her on his own about having a drink. Her friends insisted that she accept, and everyone had something to say about what she should wear. It was like getting ready for a prom. They all laughed so hard she didn't think she'd be able to walk to their designated meeting place. She wasn't sure how she felt about this, but her friends encouraged her, telling her it would be good for her. She didn't even know what she would say to a man at this point in her life. She felt strange but decided to go ahead with the meeting anyway.

When they met, she learned that Lionel, the man in question, was a recently retired corporate executive whose wife had died two years ago. She had also died following a lingering illness, which gave them something in common. In addition, he was charming and witty. He had lived in Atlanta, Georgia all of his life and had four grown children, busy with their own lives. As Lionel spoke about his feelings following the death of his wife, Marian, Audrey began to realize that he had had some different adjustments to make than she had. He obviously understood his financial situation, but he was at a loss as to how to manage anything in the home. He shared with her his sense of inadequacy as to what to do about simple things, such as their cleaning woman asking him what he wanted to do about the rug-cleaning service. Apparently his wife had the rugs professionally cleaned once a year, but he had no idea whether or not he should continue with this service and, if so, when to have it done. He was embarrassed by the question because he felt the woman must have realized that he didn't even know what she was talking about. He remembered feeling like a fool and felt he had stood before her for an interminable amount of time, staring at the floor with his arms dangling at his sides. Finally, he told her to go ahead as usual, but both of them knew he didn't have a clue what that meant.

Marian had always made things appear effortless, and the house-hold had run smoothly, something he accepted without question. Lionel said that in an odd way he felt he had been excluded from her life, which intensified his loneliness and sense of being at a loss as to what he was supposed to do. He mused to Audrey that somehow that moment with the cleaning woman humbled him in terms of all Marian had done managing their home and the children's lives which he never questioned. He also realized he had never tried to be an active participant in that aspect of the family's life. Audrey wondered whether John would have been able to share something like that with anyone or whether he had ever been aware of all she had done to make their home run smoothly.

As they shared their mutual experiences regarding their spouses' illnesses and the early days following the funerals, Audrey became aware of another disparity, yet also a similarity, in their social experiences. Lionel too had not known what to do about the couples who were mutual friends—but from a different perspective. As in her own case, Marian had managed the social calendar. When she was well and even toward the end of her life, if she was well enough to see friends, it just seemed to happen. He wasn't quite sure how. After Marian's death he didn't know what to do with their friends. He didn't want to impose on them and invite himself over to their homes. He didn't want to become the extra man to be paraded before a series of "wonderful" divorced, widowed, or never married women. He didn't want the women to feel sorry for him and feel he needed to be included because he didn't have the ability to prepare his own food, even though it was true that he was hopeless in the kitchen. He wasn't a hermit, and he hated eating alone. He found that he couldn't bear to be at home with the silence of the home crashing down around him. There was always this pervasive sense that he didn't belong anywhere.

Lionel found that his role even with his male friends had changed in subtle ways. For instance, he played golf with the guys on Saturdays, as he had done forever. However, now after having something to eat with them following the game, his friends would go off to do something else with their wives, and he would remain to linger over another glass of beer or cup of coffee and feel disconnected from life. He was no longer part of the group, nor was he removed from it. He described it as always feeling in limbo, of not quite belonging, of not being fish or fowl. It was odd, but until this moment Audrey had never given much thought to how the loss of a spouse might impact a man's life. He was never concerned with issues surrounding paying his share of the bill after a dinner out with mutual friends, as she had been, yet he too had concerns. Clearly, he had some different adjustments and some similar ones. Was it possible to determine which was more difficult? Probably not!

She found she was quite comfortable with Lionel, and drinks led to dinner. Her friends told her they had bet she would end up having dinner with him, but she had said the idea was ridiculous. They'd have a thousand questions for her when she got back to the suite, as well as "we told you so's." Before dinner was over, she had agreed to see Lionel again during her stay at Hilton Head. His interest in her was flattering, but she wasn't sure she was ready for a relationship or even that she wanted one. She guessed she hadn't expected anyone to be interested in her, so she hadn't focused on such an eventuality at all. She knew she would give the whole area of relationships more thought when she got back home.

So much had taken place since John's death. She was still dealing with all the changes in her life and attempting to make good decisions for herself as to how she spent her time. She was very positive about her current relationships with her children and grandchildren. She was closer to Joanne than she had ever been, and both women had benefited from the opportunity they had created to get to know each other better. The weekly lunches had really been a plus. They now shared things with each other they had never shared before. Audrey tried to be as supportive as she could to her daughter with regard to her marriage. She knew there was ongoing tension between the couple because of their financial situation.

She adored Joanne's children, and they felt the same about her. All of them looked forward to her day with them. Because she now had more time to spend with Heidi and Noah, she also made a point of doing extra things with the oldest child, Jamie, who was usually in school during

Audrey's visits. She and "Gran Gran" had some special sleepovers. Audrey always got a thrill out of having the chance to personally watch her grandchildren acquire new skills and proudly demonstrate them for her. Children learned so much in such short periods of time.

She was also pleased with her current relationship with John Jr. In his high school and college years, he and Audrey had been fairly close. It was common for him to come to her with a question about which course might be better for him or, more likely, a question related to a relationship he had with some girl. Their relationship changed when he entered medical school, as did his overall attitude. Audrey couldn't pinpoint when he developed what she called his superior attitude, but she hadn't found it attractive. It created more distance between them. The conversation she had with him in the kitchen about her financial situation had brought them back to where they had been in the past. She thought they both realized this was a turning point for them. John Jr. had gone with her to Mr. Silver's. He liked his approach to his mother's situation as well as his mother's understanding of her financial affairs. He realized he had never given much thought to his own financial affairs, and this type of approach would also be of value to him. Before he left the office with Audrey, he had made an appointment for himself and his wife to meet with Mr. Silver and took home with him various forms that Mr. Silver requested be completed in order to give him a full picture of his financial status.

After this, there were more invitations from her daughter-in-law, of whom Audrey was fond, for dinner or an activity involving her grandchildren. She hadn't seen much of John Jr. and his family before now and felt she was just getting to know them. J.T., the older son, was a freshman in high school and all boy. His younger brother, Casey, was more sensitive and serious, spending all of his spare time poring over computer books and doing scientific experiments. She had both of them over to spend the night and was pleased with the way things turned out. They all seemed to be discovering one another.

Audrey was basically comfortable with her social life too. Some of the couples from her married days had remained friendly with her. They included her in their dinner get-togethers and other activities. There had been some rocky times in the beginning over money, but these had been resolved. At first the men didn't know what to do about her when it came to buying a ticket or paying a restaurant bill. They had tried to pick up her share and split it among them, but that made Audrey feel like a charity case. She had told them as firmly as she could that she wanted to join them but couldn't do it if they would not allow her to pay her own way; it was uncomfortable for her not to do so. They finally got the message and now treated her as an equal on that level. She realized she was the first widow in their circle of friends, so it was like breaking ground. Walter and Jane were still a problem sometimes because of Jane's reaction to her husband's attention to Audrey, but Audrey paid less attention to it, as did everyone else in their group.

Her new friends were more diversified and exciting to her. She had become quite friendly with Heather, whom she had met through her symphony volunteer work. She too was a widow, and they had gotten into the habit of getting together one evening a week to take in a movie, have something to eat together, go shopping, or whatever else appealed to them. She was probably her closest friend now, mainly because they were both widows. It did make a difference! She could discuss things with Heather that her other friends wouldn't understand. Heather was the one who had suggested the London theater trip, which Audrey was considering.

Audrey was most pleased with the friends she had made through her work with the Reading Is Fundamental (RIF) program. All the volunteers were concerned about motivating young children—particularly disadvantaged children—to read. They worked tirelessly to make sure the program worked in their community. Audrey realized what a relatively sheltered life she had previously chosen to lead and enthusiastically embraced this new activity. Although initially intimidated by the group, she responded positively to their acceptance of her. They made her feel welcome very quickly, and she realized that her organizational skills were helpful to this involved group of women. They were also very complimentary to her about her contributions to the program. All this made her feel good about her decision to become active with this group.

Elizabeth

Reactions to Identifying Today's
Personal Attitudes and Realities

Elizabeth completed her "Who Am I Today Personally?" form as follows:

Who Am I Today Personally?

Personal Strengths

1. Becoming more outgoing
2. Beginning to make personal decisions
3. Recent ability to envision major lifestyle change without guilt or fear
4. Openness to new friendships

Personal Weaknesses

1. Lack self-confidence
2. Still dependent on the approval of others
3. Slow to change
4. Afraid of making mistakes

Personal Needs

1. To have more social contacts
2. To be self-sufficient
3. To be physically closer to Abigail
4. To be more responsible about personal health

Elizabeth had a difficult time completing her "Who Am I Today Personally?" form because she wasn't sure she really knew who she was anymore. She wasn't the same person she had been when Ben was alive, but she hadn't changed a great deal either. She had amazed herself on the cruise she had taken with Abigail; she had participated in almost everything. She thought it was the most exciting experience she had ever had. She wished she had been brave enough to insist Ben take her on a cruise after he had retired. She had made comments about cruises, but he never picked up on the idea as something she really wanted to do. She wondered if he would have gone if he had known it was important to her. Well, she'd never know. She thought about the expression on Abigail's face when one of the crew members asked Elizabeth to dance and she had accepted. She smiled to herself just thinking about it.

The ports they visited were all interesting, and the heat hadn't bothered her. By the end of the first full day on board, she and Abigail found themselves socializing with a small group who shared similar interests. She was surprised at how close they had all become in the course of one short week. She had discussed a variety of topics with these people, topics she had never discussed with the few friends she and Ben had had in Boston in all the time they had known them. One of the couples she had become friendly with on the ship lived near Abigail in Florida, as did another widow whose company she particularly enjoyed.

Elizabeth was giving more and more thought to relocating to Florida. Because she and Ben hadn't socialized that much, at this point she really had only acquaintances in Boston. The exceptions were her longtime friend Mabel and now her new friends the Weatherlys and Lucy. When she visited Abigail's retirement community, she was amazed at the number of activities offered to the residents. She sat in on Abigail's Wednesday afternoon bridge group and remembered how much she and Ben used to enjoy their bridge games before he became ill. She was reluctant because it had been so long since she played, and she understood that there had been many changes in how the game was played. However she thought it would be fun to play bridge again and resolved to update her knowledge of how the game was played.

Abigail had encouraged Elizabeth to attend some of the activities with her, and she had done so. She'd always wanted to take an advanced quilting class but had never gotten around to it. The class she visited at the retirement facility seemed perfect—it was neither beyond her sewing level nor too simple. The young woman teaching it seemed to be very pleased to answer any and all questions. When she saw other women about her age participating and asking questions, she felt more comfortable about undertaking such an activity herself. She was beginning to get frustrated with herself for always needing support from someone else. The senior citizens she saw in Florida didn't seem to need the same kind of approval and support she appeared to need. A part of her was tired of being this way, worrying about who she was, what others would think, and what she was going to do. Another part was reluctant to change. Elizabeth realized she had been encouraged to be dependent on her parents and Abigail as a child. She now understood this had done her a major disservice.

Mabel and Lucy had suggested to her that she visit some continuing care retirement communities (CCRC) in the Boston area before she made a final decision about moving to Florida. Elizabeth thought this was a good idea. Mabel had a widowed friend living in a CCRC, and she suggested they go over for lunch. Mabel made the necessary arrangements with her friend, Caroline, who turned out to be very gracious. They had had a delicious lunch as Caroline's guests in the light, airy dining room. Afterward, she gave them the grand tour of the clubhouse complete with an indoor swimming pool and the grounds. She showed them the week's schedule of events and the menus. Elizabeth noticed that the day they were there a lecture by a well-known Boston antiques dealer was scheduled. Caroline's apartment was surprisingly spacious and tastefully decorated. Her son and daughter lived nearby, and the location enabled her to spend time with her children as well as on her own.

Elizabeth thought such a place would clearly be an option if she stayed in Massachusetts. Although, if she stayed in Boston, she didn't know if she was quite ready to give up her home—all these decisions! There was something about Florida that was more appealing, but she wasn't quite sure what it was.

She decided to invite Pastor Appletorn to tea. She thought it would be helpful to discuss her dilemma with him. She hadn't had much of an opportunity to talk with him personally since she had returned from her cruise. She attended church faithfully on Sundays, but that wasn't the same as speaking with him one to one. She thought about how much more comfort she had derived from his sermons these past few weeks, and all because she had been fitted with a hearing aid. Now that she had adjusted to it, she readily admitted that she had needed one. Funny, she hadn't realized how much her hearing had deteriorated until Abigail had brought it to her attention.

When Elizabeth had gone for her physical, her doctor, Dr. Longworth, had said he hadn't seen her in so long he had forgotten what she looked like. She was glad he had referred her to the audiologist to address the hearing problem. The hearing aid had made a world of difference!

As she greeted Pastor Appletorn at the door, she was glad to see his smiling face. He had a way of making all of his parishioners feel special. They had tea with some scones she had baked for the occasion. He complimented her on how good they were. He asked about her cruise and her sister. She told him all about the cruise, her sister, and where her sister lived. She made a special point of telling him she had attended church with Abigail in Florida and had enjoyed the sermon but assured him it wasn't the same as attending his church. He reminded her that it didn't have to be just the same to be valuable—he was sure the Lord appreciated diversity among his flock. He added, as she knew all too well, that nothing stayed the same forever. Toward the end of the tea, Pastor Appletorn surprised her by saying, "Elizabeth, I've known you for a long time, and I hear something different and new in your voice when you talk about Florida. There is a spark, a greater sense of self-confidence that I have never heard before. I can't tell you what to do. If you do move, it will be a loss to our congregation, but I think you should give it some serious thought."

After he left, Elizabeth sat in her familiar comfortable dining room for some time. Mittens jumped up and sat in her lap, purring away. She really did enjoy having him. She would have to inquire as to whether or not they allowed pets at Northern Palms. She thought they did but wasn't positive. What really was keeping her in Boston? She guessed she felt disloyal to Ben because they had always lived here, and Ben was buried here. It was as if she had decided Boston wasn't good enough for her anymore. But Ben was no longer with her, and she was all alone. The winters were really hard on her, and she knew she would have to increasingly depend on Pastor Appletorn and other members of the congregation for one thing or another when the weather was bad. In Florida, she had been able to be something more than Ben's wife. She was Elizabeth in her own right, and she liked the feeling. She wasn't sure who she was quite yet, but she liked the way she had felt in Florida. Besides, she did want to be close to Abigail. She was getting closer to making a final decision every day.

PART THREE

Building a Secure and Rewarding Future

CHAPTER ELEVEN

Developing Your Long-Term Financial Plan

When you become a widow, you need to understand your total financial situation and manage your own money in order to survive and even thrive! The recognition and acceptance of the fact that financial decisions now rest in your hands may require an adjustment in mind-set. It is not that you are incapable of handling finances; it is more often likely that you might not have been involved in the process—either by your choice or your husband's. Given that you might have been accustomed to your husband's assuming responsibility for your family's finances, you might try to find someone else to assume that role.

Delegating total responsibility to someone else frequently causes widows to run into financial trouble. It is understandable that the widow wants to rely on someone else in the way she relied on her husband. Many new widows assume the "child widow" role because it is familiar, and they resent the fact that they are forced to manage their own money. Others resist dealing with finances because it is symbolic to them of the fact that they are widows—a state they did not choose and don't like. Perhaps not taking charge of their finances allows them to cling to the myth that their life has not really changed or to the unhealthy approaches to money established during their childhood.

Regardless of how you felt about money management in the past, as a widow you must now accept the fact that you and you alone have the ultimate responsibility for your financial future. To do this, you have to understand your financial situation from a short-term as well as a long-term perspective. Ultimately, you may decide to delegate all or part of the management of your money to someone else, but before you take that step you need to understand your situation.

It is important to recognize that having a team of advisors consisting of your lawyer, financial planner and accountant working together will provide you with the best long-term results.

Updating Your Budget and Balance Sheet

Now that you have been living on your own for a while (six months or more), you have a better idea of what you are actually spending as opposed to what you estimated you would spend. In chapter 7, we presented a format to help you estimate the amount of money you need to cover your expenses. You might be tempted to go through this exercise initially and then ignore it. However, it is essential to keep monitoring your expenses and income periodically to make sure you are not spending your principal. This is not easy to do while the estate is being sorted out. In those early stages, the difference between income and principal is not always clear.

As we have mentioned many times, the first year of widowhood is one of transition, one during which many mistakes may have been made inadvertently. We have tried to show you how to avoid these mistakes. After you have gone through this initial stage of dealing with crises—both emotional and financial—your life should become more predictable, and new patterns will be established. Now is the time to look at your budget again. Are all your expenses necessary? We hope that you are past the splurges you might have indulged in initially—the special vacation, the clothes you bought, or the redecoration of the home—most of which were designed to cheer up you and your family. Are things costing more than you expected or less? Is your income sufficient to cover your expenses?

It is also advisable to update your balance sheet. Now that your husband's estate is settled or is closer to being settled, you should have a better idea of what you actually own and what debts you still owe.

It is a good idea to compare your current net worth with what it was last year. After this year, we recommend you calculate your net worth at least annually to see where you are. Note if you are making progress or losing ground. By now you should have sufficient information to make some major decisions about whether you want to sell your home or make any changes to your investments.

At this point, it is important to do some longer-range planning rather than the "getting by" approach of the early stages of widowhood. We have used the time frame of a year, but, as we said previously, we realize the time when you feel ready to plan for the future may be shorter or longer than a year. Each person's situation is different.

In the early stages of widowhood, you probably worked with your husband's advisors. Assuming that you now feel more in control of your situation, we recommend you review your relationship with these advisors. Were they helpful to you and responsive to your requests? If not, you may want to change them. If your experiences were good, make appointments with them to discuss your future financial plans.

Estate Planning With Your Attorney

Your Will

The attorney who handled the settlement of your husband's estate probably reviewed your will or created one for you to ensure your estate would be in order. However, you should reexamine the will that you approved when you first were widowed. It may not accurately reflect your intentions now that things have quieted down somewhat, and you have had more time for reflection.

Questions to consider when drafting a will include the following:

- Who will inherit your assets?
- Who will supervise the distribution of these assets and the winding up of your affairs?
- How will your assets be distributed? Outright gift or managed for the beneficiary in a rust?
- When will the distributions be made?
- Who will be the guardian for your children if they are minors?
- Do you want the personal and financial guardian of the minor(s) to be the same person?

237

On this last question, if you don't have a valid will and you have children, in most states your probate estate will be divided equally among them. If any of them are minors (the age of a minor varies from state to state), the court will appoint a guardian for them as well as an administrator to settle the estate. To avoid this, you need to designate a guardian or personal representative in your will.

Make sure the person you select agrees to assume that role. The person you have in mind may not want to take on that responsibility. Be sure that the person you ask to be trustee for your children realizes that he or she doesn't have to be an expert in investment management. In fact, you should encourage this person to seek professional help managing the inherited assets. You might even decide to name a second trustee who is not involved with the care of the children but is financially knowledgeable. To avoid disaster, you might consider naming a trust protector who can discharge a trustee under some circumstances or even veto certain trustee decisions. You also may want to allow a change of trustee should the beneficiaries move out of state. Think through all of these issues and discuss them with your attorney.

It is a common misconception that if you are single and you don't have children, you do not need a will. This is not correct. In fact, a single person's estate planning might be more complex. The purpose of a will is to make sure that your assets go to the individuals or institutions that you designate.

We recommend that you use percentages rather than dollar amounts in your will. For example, if your will specifies that your six heirs should receive $100,000 each and your total estate is less than this amount, then your personal representative has a problem. If instead you had said each heir was entitled to one-sixth of the estate, it would be easier to divide your assets.

Under current federal estate tax law, when you die, $13.61 million of your assets will be excluded from federal estate tax (for the year 2024). This estate exclusion amount will be reduced to about half of its current amount in 2026, which will be increased for inflation unless Congress changes the law before then.

If your assets exceed these amounts, your estate will be taxed according to an established formula. The amounts listed above are your federal estate tax exclusion. However, your state may impose taxes on smaller estates. Congress is able to change the Federal estate tax exclusion at any time which makes estate planning difficult.

Any assets you do not own in your own name will not be distributed according to the terms of your will. For example, assets you own jointly with another person with right of survivorship become the property of the surviving joint owner, regardless of what your will might say. Similarly, IRAs, pension benefits, and life insurance pass to the named beneficiary. If the named beneficiary is the estate and not an individual, what the will says determines how the assets are distributed. As for retirement plans and IRAs, we recommend you name individuals rather than your estate to avoid adverse tax consequences for your beneficiaries.

Some people have very good wills indicating how they want their assets distributed. However, if their stock and bank accounts are jointly titled that would negate the terms of the will for those assets. For example, your will may specify that your five children share equally in your $600,000 estate. If a part of the estate consists of a jointly held bank account of $100,000 with one of your children, this asset will go directly to that child and the balance of your estate ($500,000) will be divided equally among your five children. This probably was not your intention.

You should consider changing your will if any of the following occur: you remarry, divorce, a tax law changes, you have a child or grandchild, someone mentioned in the will dies, you move from one state to another, or the size of the estate has changed significantly. In the past, you might have added a codicil to your will to reflect a desired change. Today, signing a new will that reflects any change costs about the same and will be less subject to challenge.

One item which often is overlooked is care for your pet if you have one when you die. This can be specified in your will but should be discussed in advance with the person who has agreed to take care of your pet.

Once your will is drafted according to your specifications, your lawyer should make sure that it is signed, witnessed by the required number of people, and valid in your state of residence. There should be only one original will and It should be put in a safe place, where the appropriate people can find it. This last piece of advice seems obvious, but it is not. Often, someone dies, and the family has no idea where the will is located. Make sure your family does not have this problem. The best place to leave the original will is with the lawyer who prepared it and then make sure the family has that information.

Powers of Attorney, Living Wills, and Advance Directives

In addition to having a will, you should designate someone to have what is called a durable power of attorney (POA). This allows that person to act on your behalf should you be traveling or become incapacitated. If you become unable to make financial or medical decisions and have not given anyone your POA, a family member or friend may have to petition the court to appoint a guardian for you. We recommend that you have two durable POAs, one to handle your financial affairs and the other to cover your health-care directives. You may want the same person to have both POAs, or you may want to appoint two different people.

The financial POA allows your agent to act for your benefit when handling your financial affairs. However, check with your bank and investment manager to make sure they will accept the document prepared by your lawyer. Sometimes they will honor only their own POAs, so you should sign both.

The healthcare POA enables you to provide guidelines and instructions about the extent of medical care and intervention you would want under various circumstances. This POA will be effective if your physical or mental condition makes it impossible for you to understand, make, or communicate an informed decision about providing, withholding, or withdrawing treatment. In this document you would also appoint someone to act on your behalf. For example, the person you name would be able to talk with your doctors and nurses about your care. It is very important to have someone to represent you in this capacity. Doctors and hospitals today have to follow very strict privacy rules designed to protect your personal information, but the unintended side effect is that without your written consent they may not be able to discuss your condition with your loved ones.

In your healthcare POA you can describe what quality of life is acceptable to you, thus relieving your family and friends of the burden of making these difficult decisions. Today many hospitals require that you have one of these in place before undergoing an operation. In some states, the individual designated for this responsibility must sign an affidavit stating that he or she will in no way financially benefit from your demise.

This healthcare POA is different from a living will, in which you express your wishes to withhold or withdraw treatment if you are a candidate for life support and are considered terminal. For instance, if you were to develop Alzheimer's disease, a living will would not control medical decisions.

Rather than having a healthcare POA and a living will, many lawyers prefer to draft an Advance Medical Directive, which combines the two into a single document. In this case you would have an Advance Medical Directive and a financial POA rather than three separate documents.

We consider each of these documents as important as a will and suggest you ask your attorney to draft them at the same time as your will is being updated. Your signature on these documents should be notarized and witnessed (the number of witnesses varies among states). If you own property in more than one state, make sure the POAs will work in these states. And as with the will, make sure that there are plenty of copies in the right hands.

Living Trusts

To further confuse you, there is another legal document called a living trust—which is totally different from a living will which relates only to medical decision making. (The only similarity is they are both legal documents.) A living trust is a written agreement that is established while you are alive (thus the name living). Typically, you name yourself as the trustee of your own trust and you are the beneficiary of the trust. You would name someone else (a relative, friend, lawyer, or bank trust department) as the successor trustee. This successor trustee can distribute the assets in the trust if you die but can also act on your behalf if you become ill and are unable to manage your own affairs.

A living trust can be revocable or irrevocable. A revocable trust means the person who establishes it can change the terms of the trust at a later date if desired. An irrevocable trust, once established, cannot be changed. Setting up an irrevocable trust has tax advantages, but they are rarely used because most people don't like to set up something they can't change later.

There are six reasons why you would consider establishing a living trust for yourself:

1. Assets in the trust will not have to go through the probate process, which in some states can be expensive. Even more important, having your assets held in trust will expedite the distribution of assets to your heirs.

2. Assets held in a trust are not a matter of public record when you die.

3. A trust is less likely than a will to be successfully challenged by unhappy relatives and friends.

4. Even though we think powers of attorney are effective, a trust is less likely to be questioned than a power of attorney.

5. In some states, transferring your property into a living trust may protect it against your creditors.

6. If you own real estate in more than one state and it is titled in the name of the trust, you can avoid your estate's having to be probated in another state.

Once you establish a trust, in order for it to have the desired effect you must transfer all of your assets into the name of the trust. This procedure is fairly simple: Your bank and broker open a new account for you in the trust name, and you instruct them to transfer your current holdings into it. Real estate should be retitled in the name of the trust. You control the assets, just as you did when they were in your own name. However, some widows set up a living trust but never follow through with the next

242

essential step of titling all their assets in the trust name. If you do not take this step, then the assets will have to go through probate which you were trying to avoid by setting up the trust.

Some advisors recommend that everyone have a living trust instead of a will. We think that the living trust can be a useful device, particularly for an elderly single person with an uncomplicated financial situation, someone who is suffering from a debilitating illness, or someone who travels extensively. However, just as no one investment is a panacea, neither is having a living trust to the exclusion of other legal documents. If you and your attorney decide a living trust fits your circumstances, we think you still should have a will to take care of other matters that are not included in the trust.

Selection of the appropriate successor trustee is very important and is similar to selecting a personal representative for your will. In fact, we would assume you would name the same person to take care of both responsibilities. (See chapter 5 for the list of duties of a personal representative.) If you select an individual, it is very important that this person be honest, financially knowledgeable, and younger than you are!

Letter of Instruction

It will be helpful to your heirs to provide them with additional information they need to know after you die or become incapacitated. You can keep printed copies of this information together with your estate documents and give a copy to your personal representative. Items to include are:

- List of your debts and recurring bills
- Details of money owed to you
- List of your assets
- Copies of deeds
- List of your advisors with contact information
- List of fiduciaries named in the controlling documents (PRs, Trustees etc.) with contact information.
- List of beneficiaries with contact information.
- Copy of the cover page of each of your insurance policies
- Passwords for your online accounts/bank accounts

- List of where to find original documents (Will, promissory notes, trusts)
- Pet care instructions (if applicable)
- Personal property, specific instructions as who gets what

The Role of the Lawyer

You may be tempted to use the forms available in popular books or computer programs to set up your estate documents in order to save the lawyer's fees. We strongly recommend using an estate planning attorney to make sure that every legal aspect of your situation has been considered. This attorney will know how to prepare the appropriate documents required in the state in which you live and will make sure they stay valid if tax, probate, or property laws change. In addition, your attorney may bring up issues you should consider that you might not have thought about previously.

Comprehensive Financial Planning With Your CERTIFIED FINANCIAL PLANNER™ (CFP®)

When you were first widowed, your major concern was whether you had sufficient income to cover your expenses. Now that you are past this initial stage, it is time to look at your overall financial picture with your financial planner. A key component of your financial plan Is managing your investments.

The Role of the Financial Planner

The financial planner's primary role is to review your overall situation and recommend specific actions to enable you to better achieve your long-term economic goals and objectives. She usually charges you a fee to prepare a written financial plan.

Once you agree on a course of action, then the planner's role is to make sure that you implement the recommendations in your plan. Most financial planners will manage your portfolio themselves and charge you an annual fee. In some cases, the financial planner may also prepare your tax return, charging you an hourly fee.

During the first year of widowhood, typically you will meet and talk with your financial planner several times as you get your financial life in order. Subsequently, you should meet in person with your planner at least annually. Moving forward, you should consult your planner prior to making any major financial decisions.

Tax Planning With Your Accountant

The best time to do tax planning is in the late fall, when you have a good idea of what your income will be for the year. It is also usually the slowest time of year for accountants, so they have time to spend with clients on planning. By that time you should have enough information so that your accountant can estimate your tax liability for the current year and project it for the next year.

If appropriate, your accountant will also make suggestions about what you can do to reduce your tax bill for the current year. By visiting your accountant in the fall, you will have enough time to implement any recommendations in that taxable year and for the next year. This is also the best time of year to find a new accountant should you so desire.

Your accountant will tell you what financial information you need to keep track of during the year and how best to organize this information. As with any other professional advisor, the better prepared you are for your meeting, the lower the fee you will be charged. If you appear with a shoebox full of receipts, you will have to pay someone else to organize them. If, instead, you have kept your records in an organized way and present them to your accountant, your fee will be lower.

Sometime in the future, you might decide you would like to prepare your own tax returns without the services of an accountant. If so, there are several computer tax preparation programs available. If you do prepare your tax returns yourself, we strongly recommend that you have a professional tax advisor review them. Tax laws keep changing, and an accountant will be aware of any new action you should be taking in light of these changes. Also, if the IRS audits your return, it is very comforting to know that you have a professional who can represent you.

The Role of the Accountant

As we previously mentioned, the accountant's role is to prepare your tax return in a timely manner and give your tax advice. Some accountants may also help you with budgeting and long-term financial planning. Sometimes, because they are asked or are so inclined, they may make investment suggestions but be careful about taking this advice without consulting your financial planner. For instance, if you complain about the amount of taxes you are paying, your accountant might respond to your concern by recommending that you invest in tax free municipal bonds. By making this recommendation, she is responding to your concern. Municipal bonds do pay tax free income. However, from an investment point of view, your principal rarely grows when invested in bonds and in fact can decline if interest rates rise after you invest. If your primary investment objective is growth of principal, this recommendation might be shortsighted.

Summary and Conclusion

In this chapter we have focused on your future long-term financial plan and provided you with information about the advisors with whom you will be having a lifetime relationship. This team consisting of your lawyer, financial planner and accountant will continue to advise you about your financial future.

Diane

Reactions to Developing Her
Long-Term Financial Plan

A year had gone by since Mark had died. It was hard for Diane to believe. She had completed the first part of her paralegal refresher program. She was amazed at the new developments in the estate planning field since she last worked as a paralegal so many years ago. She had thought it would be difficult to master the different computer programs, but she found that after a while it all made sense.

Dorothy had called Diane and suggested they get together to update her budget. Diane had been able to keep fairly reliable records of what the family had spent over the past six months, using the forms Dorothy had given her. When she totaled her expenses for Dorothy, she realized that although they had spent more money in some areas than she had estimated, they had spent less in other areas, and it all seemed to equal out. She was proud of the children, who had really pitched in and helped. Adjusting to the new schools had not been easy for Jeremy and Alice, but, after an initial period, they seemed to be doing well and making new friends. It looked as if they had made the right decision to stay in their home instead of keeping all the children in private schools.

When Dorothy met with Diane, Dorothy urged Diane to review her will. She knew that Diane had put the will together in a hurry after Mark's death and thought it would be advisable for her to look at it again.

Following her advice, Diane met with Mary Sue Ryan, the partner at Mark's firm in charge of estate planning. Mary Sue reviewed the will with Diane. Diane had appointed her father as guardian for the children, and that still seemed to be a good idea. Previously, she and her dad had discussed her parents' ages in relation to the task of raising the children. Dorothy had drawn to Diane's attention the need to give consideration to age when determining a guardianship. Dorothy pointed out that sometimes it is better to have a younger family member or good friends closer to the age of the parents assume this responsibility. Because her parents were still comparatively young, Diane had decided to ask them to be guardians for her children. She viewed this as her best option, at least for the time being.

Mary Sue told her that, in addition to the will, she also needed to give her father a power of attorney so he could act on her behalf should anything happen to her. She should also have a health care power of attorney and a living will. Diane vaguely remembered that Mary Sue had mentioned these issues to her when they had met shortly after Mark's death. However, at that time, she was in no condition to comprehend the information given to her. Now, because she had covered these issues in her paralegal courses, Diane understood why these documents were important. She would have to check with her father to see if he was willing to be the designated person for these powers as well as guardian for her children, but she was sure he would agree.

Diane had initially resented her father's advice on financial matters, but now she realized how valuable it had been. She felt fortunate she had located such a good financial planner. So far, Dad had agreed with her advice and in fact was considering going to Dorothy himself. He didn't think he needed any help with his own financial planning, but Mark's death had made him worry about what her mom would do if she were widowed. He realized that she would be as ill-prepared as Diane had been to handle her finances.

At this meeting with Mary Sue, Diane took the opportunity to tell her about the estate planning paralegal program in which was enrolled. Mary Sue was interested and encouraged Diane to talk with her when she finished taking the program. They might have a job opening. If they didn't, she might know another firm that might need a paralegal. She herself had found the estate planning area very rewarding. She especially liked it because, unlike some other kinds of law, you could actually see how you helped people.

A few months later, Diane called Dorothy and told her that with Mary Sue's help, she had gone on a couple of interviews and had received a job offer to start at the end of June. The law firm would pay half her medical insurance premiums and all her disability insurance premiums. It also offered a 401(k)-retirement plan, which meant that she could contribute to her own retirement plan. She asked Dorothy to see how much her salary would improve their cash flow situation. Maybe the family could afford to take that Christmas vacation this year after all! She was concerned because she had spent part of her cash reserve as a result of her expenses during the past year.

Dorothy put Diane's new numbers into her computer. She was gratified to see that it appeared that finally she would have an annual positive cash flow. In putting together these numbers, Dorothy had factored in her health club dues, the life insurance premium, her medical insurance and even a contribution to the 401(k)-retirement plan. She knew how happy Diane would be when she finally saw a positive cash flow instead of negative numbers!

When Dorothy showed these projections to Diane, she warned her not to get too excited because there would always be unexpected expenses. She advised Diane to try to save any excess income for these expenses or a special event rather than spend it all. She might be able to start a college fund for the two younger children. Diane was really pleased to see these new budget numbers. She knew that there would be extra expenses caused by her working, but it would be such a relief not to have to worry about every penny!

Susan

Reactions to Developing Her Long-Term Financial Plan

Susan had interviewed for and had been offered the job of executive director at another association. The pay was considerably higher than her current income, and so was the responsibility. There had been many applicants and being selected for this challenging job gave her a sense of accomplishment. After considerable thought and discussion with Dr. Coleman, she decided to accept the job. She hoped she had not taken on more than she could handle.

Susan had gone back to the lawyer she and Lance had previously used, Tim Longwood. She realized that her mother would have some real problems paying for the retirement community if anything happened to her. If Susan died, the trust assets would go to Lance's children, so this income would no longer be available. Because of estate tax considerations, she decided to leave her assets to her brother, Ron. She would have to discuss this idea with him because she wanted to make very sure that he would use the money to take care of their mother as long as she lived.

She talked her idea over with Ron, and he agreed to provide for their mother if Susan died. He was somewhat concerned because he really did not have much experience managing investments. Susan suggested that he might want to use the bank trust department to help him. They both hoped this was a problem he wouldn't have to worry about, but Lance's premature death certainly had affected all of their thinking.

Susan returned to Bob O'Brien, the stockbroker, to update him on recent developments in her life. She was now clear about her investment objectives. In view of her increased salary, she no longer would need the stock portfolio to generate as much current income but instead could concentrate more on growth of principal. She told him that she intended to add $50,000 to this account using the excess proceeds from the lake cottage sale. Bob was glad to hear of her change of investment objectives and agreed to make recommendations for the portfolio she had inherited as well as the new money she was adding to the portfolio.

Susan also showed Bob the statements she was receiving from Ms. Peabody, the trust officer. He reviewed them for her and explained that she really had no control over this account because Lance had named the bank to manage the trust. It appeared the trust officer was doing a good job—the principal and the income had both increased during the time she had managed the account. Bob said he would be glad to review the account with her once a year to make sure the trust objectives were being met. He pointed out that, according to the terms of the trust document, she did have the option of moving the account to another bank trust department if over a reasonable period of time they were not pleased with the performance of the portfolio.

Audrey

*Reactions to Developing Her
Long-Term Financial Plan*

At Mr. Silver's request, Audrey had reviewed her budget one year after John died. As she had anticipated, her expenses were higher this past year than they had been when John was ill. However, she had sufficient income to cover her expenses. She felt it was time she enjoyed herself rather than focusing on the care of everyone else.

She did think she should pursue further the idea of moving to a smaller place. Because she had lived in the same home for the past 23 years and John had handled the original purchase, she really wasn't sure where to start in either putting her home up for sale or buying a new place.

One of her friends from the club, Georgia Brown, was a real estate agent with a leading firm in her area. Audrey decided to call her and talk to her about a potential move. She wanted to ask this friend how much the home would sell for and if she should look for a new place now or concentrate on selling her home first.

Georgia came to her home the following week and was very helpful. A couple of comparable homes were sold in the neighborhood recently for $500,000. After looking at her home, Georgia suggested Audrey ask for a slightly lower amount because she had concerns about the kitchen being outdated. Audrey asked if she should redo the kitchen before she put the home up for sale. Georgia said no as she thought that the additional money Audrey was likely to receive for the updated kitchen wasn't worth the aggravation. The purchasers would probably have their own ideas about what they wanted in a kitchen, and it was better to let them deal with renovating it. However, it did mean she would have to accept a somewhat lower price than if the kitchen was up to date. Despite that, Georgia thought that the home would sell quickly. The neighborhood was a good one, the garden looked particularly pretty at this time of year, and it was perfect for a young family.

Audrey knew she should talk to more than one real estate agent, but she really liked and trusted Georgia and felt she would take a personal interest in the sale because they were friends. She had accepted the maxim of not making a major move in the first year of her widowhood and had not done so, but she was ready to do so now. The question was: What type of home should she buy?

One thing she was sure about was that she wanted to stay geographically close to Joanne, her friends, and the golf club. She also wanted to have three bedrooms so her grandchildren would have a place to stay when they visited. She asked Georgia to help her find the right place. She had looked at town houses, smaller single-family dwellings, condominiums, and even retirement communities. She had made multiple lists of the pros and cons of each and finally decided that a town house would be best. She soon located one that suited her needs. The space was manageable, and it had the requisite number of bedrooms. The yard required minimal upkeep, and she could go outside and barbecue if she wanted to do so. The kitchen was well designed, modern, and cheerful. All in all, it suited her needs, and the price was right.

Audrey consulted with Mr. Silver, and he concurred that the move appeared to be a good one, both personally and financially. Knowing her aversion to debt, he recommended that she pay cash for the home.

She was surprised at how quickly her home sold. She had accepted an offer for a little less than she had asked but the young family who bought it seemed perfectly suited to the home. In addition, they were willing to settle in 60 days without contingencies. She hoped they would enjoy living there as much as she had. After she paid Georgia's commission, she would receive more than enough from the house sale to buy the town house.

Now that she knew she had the money in hand for the purchase of the town house, Audrey spent many hours deciding which pieces of furniture to move, which to replace, and which to give away. When she moved into her new home, the end result was a tastefully decorated home that combined new purchases with valued pieces from her former home. Much to her surprise and relief, Audrey found that she was immediately comfortable in her new home. It certainly was a lot easier to take care of, and she loved the fact that everything in the kitchen was brand new. She didn't have to worry about maintenance problems the way she did with the old home. Achilles too seemed to have no difficulty adjusting to his new home.

The grandchildren liked it as well, which pleased her. She was much more involved in their lives now than when John had been alive. She valued these expanded relationships with her grandchildren and always made time for them.

As soon as Audrey was settled in her new home, she made an appointment to see Mr. Humphrey, as he had suggested. She was concerned about the education of Joanne's children should anything happen to her. She was also a little worried about the stability of Joanne's marriage. Mr. Humphrey pointed out that in her will she could set up a trust for the grandchildren that specified it was to be used for their education. If anything was left in the trust after they were educated, Joanne would receive it. Audrey said that although she had a comfortable income from John's pension and Social Security, she didn't have a lot in assets to leave to the grandchildren. Mr. Humphrey explained that although it might not seem like that much now, hopefully her investments would grow over the years so he thought there should be sufficient funds to take care of the children.

Once again, Audrey expressed her wish to treat John Jr. and Joanne equally in her will, even though John Jr.'s financial situation was much better than Joanne's. Mr. Humphrey suggested that Audrey discuss her concerns with John Jr. In fact, he might be a good person for her to name as the trustee for the education trust because he was more financially astute than Joanne. John Jr. might not have as warm a personality as Joanne did, but Joanne was his sister, and if she needed financial help, Mr. Humphrey was sure that John Jr. would take care of her and the children.

Mr. Humphrey also discussed with Audrey to whom she should give her financial power of attorney as well as her health care power of attorney. She thought that John Jr. was the best choice for the financial power of attorney but wanted to give Joanne the health power of attorney because she felt emotionally closer to her. Audrey thought that as tough as the decisions Joanne would have to make would be, she had seen her father suffer and would do the right thing for Audrey. She knew that her daughter would consult with her brother, as he was a physician, before making any final decisions on her behalf. She also wanted Mr. Humphrey to prepare a living will for her.

Now that Audrey felt that her financial situation was in order, she decided to approach Joanne about spending a long weekend with her at a spa. She thought it would be good for both of them. Joanne was somewhat overweight—she had never really lost the weight she had put on during her pregnancy with Noah. Audrey thought a trip to a spa would help her get started on a weight loss program and would be a good break from her daily routine. Audrey was doing well with her walking regimen and her golf, but the latter was seasonal, and sometimes they used the golf carts instead of walking the course, which she preferred. She thought she might want to buy a treadmill or stationary bike so she could exercise at home in the winter. Spending time at a spa would help her learn more about the various kinds of exercise equipment available to her.

Audrey was going to suggest that perhaps Keith's parents could take care of the children on the two weekdays involved and Keith could manage them on the weekend. If necessary, Audrey would offer to pay for a sitter for the weekdays if Keith's parents were not available.

Elizabeth

Reactions to Developing Her Long-Term Financial Plan

Elizabeth had spoken to Mr. Grossfeldt about the possibility of moving to Florida. He had given her a list of questions to ask the director of Northern Palms, which was the continuing care retirement community (CCRC) in Florida where Abigail lived. The idea of a CCRC appealed to Elizabeth because it provided both housing and access to health care on three levels:

- **Independent living**, where she could initially live in an apartment as long as she was physically and mentally able
- **Assisted living** *when* she needed more help with daily activities (dressing, bathing, etc.)
- **Nursing home care,** available in the same community if she ever needed it

Mr. Grossfeldt told her she should ask for an audited financial statement. He said that this statement was important because she needed to be sure that the community would not go bankrupt if she was intending to live there the rest of her life. This could be 15 or 20 years. Elizabeth was taken aback with the thought she might live that long but Mr. Grossfeldt told her that according to the American Academy of Actuaries that a female her age (76) in good health who had never smoked had a 54 percent chance of living to 90, a 30 percent chance of living to 95 and a 10 percent chance of living to age 100.

She should also obtain a copy of the contract Northern Palms wanted her to sign that would spell out what she would pay and what she would get in return. Elizabeth needed to know how much the facility would charge as an entrance fee and how much of that fee was refundable if she changed her mind. She should ask for a written schedule of costs for the independent living apartment she liked but also should ask what the fees would be if she had to move to the assisted living or to the nursing home section of the CCRC. This schedule should spell out what her costs would include (meals, housekeeping, etc.).

Once she had obtained this information from Northern Palms, Elizabeth met with Mrs. Greenfield, her accountant. Together they went over the projected costs to move. She reviewed her current budget and then tried to figure out how these expenses would change if she moved. She also needed to make sure she had sufficient money for moving expenses.

Elizabeth realized she would probably spend more on clothes in Florida—at least initially—despite the fact she wouldn't need winter clothes. Since she and Ben had not socialized much, there had not been much need for many new clothes. She expected the amount she spent on entertainment and travel to increase. She had enjoyed the cruise so much that she wanted to make sure she had sufficient money to travel every year. She probably should budget more for gifts for the wider group of friends she anticipated having than she did in Boston.

On the other hand, she wouldn't spend as much on food because one meal a day would be provided for her at the retirement community. She would have no home maintenance expenses or real estate taxes to pay. After giving Ben's car away, she had spent a fair amount on cabs and other transportation for hire in Boston. However, transportation should be less of an expense in Florida since Northern Palms had shuttle buses which went to most places. Altogether it appeared her annual general living expenses would be reduced.

The director of Northern Palms had told her that there were three different monthly fee programs depending on the contract type. A "Life care" contract would charge her the same amount per month whether she was in the independent unit or the assisted-living or skilled-nursing unit. The "modified" contract would cost less but would only cover limited health-care services. When she needed more help, then the fees would increase. "Fee-for-service" contracts would require payment for all health-related payments. Elizabeth decided that she would opt for the modified contract as she didn't know when she would need additional care—if ever—and didn't want to pay for it in advance.

Mrs. Greenfield told Elizabeth that Florida had no state income tax. That would be a nice contrast to the high taxes in Massachusetts. Also, part of her monthly fee would be considered a medical expense and would be deductible on her federal income tax return.

Elizabeth did not need to be concerned about estate taxes in the state of Florida because Florida did not tax estates. She didn't need to worry about federal estate taxes either because her total assets were less than the legal limit. Mrs. Greenfield suggested Elizabeth consult with Mr. Grossfeldt for more details about the legal issues of estate planning if she became a Florida resident.

Mrs. Greenfield reviewed the audited financial statements as well as the history of past annual increases in the monthly fees at Northern Palms that Elizabeth had given her. She explained that Elizabeth should expect these fees to go up annually as costs increased. When Mrs. Greenfield looked up the facility, she was pleased to see that this community had good ratings.

Elizabeth called Mr. Grossfeldt and told him about her meeting with Mrs. Greenfield. He said if she became a Florida resident, he would make sure that her existing living will, and powers of attorney conformed to Florida state law. Because she had put most of her assets in a living trust at the bank, most of her estate would avoid probate fees. He recommended that eventually she should have all her assets in the living trust.

Mr. Grossfeldt asked Elizabeth if she had thought about to whom she wanted to leave her assets when she died if her only heir, Abigail, predeceased her. This was a difficult question. She thought she might like to leave some money to her longtime friend Mabel, who certainly could use it, but she really didn't have any other living relatives or close friends. Mr. Grossfeldt suggested she might consider dividing her assets between two charities: Pastor Appletorn's church and Ben's college. This suggestion of giving all her assets to charity if Abigail died first appealed to Elizabeth because the charities selected represented important aspects of her life with Ben.

Mr. Grossfeldt said she could arrange to have Abigail be the beneficiary of her trust in the event that Elizabeth died before Abigail. This would mean Abigail would receive income from the trust as long as she lived. When Abigail died, the assets in the trust would go to the named charities. Mr. Grossfeldt also told Elizabeth that although she named these two charities now, she could add or delete charities later or change the beneficiaries totally if she wished.

Elizabeth really liked these ideas and said she would consider them seriously. In the meantime, her conversations with Mr. Grossfeldt and Mrs. Greenfield were very reassuring. It appeared that the information she had gathered so far seemed to support her decision to move to Florida. She could hardly believe that she was involved in all these financial decisions. She considered herself fortunate to have such informed and empathetic advisors to help her make these monumental decisions. Quite a change from leaving all the financial decisions to Ben, as she had done during their married life!

CHAPTER TWELVE

Protecting Your Assets

A s a widow, having sufficient income and investing wisely are of paramount importance to you. Of equal importance is insurance, which protects the assets you have already acquired. Most people think of life insurance when they hear the word insurance, but others you should also consider are health, long-term care, disability, car, household, and liability insurance.

Life Insurance

Psychologically, many people resist the idea of buying life insurance because it is connected to the concept of death, and most people do not want to accept this inevitable event. They prefer instead to invest money in assets that provide current income or growth of principal, which they can see and enjoy. The problem is that they may not have enough time to accumulate sufficient money to provide for their dependents or to pay estate taxes should they die before they have amassed sufficient capital.

How Much Life Insurance Do You Need?

The question most often asked is, how much insurance should I carry? You recently completed the exercise of determining if you have sufficient income on which to live. If you are over 65 and your children are relatively self-sufficient, you may feel you don't need any insurance. On the other hand, although you may not need insurance to provide for your children, you may need it to pay estate taxes when you die.

If you are a younger widow with dependent children and limited assets, we think you should buy insurance on your life so there will be enough money to take care of your children if you die before they reach adulthood.

There are other dependents to consider besides your children. You may also have siblings who are less economically fortunate than you are or parents who need your financial help. To determine how much life insurance you need, review your situation with your financial planner so that you can determine the amount of coverage to carry.

What Kind of Life Insurance Should You Buy?

Also influencing the decision of how much is enough is the cost factor. When you are younger, insurance is less expensive—logically so, because the chances of your dying at this time in your life are less than when you are older. The cheapest form of insurance is term insurance. This type of insurance will cover you for a certain time period and the cost will increase annually. For those of you who will have a need for cash for a limited period of time—such as until your children are through college—term insurance might make the most sense.

For those who want more than a death benefit policy, whole life insurance, universal life insurance, and variable life insurance are also available. With whole life insurance, you pay a predetermined premium presumably for the rest of your life. Part of the premium pays for the death benefit, and part is invested within the insurance policy.

Universal life insurance is similar to whole life insurance, but, instead of the cash in the policy earning a fixed rate of interest, the interest rate varies annually according to what interest rates are available in the marketplace. The portion of your annual premium that is greater than the amount necessary to cover your annual insurance cost is invested for you, building up a cash value that is tax sheltered. Universal life is less expensive than whole life, but it is also riskier because the interest rate that the cash value of the policy earns is not as predictable as in whole life and the cost to you to maintain the policy is not fixed.

In a variable life insurance policy, the cash portion is invested in separate accounts, which in turn are invested in stocks and bonds.

Which Insurance Company Should You Use?

If you and your financial planner determine you need life insurance, then you should select what kind of insurance and which insurance company is best for you.

Two primary indicators of a good insurance company are its long-term dividend performance and the strength of its financial ratings. Whether an insurance company is a good one may be determined by comparing the dividends it actually pays to policyholders with the dividends the life insurance agent projected it would pay.

Insurance companies are rated by A. M. Best, Standard & Poor's, and Moody's. You can check their ratings online. Be aware that costs may vary from company to company, even for term insurance. For instance, a company that wants to build its term insurance business might offer very low costs for these policies but may not be competitive in other kinds of insurance.

Another issue to consider is whether you should buy a waiver of premium. This term means that if you become disabled and are unable to pay the premium, the insurance company will continue to pay the premium to keep the insurance policy in effect. This adds to your cost.

These are all issues your financial planner should check before recommending the best company for your particular situation. As with other investments, the track record and a strong balance sheet of the insurance company you select are very important.

Health Insurance

As we mentioned in Chapter 6, health insurance is a major concern for widows, particularly if they have witnessed the major expenses incurred by their husband's illness. If your husband had health insurance through his employer, the COBRA regulations issued by the Department of Labor require his firm to continue to offer insurance coverage to you and dependent children for 36 months. Your cost for this coverage will be higher than your husband paid. You will pay the group rate for yourself and your dependent children. It is likely that while your husband was employed, the firm contributed to or paid for this coverage. However, after 36 months, you must find your own insurance, and this can be very expensive.

You can sign up for your own health insurance coverage via *www. healthcare.gov*. This platform was launched in 2010 under the Affordable Care Act and it mandates health insurance companies to provide certain levels of coverage with every plan for people younger than age 65. The portal asks you for the estimated household income in the current year and may offer you subsidized rates if the income level is below a certain threshold (can vary by state), otherwise you will pay the full unsubsidized premium cost. In some cases, particularly if you are concerned about your own health condition, you might want to go ahead and apply for your own insurance so that you are not in the position of coming to the end of the COBRA protection and find your health will not permit your being insured privately—or at prohibitive rates. If your husband was retired, health insurance may have been one of his retirement benefits. If he was over 65, Medicare may have been covering him. He also may have had some kind of supplemental (Medigap) coverage.

What Coverage Should You Have?

As a general rule, if you are able to participate as part of a group, the rates are cheaper, the service is better, and you have fewer problems with claims. As far as guidelines go, a comprehensive major medical plan should pay the majority of your medical bills after deductibles. As with other kinds of insurance, the higher the deductible (the amount you will pay out of your pocket), the lower the premiums you will pay.

The lifetime minimum benefit under the policy should be at least one million dollars. The policy should be guaranteed renewable and noncancelable. Most insurance is less expensive if premiums are paid annually. Be aware that having dental and psychiatric coverage, while desirable, raises your premiums.

HMO (health maintenance organization) and PPO (preferred provider organization) coverage has become more broadly used. HMOs require you to use their doctors and their facilities. PPOs allow you to use either their doctors and facilities or your own doctors and facilities (you pay more for the latter). There are advantages and disadvantages to each kind of plan. Above all, you want to make sure that if you become ill, at least your major costs are covered.

Medicare Insurance

Understanding Medicare is not easy. The subject is covered thoroughly online at *www.ssa.gov*. You can also obtain the information from Medicare customer service at *www.medicare.gov*.

In 2024, Medicare Part A pays all hospital costs during the first 60 days aside from the $1,632 deductible. If you need to stay longer than 60 days, your share of the cost will be higher. Medicare Part B pays doctors' bills. You have an annual deductible of $240 (in 2024) and then you pay 20 percent of the remaining fees (more if your doctor does not participate in Medicare).

Even if you plan to keep working, when you turn 65 you should sign up for Medicare Part A since it is free. However, if you continue to work past age 65 and you have adequate health insurance coverage, you may want to wait to enroll in Medicare Part B for two reasons. First, there is no reason to pay for insurance coverage you do not need. Second, there is a six-month period during which you cannot be denied benefits or charged extra by a Medigap insurance provider for preexisting health conditions. The six-month period begins with the month you enroll in Medicare Part B. Therefore, you do not want the six-month period to expire before it is time to apply for Medigap coverage. However, if you do not enroll in Medicare Part B when you first become eligible you may owe a penalty if you enroll later.

Starting in 2006, Medicare began to offer a third type of coverage (Part D) which provides prescription drug coverage. There are several Medicare prescription drug plans to choose from, and you will pay a monthly premium to join one of these plans. The plans are provided by private insurance companies who contract with the federal government. All Part D plans must meet a federal standards, but the plans available to you depend on the state in which you live.

The cost of a Part D plan depends on which plan you choose. You can choose a plan with a low premium, but benefits may not be as comprehensive as those in the other plans you could choose. To find the plan that best suits your needs, you will need to compare the total out-of-pocket costs you're likely to incur, and the medicines you need covered.

At the Medicare website *www.medicare.gov* you can input your list of medications into the "Formulary Finder" to determine which plans cover your medications and whether there are any limitations. Also use Medicare's online "Drug Plan Finder" for the estimated annual out-of-pocket costs for all the plans available to you. Phone numbers for each insurance company are shown so you can call them directly to confirm that you understand the benefits as well as the costs of any plan you're considering.

Enrollment in Part D is optional, but as is the case with Medicare Part B, if you do not enroll when you first become eligible, you may owe a penalty if you enroll later. If you choose not to enroll because your current health insurance plan provides good drug coverage, you should ask your health insurance plan administrator for a written statement saying that your current coverage is at least as good as Medicare's. With this letter you will be able to avoid a late enrollment penalty if you decide to enroll in a Part D plan at a later date. You should enroll in Medicare Part D as soon as you are eligible if you do not have any other prescription drug coverage.

Note that there is an annual Open Enrollment Period from October 15th–December 7th which allows you to switch from one Medicare Drug Plan to another, if needed, or switch from Original Medicare to a Medicare Advantage Plan. Any selections made during this time will start coverage on January 1st of the following year.

Medigap Insurance

Medigap insurance is supplemental insurance provided by insurance companies to cover what Medicare doesn't cover—costs related to deductibles, copayments, coinsurance, and more. You will have a six-month open enrollment period that begins when you initially apply for Medicare Part B. This is the best time to buy a Medigap policy.

A variety of Medigap policies are available to you. There are actually 10 standardized model coverages labeled A, B, C, D, F, G, K, L, M, and N. Every insurer must sell the basic A coverage, which picks up most out-of-pocket co-payments for hospital charges and doctor bills. Policies B through G provide increasingly comprehensive coverage. Policies K and L are newer and are designed primarily to cover catastrophic expenses. The premiums for policies K and L may be lower than they are for the other types of Medigap plans, but your out-of-pocket costs will be higher. As you might guess, the price increases as the benefits increase, and the rates vary among insurance companies, so comparison shopping is necessary. (Note: The standard Medigap policies differ for residents of Massachusetts, Minnesota, and Wisconsin.) For more information about insurance to supplement Medicare, you might find helpful a free booklet titled *Choosing A Medigap Policy: A Guide to Health Insurance for People with Medicare*, published by the Centers For Medicare and Medicaid Services.

We recommend comparing the coverage offered by three companies. Once you and your financial planner have selected a company and you have paid the initial premium, you have 30 days to receive a full refund if you decide to cancel. When you apply for Medicare Part B, there is a six-month "window" when Medigap insurers must accept applicants regardless of existing health problems (as long as you have had continuous health insurance coverage for the six months before enrolling), so timely application is important.

Medicare Advantage Plan (Part C)

Medicare Advantage is a Medicare approved plan from a private company that offers an alternative to Original Medicare for health and drug coverage. These "bundled" plans include Plan A, Part B, and usually Part D. These plans may offer extra benefits that original Medicare doesn't—dental, vision, hearing and/or health & wellness services. The plan also requires you to visit doctors who are within their plan network.

Note that you buy a Medigap policy in combination with Original Medicare coverage or you can purchase a Medicare Advantage Plan. One cannot hold both at the same time.

If you ever want to switch from Medicare Advantage to Original Medicare, you will have to check with your Medicare Advantage plan to check If you can disenroll.

Disability Insurance

Most people don't realize the frequency or impact of disability. It is the greatest cause of mortgage foreclosures in the United States. If you are working, we think disability insurance is as important as health or life insurance. It provides needed income during periods when you are incapacitated because of sickness or injury and can no longer work and receive a salary. Unemployed individuals cannot be covered.

Most employers provide disability benefits, but they are not generally sufficient to cover all your expenses. What is particularly important is how the insurance company defines disability. Would the insurance company refuse to pay if you could do any kind of work (such as sweeping floors)? The desired coverage, which is called own-occupation coverage, would pay if at the time of your disability you could not perform the duties of the profession for which you are trained.

You can buy your own disability coverage that is renewable each year at a cost fixed at the time of purchase. This disability coverage cannot be canceled by anyone other than you. It has a more liberal definition of disability and in most cases will pay benefits even if you are only partially disabled and working on a limited basis. This type of insurance is more expensive than group insurance, but the longer you wait before you receive the benefits (90 days versus 30 days), the lower the premium will be. Coverage, whether group or individual, is usually limited to 60 percent of your current income. The amount of coverage you should purchase depends on your occupation and income level.

When you are reviewing your other insurance needs, make sure you don't overlook disability insurance. It is more difficult to obtain if you are self-employed, but, here again, if you are unable to find individual coverage, some coverage is usually available from groups (such as an organization you may belong to). There are insurance companies that specialize in providing disability insurance. Your financial planner will help you select the right one for your circumstances.

Key Decisions
Long-Term Care Insurance

One of the major concerns among older people is the possibility that as they grow older, failing health and dependency will require long-term care either at home or in a nursing home. This is also an area of concern for adult children with elderly parents.

According to *LongTermCare.gov*, someone turning age 65 today has almost a 70 percent chance of needing some type of long-term-care services and support in his or her lifetime; 20 percent will need it for longer than five years. According to Genworth's Cost of Care Survey (2021), the national monthly median cost for an assisted living facility was $4,500 and a semiprivate room in a nursing home was $8,000 a month.

What are the odds you will need this type of insurance? This depends on your sex, health, family history, and family relationships. But the fact is that most people don't want to be dependent on family or charity if they require this type of care.

Many people think Medicare will pay for these costs. Medicare is supposed to pay for 20 days in a skilled nursing home after hospitalization and then a small percentage of the next 80 days.

However, it is difficult to meet the many requirements to qualify for this coverage. Medicaid could pay the balance of payments, but to qualify for Medicaid you must first have exhausted your personal resources. It is our experience that Medicare and supplementary medical policies provide very little coverage in this area as the care needed is supportive rather than skilled.

Increasingly, individuals are purchasing long-term care insurance before a crisis develops. You hope that you will never need it—but you want to be covered. Unlike medical policies that reimburse you for a portion of a covered medical expense, long-term care insurance pays a daily benefit to help offset costs. You choose the benefit amount you want, the time you wait until the payments start and the length of time it will be paid. You can also choose inflation protection, which provides an annual increase in the daily benefit.

The long-term care coverage offered today has fewer restrictions and offers more types of care than what was offered a few years ago. Now, the major insurers in this field cover not only nursing home expenses but also home care, adult day care, and assisted living.

To qualify for long-term care insurance, you must be relatively healthy when you apply. As you grow older, the chances increase that you may be rejected for coverage because of a medical condition. Also, like whole life insurance, the younger you are when you buy this coverage, the lower the annual premiums. The coverage you buy should be renewable for life and noncancelable except for nonpayment of premiums.

According to the American Association for Long-Term Care Insurance the rates for insurance are most favorable between the ages of 55 and 65. Although those with family history health concerns should consider it at an earlier age.

Kinds of Long-Term Care Insurance

There are two broad types of Long-Term Care insurance policies: the traditional stand-alone policies and the newer hybrid policies which combine life insurance with long-term care. While the latter could be more costly, these plans guarantee a payout, whether as a long-term care benefit or a life insurance or annuity distribution and generally have less stringent underwriting standards than traditional LTC plans.

It is important for you to understand that the life insurance rider which would be attached to a whole life insurance policy allows you to use part or all of the policy's death benefit amount for long-term care while you are alive, but it would deplete the potential inheritance to the beneficiaries if much of the death benefit is used prior to the policy holder's death. So, a basic question to ask yourself is what the intended purpose of the life insurance is—current long-term care coverage or providing a legacy for a beneficiary.

As long-term care policies have significantly risen in cost over the past few years, a hybrid policy that combines long-term care (as a rider) with life insurance benefit may be a good way to provide you with some coverage rather than none.

Selecting Long-Term Care Insurance

When selecting a long-term care insurance policy you need to consider several factors see below:

- **Daily benefit.** The daily cost of staying in a nursing home varies in different parts of the country. These costs will differ according to the type of facility and amenities offered. For instance, a private room costs significantly more than a semiprivate room. Decide how much of your own money you are willing to spend for your room.

- **Elimination period.** This is the length of time you have been in a nursing home or receiving home care before the insurance company starts paying benefits. The shorter the elimination period, the higher premium you pay. This decision depends on how much of your costs you want to, or are able to, personally pay. We recommend if you do have other income which can pay your initial costs, you should select a longer waiting period.

- **Length of coverage.** Typically, you can select to receive benefits for three years, five years, ten years, or lifetime.

- **Inflation-adjusted coverage.** The cost of nursing homes increases annually. Typically, you might sign up for the policy when you are 55 and not need the care until you are 80 or older. Most policies allow you to buy the option that increases the daily benefit each year in line with a certain inflation rate. We recommend that you take this option. Compound inflation coverage provides more protection than simple inflation coverage.

- **Selection of the insurance company.** We think it is crucial to seek the opinion of a financial planner or insurance agent who specializes in understanding this type of coverage. This advisor will be looking at insurance companies that have been working in this market for at least five years. Certain companies are known for paying benefits promptly, while others put the policyholder through a lot of red tape before paying the benefits.

- **Payment of benefits.** The two methods of payment are reimbursement and indemnity. Almost all policies are reimbursement policies, under which the owner incurs an expense, submits the bill, and is reimbursed. In most cases, any unused benefit will be credited to your account. With the indemnity method, you receive the daily benefit even if actual expenses are lower.

  It is important to consider the conditions which must occur before the insurance company will approve a claim. These conditions are sometimes called "gatekeepers" and they will be outlined in a long-term care policy. For example, benefits may not be payable unless you need help with at least two activities of daily living, which include tasks such as dressing, bathing, and eating. The specific words used in the definitions within a policy might narrow your coverage and this will be recognized only by an experienced reviewer. The fewer gatekeepers required by the policy, the sooner the insurance company will start paying your bills.

- **Type of care to be reimbursed.** Assisted-living coverage is important because these facilities are a transitional alternative between your home and a nursing home. This type of care may be sufficient for many elderly who would otherwise be forced into a nursing home. Coverage should also apply at home or in an adult day care center. Coverage for hospice care in a hospice facility or at home can be an added benefit.

- **Group or individual coverage.** As with most kinds of insurance, individual coverage is more expensive than group insurance, but group coverage tends to cover less. Specifically, group insurance tends to include more gatekeepers. It is more stringent about which preexisting conditions it will accept before it insures you and what it will pay for when you do need assistance.

Not everyone needs long-term care insurance coverage. Since the chances are you won't need the coverage until after you are retired you need to consider what your retirement income will be and if it would be sufficient to cover your long-term care costs. If you wish to preserve your assets for your heirs and not spend them on nursing home costs, you may want to buy at least some long-term care insurance.

In any case, we think it is worthwhile to consider getting this insurance to cover all or part of your potential needs. Insurers are continually upgrading the policies they offer, so we would recommend asking your financial planner whether this coverage makes sense for you and, if it does, to help you find the best coverage currently available.

Preplanning Your Funeral

On a separate but related subject, just as people resist buying life insurance, they also avoid planning for their funerals. Unfortunately, none of us can avoid death. Recent statistics indicate over 50 percent of people preplan their funerals. Both prearranging and prefunding your funeral and burial plot can lift a great financial and emotional burden from your family when you die. On the other hand, do not feel that you must do this kind of planning. You need to make a personal choice in keeping with your existing religious practices and personal preferences.

If you were happy with the arrangements for your husband's funeral, you may want to work with the same funeral director. If you want to make a change, ask for recommendations from well-informed relatives and friends for the name of a well-established firm with a good reputation in the community.

When you meet with the funeral director, you can discuss all aspects of your eventual funeral service, make the appropriate decisions, file your prearrangement instructions at the funeral home, and inform your family where to call when you die. You also may choose to fund your funeral when you make the arrangements. This prepayment plan will freeze most of your costs at today's levels and is generally transferable to other states.

Burial arrangements are separate. The arrangement with the cemetery would include buying the plot as well as its perpetual care and maintenance. These costs can also be prepaid, and you can take title to the plot.

You also might decide that it might be helpful to your heirs to provide them with information about your life pertinent to your obituary or even write it yourself. Often at the time of your death, members of the family are unable to recall the history of your life as well as you can now—after all, who knows the details better?!

Homeowners Insurance

We recommend that you review your homeowner's insurance annually. It is important that you have your home (the physical structure) insured for 100 percent of the replacement value. If you have lived in your home for many years, your policy limits may no longer cover the actual replacement value. Your insurance agent can help you determine what your coverage should be. It is important to keep this replacement-cost evaluation up to date.

We also recommend personal property replacement-cost coverage. Then, if you have a fire and your sofa is destroyed, you will get enough money to buy a new sofa that is comparable to your original one. A comparatively simple way to keep records is to save receipts for more expensive purchases.

To cover your valuables, you need an additional policy attachment called a valuables floater, which requires an appraisal of your collectible items (art, silver, antiques, stamps, jewelry, and furs).

To add insult to injury, if you do not have this coverage and lose a valuable piece of jewelry, not only would you not receive adequate compensation, but it is unlikely that you would be able to deduct the loss on your tax return. Unreimbursed theft and casualty losses must exceed 10 percent of your adjusted gross income (AGI) to be deductible, subject to IRS rules.

Car Insurance

Your car insurance coverage includes five major areas:

Liability

Liability insurance covers injuries you cause to pedestrians and occupants of other cars as well as damages to someone else's property. We recommend that you have at least $300,000 for bodily injury suffered by one person in each accident, $500,000 for injuries suffered by all persons in the same accident, and $100,000 for damage to property. This may appear on your policy as 300/500/100. Some companies offer a more flexible single-limit policy covering total payments for both property damage and bodily injury that will show one number instead of three.

Medical Payments and Personal Injury Protection (PIP)

This insurance covers medical bills resulting from accidental injury to you or passengers in your car regardless of who caused the accident. It also covers you if you are injured in any motor vehicle accident such as when you are riding in someone else's car or when you are out walking.

If you have no-fault insurance (which some states require) or other medical insurance, you probably do not need this insurance. However, some reasons to consider it are that it may cover your lost wages, funeral expenses, and the medical bills of your passengers who may not have adequate health insurance of their own.

Uninsured Motorists

Accidents involving uninsured motorists are always a potential threat. Uninsured motorist coverage covers losses you incur when involved in an accident with a motorist who is uninsured. We recommend coverage of at least $100,000 per person and $300,000 per accident. This coverage is inexpensive, worthwhile, and mandatory in many states.

A variation on the same theme, underinsured motorist coverage protects you when you are involved in an accident with a motorist whose limits are too low to compensate you adequately for your damages. It may be part of the uninsured motorist coverage, or it may be offered separately.

Collision Insurance

This covers damage to your car as a result of a collision with another object. You can collect it no matter who caused the accident. This coverage usually does not pay more than the current value of the car. A higher deductible will reduce your premium, but the deductible should be set at an amount that you are willing to pay in the event your car is damaged.

Comprehensive

This section of the policy insures you against theft as well as damage to your car from falling objects, vandalism, and so forth. Again, to keep premiums low, set the deductible at the highest level that you would be willing to pay.

Also keep in mind that when you rent a car, a collision damage waiver (CDW) is not necessary if your own car policy covers you. Dull reading as it may be, read your policy carefully or call your agent before you find yourself standing at the rental car counter faced with the expensive CDW option. Many credit card companies also offer collision damage protection.

Umbrella or Excess Personal Liability Policies

These policies protect you in the event of a claim against you by someone who holds you responsible for an injury. For example, a friend slips on a stair in your home, falls down the full flight of stairs, and breaks both arms and legs. Even a good friend might feel the need to sue you. These policies usually apply to family members and include residence and personal injury liability.

You may have limited personal liability coverage through your existing home or car insurance, but this coverage is usually insufficient. You should have a separate liability policy that provides supplemental coverage. We recommend that you have total liability coverage equal to your net worth to reduce your risk of catastrophic contingencies. As your net worth increases, you should increase the amount of your liability coverage. This coverage is inexpensive and very cost-effective for reducing risk exposure. You can usually obtain it from the carrier of your car or homeowners' insurance.

Increasingly, insurance companies are insisting on covering both your car and your home. Using the same company is often more convenient and less expensive; it also prevents duplications in your insurance.

Identity Theft

Another essential way to protect your assets is to protect your financial identity. Identity theft happens when a criminal uses your personal information to obtain credit or make purchases. In the past, you could protect your identity by keeping an eye on your wallet or purse and by tearing up the carbon copy imprint of your credit card when you bought something on credit at a store. Unfortunately, identity protection takes a lot more work today. Identity theft is not just something that happens to other people

Monitoring all activity on your bank statements and credit card statements is the best way to know if there has been any illegal activity, but you want to avoid the problem from occurring in the first place. We suggest you buy a shredder and use it to shred any financial documents you want to throw away. Never give out personal information over the phone unless you are certain you know with whom you are speaking. Emails are especially tricky, because criminals can design their emails to look as if they are coming from a company with whom you normally do business. The safest way to conduct business over the phone or over the Internet is to initiate the contact yourself using the contact information that appears on your monthly statement.

Reviewing your credit report regularly is also important. There are three credit bureaus that keep information about you and your credit accounts in their files: Equifax, Experian, and TransUnion. You should obtain copies of your three credit reports and review them to make sure all of the information is correct and that there are no unauthorized accounts listed. Each agency keeps its own records, so you'll need to review all three reports. All Americans now have the right to receive free credit reports annually from each of the three bureaus. To get your free copy, visit *www.annualcreditreport.com*.

The reports also show a credit score which tells lenders how likely you are to repay a loan, so they use it to determine whether you qualify for a loan and what interest rate to charge you. The higher your score, the better your credit rating will be.

If you think you may be a victim of identity theft, call your bank and credit card companies to notify them of the problem. Place a fraud alert on your credit files by calling one of the credit reporting agencies. Also call the Federal Trade Commission (FTC) Identity Theft Hotline to learn what else you should do (1-877-438-4338) or online *www.consumer.gov/idtheft*.

Even if you haven't been a victim, it is a good idea to freeze your accounts, which you can do by calling one of the credit reporting agencies. They will give you a pin which will enable you to lift the freeze if you want to open a new account. Be sure to put this information in a safe place for future use.

Something else to consider at this point is putting together a list of your passwords and making sure that a trusted member of the family or friend knows how to locate it should something happen to you.

Summary and Conclusion

As tedious as it is, making sure that you have enough insurance as well as the right kind with the right kind of insurance company is essential to your future financial welfare. We cannot sufficiently emphasize how important it is to make sure your insurance coverage—all of it—is adequate for your personal circumstances should you suffer any kind of loss—life, disability, health, home, or car. You need to have appropriate compensation available to you. This is an area where many procrastinate, questioning whether they will really need this coverage. The policies often appear too complex to read, but when disaster strikes, it is too late.

Diane

Reactions to Protecting Her Assets

When Diane met with Dorothy about the implications of her new job, Dorothy suggested that they review her insurance in greater detail. Earlier, Diane had followed Dorothy's recommendation to buy a $1,000,000 life insurance policy on herself. The policy was owned by and payable to an insurance trust set up for the benefit of the children. At the time, Diane had agreed but did not really understand the implications of the trust, so she asked Dorothy to explain the trust to her again.

Dorothy told Diane that when she died, under current law no federal estate tax would be due. However, the state of Maryland taxes estates valued over $5 million. Therefore, if the $1,000,000 insurance proceeds were added to her estate assets, Maryland would tax the estate. By having the trust buy the insurance policy and pay the premiums, this would remove the $1,000,000 insurance proceeds from her taxable estate, thus potentially leaving more to her children.

The firm for which Diane was going to work had said it would pay one-half of her medical insurance premiums. This would be particularly helpful when Mark's firm's coverage would no longer be available to them. With Dorothy's help, she had looked into the costs of individual health insurance coverage and found that once she was no longer covered by Mark's plan, the premiums would be much higher. When Diane started working, her premiums would be reduced. This meant in addition to having income from her salary, Diane would lower her annual expenses because the firm would provide her with group health insurance coverage.

Diane also asked Dorothy about her disability insurance. Dorothy told her this insurance would be available to her through the law firm when she started working. She said she would be glad to review the coverage to make sure it was adequate for her circumstances.

Dorothy reviewed Diane's household, liability, and auto insurance and recommended that she consider using the same company for all three.

In this way, she might be able to lower the premiums. Diane reminded Dorothy that Erin was about to turn 16 and would need to be covered by Diane's car policy when she got her driver's license. Dorothy told her that the increase in premiums would probably not be that great because Erin was female, a good student, and would not have a car of her own. Diane would have more of a problem when Jeremy required insurance. Based on accident statistics, insurance companies consider young male drivers to be more of a risk than young females and therefore charge a higher premium for them. Premiums for younger drivers generally decrease once they reach age 25.

Diane was really pleased with her meeting with Dorothy. She felt that she understood her current insurance situation better. What a good feeling that was!

Susan
Reactions to Protecting Her Assets

The benefits at Susan's new job were not as good as they were at her old job. Her former employer paid for all of her benefits; the new one paid only part of her benefits. However, she was earning considerably more, and if she had to spend part of it for benefits, so be it.

Under tax law (2024) Susan could contribute as much as $23,000 per year to this retirement plan and receive a tax deduction for the amount she contributed. In addition, the money would accumulate for her, tax deferred. She thought she should take advantage of contributing more to this retirement plan than she had at her last job. She didn't think she could contribute the full amount allowed, but she certainly would do as much as she could to help reduce her tax bill. Also she needed to start being responsible for building her own retirement assets.

At her new job she would have to pay one-half of the medical insurance premiums; however, this was certainly a necessary expense. Susan saw little reason to buy life insurance in addition to the $50,000 coverage provided by the association—the only person she really had to worry about was her mother. If Susan died, she thought her other assets would be sufficient to take care of her mother.

When she called the homeowners insurance agent to ask him to remove the coverage on the cottage, she remembered to ask if her current policy included replacement coverage on the contents of her condominium. After checking, he said it didn't, so she asked him to add that coverage to her existing policy. The agent asked her if she needed a valuable-items rider on her policy, explaining that if she owned any expensive jewelry, rugs, or paintings, they should be separately insured. Susan and Lance had bought some paintings and an Oriental rug when they were married. Lance had also given her a few pieces of fairly valuable jewelry, which she cherished. The agent told her to have these items appraised so he could provide her with appropriate coverage.

He also told her she had no personal liability insurance and recommended that she have about $1,000,000 personal liability coverage, which would be equal to her net worth. He could add this coverage to her existing coverage for a relatively small amount. In view of her financial responsibilities, Susan thought this was a good idea.

These were the sort of issues Susan had not been able to face in the early stages of her widowhood. It felt good to be able to focus on these details once again. She no longer was battling against a strong current to merely keep afloat. Finally, she was moving forward.

Audrey

Reactions to Protecting Her Assets

Audrey had been approached by an insurance agent about buying life insurance. The same agent had talked to her about purchasing long-term health-care insurance. She really didn't know this agent, so she decided to call Mr. Silver and ask him what he thought about these ideas. He suggested that she come in with the information the agent had provided her with, and they could discuss the ideas further.

When they met, Mr. Silver said that her primary reason for purchasing life insurance would be to provide a larger inheritance for the grandchildren. However, at her age—and he struggled to be diplomatic as he discussed this with her—it was expensive to buy life insurance. He thought it would be better to focus on building her current investments.

He suggested instead that Joanne should have some life insurance, which Audrey could fund at least until the grandchildren were through college. If something happened to Joanne, Keith might have a problem financially taking care of the children. Mr. Silver also recommended that, in view of Audrey's concern about Keith's financial stability, it might be a good idea to set up an insurance trust. If Joanne died, then the proceeds of the policy would go into a trust to be managed for the children, as Audrey had provided in her own will. Audrey thought this was a good suggestion and decided to discuss it with Joanne. Knowing how tight their budget was, she would make sure Joanne knew that she would pay the premiums. Should Joanne prematurely die, that would provide support for her children until they had completed college.

Next they discussed the long-term care insurance. Audrey had excellent medical coverage through John's company. After hearing some of the horror stories of other widows, she was exceedingly grateful for this coverage. However, the idea of buying long-term care insurance appealed to her because it would prevent her from being a burden to her children if she became unable to care for herself.

Audrey mentioned to Mr. Silver that a friend had told her if she needed to go to a long-term care facility, she could apply for Medicaid coverage. Mr. Silver told her that wasn't actually accurate since in order to qualify for Medicaid she would have to give away most of her assets and he didn't think she would want to do that. He was also concerned that Medicaid might not offer the same coverage if and when she had to go to a long-term health care facility some 20 years hence.

Audrey readily agreed with Mr. Silver and asked him to look into how much long-term care insurance would cost her. After receiving this information and looking at her budget, it appeared that she could afford it, although Mr. Silver reminded her that her premiums could increase in the future.

When Audrey had moved into her new townhouse, she had obtained replacement-value insurance on the home and its contents. At the same time, she combined this insurance with her car insurance and bought an umbrella liability policy. It looked as if she had protected herself as well as she could with insurance. She was particularly pleased with the decision she had made about the long-term health-care insurance. She was adamant about being able to take care of herself now and in her old age!

Talking about her future led her to thinking about planning for her own death. She decided to make an appointment to meet with Mr. Brown, the funeral home director who had been so helpful to her when John died. She had a pretty good idea of what she wanted for a funeral service and thought it would be helpful to her children for her to make the arrangements ahead of time. In fact, after meeting with Mr. Brown Audrey thought she would take it a step further by prefunding the costs. By doing so there would be no questions as to how and by whom she wanted to be buried. Audrey and John had previously purchased adjacent plots in the Oak Tree Cemetery, so she didn't have to worry about that decision.

Audrey was pleased with all the planning she had done this past week and shared what she had done with Joanne when they were at the spa the following week. Joanne actually had jumped at the chance to go with her mother for the long weekend. She was exhausted from caring for her family and knew she was overweight. Her family hadn't had sufficient funds to take a vacation in years. Her father's death had also taken its toll on her, and she missed him sorely. Earlier in her marriage, before he had become ill, her father had given her a little extra money to purchase something for herself because, as he used to say, she would always be "his little girl." Thinking of those days always brought tears to her eyes.

While they were away, Audrey made sure Joanne understood her feelings about being able to provide for herself. Even though it was a painful subject, she also shared with Joanne her feelings about her own life and why she had requested that Joanne be given her health power of attorney. She told her daughter that she trusted her to make the right decision regarding medical treatment should she be unable to do so. Joanne got all choked up at this thought but understood what her mother was telling her. Mother and daughter hugged each other and wordlessly acknowledged the significance of the moment.

Elizabeth
Reactions to Protecting Her Assets

After reflecting on her conversation with Mr. Grossfeldt, Elizabeth asked him to change the terms of her living trust so that if she predeceased Abigail, Abigail would receive the income from the trust until she died. Given Elizabeth's age, there didn't seem much point in her applying for life insurance. If Elizabeth predeceased Abigail, Abigail would receive annual income from the trust, which should be sufficient for her needs. The charities would receive the trust assets when Abigail died.

Elizabeth had never given much thought to her health-care coverage because she knew she was covered by Medicare. However, she had recently seen a television program in which Medigap insurance was discussed as something you should have to cover what Medicare did not provide. She was totally confused and a little frightened. Perhaps Medicare did not provide her with sufficient medical coverage? As always in these matters, she found herself turning to Sam Weatherly for help.

Sam had already reviewed and selected Medigap insurance coverage for himself and his wife, Sarah. He explained to Elizabeth the purpose and various options of this type of insurance. He then recommended a comprehensive Medigap insurance policy that would provide sufficient coverage for her needs.

Elizabeth also asked Sam about long-term care insurance. He pointed out to her that it would be pretty expensive for her to buy at her age. He suggested that she discuss this matter with the staff at Northern Pines and obtain details regarding the costs of nursing-home care should she need to move to that section of the retirement community at a later date.

Elizabeth reflected that this was another reason for her to make the move to Northern Palms. Not only would she be near her sister and have better year-round weather, but she could also receive necessary nursing care when and if she needed it.

She had now inquired as to whether or not Northern Palms allowed pets and was pleased to learn that they did. They did not allow large dogs, but that was no problem—Mittens only weighed eight pounds and was a cat! She wondered how he would handle the move. She was quite attached to Mittens now and did not want to leave him in Boston.

CHAPTER THIRTEEN

Basic Investment Guidelines

There are several good books about investing, some of which we have listed in the financial bibliography. In this chapter we will not try to cover everything you need to know about investments but rather will try to highlight what we consider to be the basic guidelines to successful investing.

Some of you might not have ever been particularly interested in investments, but now circumstances have forced you to pay more attention to your financial situation. Acquiring knowledge about investments is just like learning in any field. First, you start with a little information. After a while you learn more, and as time goes on your overall knowledge increases. Unfortunately, this is a field that changes constantly. Just when you think you have grasped all you need to know, the tax laws change, a new kind of investment is introduced, or your personal situation changes.

After your husband's death, you may have been overwhelmed by all you needed to know. Initially, you dealt with the basics—making sure you had enough income to cover your expenses and determining your assets and liabilities. Then you identified and prioritized your financial objectives. In the process, some of you may have decided you enjoyed understanding your investments and actively pursued this new interest. Others of you tolerated it because you knew you needed to know enough to survive. Whichever group you fall into, let us share with you what we think are some basic guidelines to successful investing. These are based on our experiences working with clients over many years. Utilize them as you see fit based on your need, comfort level, and interest.

No. 1: Don't Spend Principal
Now that You May Need Later

When you are first widowed, you should avoid any and all large discretionary expenditures until you and your advisors have looked at your total picture. Initially, your inheritance may seem to be more than you will ever need, so you may be tempted to splurge and spend some of it immediately on various items such as redecorating your home, buying a new car, or taking an expensive vacation. We have seen widows go through substantial sums of money in five or ten years by withdrawing money periodically from their principal.

Fortunately—or unfortunately—all of us are living longer. As we previously stated, if inflation continues to average 3 percent a year, as it has over the past 10 years, your expenses will double every 24 years. Although 24 years from now may seem a long way off, the point to keep in mind is that the cost of living is not declining and will in fact increase in the future. You need to make sure that you have enough money to cover your expenses later. Your principal cannot grow, nor can your income increase if you are spending your principal as well as income to cover costs. Money may not buy happiness as you grow older, but it certainly can make you a lot more comfortable!

No. 2: To Keep Pace with Rising Costs, Invest
for Total Return as Well as for Current Income

The difference between these two kinds of returns is often confused in many investors' minds. The terms total return and current return are often used interchangeably, but they should not be. The current return (or yield) provided by an investment is the annual income you receive each year divided by the current market price of the stock. For instance, a stock that pays an annual dividend of 50 cents and sells for $10 per share yields 5 percent.

Total return represents the change in price of a stock over a stated period of time, as well as any income paid by the stock. For instance, taking the example above, if you paid $10 per share for a stock at the beginning of the year and by the end of the year it was selling for $12 per share, you would have a $2 gain. In addition, during the same year you received a dividend of 50 cents. If you add the gain in value of the asset ($2) plus the dividend paid (50 cents), your total return was $2.50. If you divide this number ($2.50) by the original cost of $10, your total return equals 25 percent.

While it is important for you to receive good income from your investments in the form of interest or dividends, it is also important for your assets to increase in value to keep pace with inflation. Thus, you should focus on the total return of your investments as well as the current return.

No. 3: Invest In Stocks as Well as In Fixed-Income Investments

If you need your investments to increase in value over time, we think you should invest at least some percentage of your assets in stocks. Some widows want to invest only in fixed-income investments that provide current income, thinking they are avoiding risk. Actually, these widows are taking more risk by confusing certainty with safety. The fact that a U.S. Treasury bond, a certificate of deposit, or an annuity will pay a fixed rate of income for a certain period of time is very appealing. However, as we have previously stated, fixed-income investments don't grow in value unless interest rates are declining. If you want to keep pace with increased costs of living we think you need to own both stocks and bonds.

We have seen some advisors recommend the "Rule of 100" when deciding what percentage of your portfolio should be in stocks and what percentage in bonds. According to this rule, you subtract your age from 100, and the resulting number is the percentage you should hold in stocks. This would mean if you were 70 years old, you would have 30 percent of your assets in stocks and 70 percent in bonds. We think such arbitrary rules don't work. Every person's circumstances are different, and effective asset allocation is more complex than using such a simplistic formula.

No. 4: Don't Put All Your Eggs In One Basket— Diversification[1] Reduces Risk

Diversification—investing in several different types of assets—reduces risk. For example, let's compare two individuals who invest $100,000. The first person selects an investment that earns 8 percent annually. At the end of 20 years, her investment is worth $466,096. Not a bad record!

The second person divides her $100,000 among five different investments—$20,000 each. After 20 years, the first investment is a total failure, and she loses all her money. The second investment breaks even, and she gets her $20,000 back. The third investment earns 5 percent, the fourth 10 percent, and the fifth 15 percent. Interestingly enough, this person would have $534,947 at the end of 20 years—almost $100,000 more than the first investor! Diversification lowered the second person's overall risk while allowing her to realize an even higher total return than she would have otherwise.

	Initial Investment	Average Annual Return	Value after 20 Years
Investor A	$100,000	8%	$466,000
Investor B	$ 20,000	(total loss)	$ 0
	20,000	0	20,000
	20,000	5	53,066
	20,000	10	134,550
	20,000	15	327,331
Total			$534,947

No. 5: Diversify Within Asset Classes, But Don't Overdo It

To reduce your risk further, we think you should diversify not only among different kinds of assets but also within asset classes. For instance, in the fixed-income asset category, you might own both government and corporate bonds. If you are in a higher tax bracket (28 percent or higher), we

---

1. Diversification does not guarantee against loss or guarantee a profit. It is a method used to help manage risk.

think you should consider investing in tax-free municipal bonds. With respect to stocks, we think you should own both U.S. and international stocks.

By diversifying your assets among different types of assets as well as within asset types, the likelihood is that you will keep pace with inflation as well as reduce the fluctuations of the overall value of your portfolio. At any given time, one group of assets may do poorly while another does well, so they offset each other. This is why we recommend this approach.

Although diversification among and within asset classes is important, you should not over diversify. If one-half of a $100,000 portfolio is in two stocks and the other one-half is invested in 23 stocks, the portfolio lacks balance. Let's say 25 percent of your portfolio is in one stock. If it doubles in value, you will be very happy, but if it loses 50 percent of its value, you will be very upset. On the other hand, if one of your smaller positions triples in value, it won't make much difference to your total wealth. Thus, you should have a balance among different kinds of assets as well as within asset classes.

No. 6: Buy Good-Quality Investments

It is difficult to predict exactly when a particular asset class is going to do better than another. Therefore, to reduce risk we recommend that you diversify your investments among different kinds of assets, balance your assets so that no one position dominates your portfolio, and select only good-quality investments in every asset category. In the investment field, good quality refers to investments that have a demonstrated record of consistent success over a number of years.

When you are buying bonds (either municipal or corporate), you are safer buying ones with a credit rating of A or better. If you buy less financially sound bonds with lower ratings, you will receive more income than you would from a better-rated company, but you are also taking more risk with your principal.

If you are selecting a good-quality stock, you want to buy a company that has a history of increasing earnings and dividends. You also want a stock with a reasonable price-earnings ratio. (The price-earnings ratio is the current market price of the stock divided by the last 12 months' earnings per share.) As a general rule, the lower the price-earnings ratio, the less risk you are taking. The higher this number, the more risk you are taking.

If you are buying a mutual fund, ask to see its long-term performance record. Look at last year's record, then the average performance over the last five years and over the last ten years. You want to see how the fund has performed in both good and (more important) bad markets. You also want to make sure that the manager or managers who created the record are still managing the assets in the fund.

Does this mean a fund which was started recently is not a good investment? Not necessarily. It really depends on the previous track record of the manager.

It is also very important to compare apples with apples. In other words, compare a particular fund's record with other funds with similar investment objectives (such as growth or income) or composition (such as international stocks).

No. 7: Don't Chase Performance

You'll usually make more money with a stock that produces consistent modest gains year after year than with one that has big gains most years and big losses occasionally. For example, would you rather invest $10,000 in Stock X, which returned 10 percent annually each year for five years, or the same amount in Stock Y, which gained 20 percent the first year, 15 percent in the second year, and 20 percent in the third year, lost 20 percent the fourth year, and gained 15 percent the fifth year?

Most people would choose Stock Y because Stock Y did better than Stock X every year except the fourth year. However, if you look at the chart below, Stock X would have been the better choice (remember the tortoise and the hare fable!).

With $10,000 invested in Stock X, at the end of the fifth year you would have $16,105. With Stock Y, at the end your $10,000 would have been worth $15,235. In other words, it is more important to seek consistent performance than spectacular gains that entail taking more risk.

	Stock X Value		Stock Y Value	
	Annual Gain	Annual Year-End	Value Gain (Loss)	Year-End
Starting Value		$10,000		$10,000
Year 1	+10%	11,000	+20%	12,000
Year 2	+10%	12,100	+15%	13,800
Year 3	+10%	13,310	+20%	16,560
Year 4	+10%	14,641	-20%	13,248
Year 5	+10%	16,105	+15%	15,235

No. 8: Avoid Risky Investments

We have told you that you can reduce risk by investing for total return, diversifying your investments, and selecting good-quality investments. In addition, you should avoid investments that are generally considered speculative, such as commodities futures, put-and-call options, and penny stocks.

What may not be as obvious a risk is investing in collectibles such as art, antiques, jewelry, Oriental rugs, and stamp or coin collections. Collectibles do not pay you current income. They may or may not grow in value, but if you need money, you might have to sell them. Often you will find that you are unable to sell your collectibles for what you paid for them or for what you think they are worth when you need the money. We are not saying you shouldn't buy collectibles for personal enjoyment, but don't confuse buying collectibles with making solid financial investments. Stock and bond certificates may not provide you with pleasure, but, properly selected, stocks and bonds will provide you with the income you need to support a comfortable lifestyle! Buy collectibles with your surplus money.

No. 9: If Something Sounds Too Good To Be True, It Is!

The papers are full of stories of unscrupulous con artists who take advantage of a widow's lack of investment knowledge or loneliness. The problem is that clever salespeople can make a risky investment sound safe.

Keep in mind that any time you are promised a higher return from an investment than is available from a good-quality investment, you are running the risk of losing all or part of your money. For instance, if a 30-year U.S. Treasury bond is paying 5 percent and you are offered an investment that pays 12 percent, this is a red flag. There is a strong possibility that such an investment involves taking unnecessarily high risk.

Our best advice: If someone you don't know and hasn't been personally recommended to you calls you on the telephone to offer a high-return investment, hang up!

One final word of caution: Widows are often lured into investing in lotteries or buying magazines with the hope they will win the big cash prize. Statistically, your chances of winning are very slim. Don't spend your money this way—unless you can afford to lose it!

No. 10: Understand That There Is No Perfect Time To Invest

Many investors worry about the market being too high when they invest. They are concerned that once they invest, the market may go down and they will lose money. Unfortunately, whether your investments immediately go up in value after you buy them is really a matter of timing. As you will see in the examples given here, if you are investing for the long term (as you should be), selecting the perfect time to invest really doesn't make that much difference to the ultimate outcome.

For instance, we looked at what would happen if an individual had invested $10,000 a year in the stocks in the Standard & Poor's 500 Composite Index for a 20-year period ending December 31, 2022. Each year, in this scenario, the widow had invested her money on the worst day (when the market was selling at its highest level). Over the period studied, she invested a total of $200,000. At the end of 2022, her investment was worth $549,645, which was an average annual compound rate of 9.48 percent.

Next, look at what would have happened if the same widow had made her investment each year on the best day (when the market hit its low point for the year). In this case, after 20 years her account would have been worth $723,233 at the end of 2022, for an average annual compound rate of 11.43 percent.[2] Obviously, she would have been happier with the second result, but certainly she still should have been pleased with the first.

In summary, there are good times and bad times in the stock market, but, over the long haul, any day is a good day to invest!

No. 11: Don't Panic and Sell at the Wrong Time

It is difficult to stay calm when the stock market goes down, but it is important not to panic and get out of the market. Generally speaking, history has demonstrated that the longer you remain invested in stocks, the greater the chance that your investment will grow. (Of course, this assumes you have selected good-quality stocks in the first place!)

The chart given here demonstrates the benefits of buying and holding, assuming you had invested $10,000 in the Standard & Poor's 500 Composite Index in January 2003 and held it for a twenty-year period. Amazingly enough, this chart[3] shows that if you had missed the 40 best days, you would have actually lost money!

If you had held the stocks for:	Your Investment would be worth:
The whole period	$64,844
Missed the 10 best days	$29,708
Missed the 20 best days	$17,826
Missed the 30 best days	$11,701
Missed the 40 best days	$8,048

Although it is sometimes easier said than done, keep in mind that you are investing for the long term. Try not to be concerned about short-term volatility. Remember, investing is a marathon, not a sprint.

No. 12: Sometimes It's a Good Idea to Sell an Investment

Although we are big believers in buying good-quality assets and holding them for the long term, there are times when you should sell investments.

2. Source: Capital Group/American Funds
3. Source: Capital Group/American Funds

When major changes occur within a company or within an industry that negatively impact your investment, you need to consider selling your holdings. For example, a company that once was very good in its field may have new management that is not as strong as previous management. A product that once was dominant in its field may no longer have the same dominance. A manager of a particular mutual fund who did very well might have moved to another fund, or the manager of a smaller fund that did well might not do as well after the fund grew in size.

Let's refute some of the various excuses we hear for not selling an investment:

- *Excuse 1: "I can't sell it—my mother gave it to me."* This excuse is based on emotional attachment to a particular investment. It might be stock in the company your father worked for or stock that your mother gave you or stock that did well for you in the past. Recognize that what was good in the past may still not be good in today's rapidly changing environment.

- *Excuse 2: "I don't want to sell it because I will have to pay too much in taxes on the gain."* Although we recognize that people don't like to pay taxes, if you don't follow your advisor's recommendations to sell, you may find that a year from now you no longer have any taxes to pay because the gain has evaporated! (If you are concerned about not having money to pay taxes, we recommend that if you make a profit when you sell an asset, put aside enough money from the proceeds to pay capital gains taxes and reinvest the difference.)

- *Excuse 3: "I want to wait for it to go back to the price I paid for it before I sell it."* This third excuse is used by those who don't want to admit they have made a mistake. Actually, your advisor is not happy telling you that you should take a loss on something she recommended, but if there is bad news about a stock, such as fraud on the part of the management or a disastrous earnings decline that looks as if it may be sustained, it is time to sell and reinvest in something that looks more promising. Remember, not every one of your stocks or funds will go up (see the example in Rule No. 2); what is important is that the total portfolio increases in value.

- *Excuse 4: "The last time I sold a stock, it went up after I sold it."* It is true that sometimes after you sell a stock it continues to go up despite what appears to be bad economic news. This happens, but what is more important is to review what you did with the proceeds from the sale. If you put it under a mattress, the sales decision was not a good one. On the other hand, if you reinvest this money and your new investment does as well as or better than the asset you sold, then you have made the right decision.

No. 13: Don't Let the Tax Tail Wag the Dog

While you should be aware of the tax consequences of investments you make, you shouldn't let saving taxes be your only concern. For example, widows who are concerned about receiving as much income as possible might think the best solution is to buy bonds which pay tax-free income. This inclination is understandable but not advisable. After determining your tax bracket, your advisor will discuss with you whether investing part of your money in tax-free bonds makes sense for you.

Some widows are concerned about the potential estate taxes their children might have to pay on their estate when they die. The obvious solution is to give away your money while you are alive to ensure that the size of the estate at your death will be low enough that no estate taxes will be due. This is an admirable goal, but one that needs to be made based on your total financial situation and estimated personal future needs. You may need this money to support yourself.

No. 14: Educate Yourself

Regardless of your interest in investments, try to become more informed. You don't need to know all the answers, but you should know enough to ask the right questions.

There are various ways to become more knowledgeable. Go to your public library or nearby bookstore to find personal finance books. Given how often the economic climate and tax laws change, be sure the books you select are still relevant (see our financial bibliography at the end of the book). Taking adult education courses on financial planning and investments offered by your local community college or university can be helpful. You also might find it helpful to subscribe to a personal finance magazine which provides current information. If you want more detailed financial information, subscribe to the *Wall Street Journal* (also available online).

If you want to learn more about stocks, if only to better understand what your advisors are telling you, consider joining an investment club. These clubs provide a social setting in which you can learn more about the fundamentals of investing. It is a good way to meet other people who are interested in educating themselves.

For additional information, the contact information for the National Association of Investors Corporation (NAIC) can be found at *www.better investing.org*. The association's approach to investing is a disciplined one. If you are not ready for a club, you can join the NAIC as an individual member and receive its monthly magazine, which focuses on stock investing. An informed investor is a better investor.

No. 15: Review Your Investments Regularly

You may have little interest in your investments other than in the income they generate. If your investments enable you to maintain a comfortable lifestyle, you might be lulled into complacency. However, you must take the time to sit down with your advisor at least once a year to review your investments. Most advisors will provide you with a quarterly or semiannual report that gives you current market values as well as a commentary on your holdings.

Ignorance is not an excuse. Preservation and growth of your assets is the key to your comfort now and in the future, and you can't afford to ignore them. Learn how to read the statements you receive from your advisor. If you don't understand them, ask your planner to explain them to you, and if the explanation is not clear, ask again. Don't be embarrassed—the statements are often more complex than they need to be. After all, it is your money, and you need to know what is happening to it.

Economic conditions change, investment options change, and your personal investment objectives may change during the course of a given year. It is important that your portfolio be adjusted accordingly. However, your advisor won't know your situation is different unless you tell her. If investments are not your strong suit, bring a more knowledgeable family member or friend with you to your meetings with your financial advisor.

On the other hand, don't obsess about your investments. If you want to monitor them regularly, we suggest you update your records on a monthly or, at the most, weekly basis. Keep in mind the big picture. Long-term trends, not short-term fluctuations, are the key to success.

No. 16: Get Professional Advice

Although it is important to be a knowledgeable investor, be aware that the field of finance is complex and continually changing. It is not an area for amateurs, particularly when your current and future livelihood depends on your investment results. It is important that the financial planner you select to assist you with your investments have experience, expertise, integrity, and empathy.

We think you need a professional financial expert to guide you throughout your life, but it is also important for you to assume the ultimate responsibility for your decisions. Ask your financial planner to put all recommendations in writing with supporting documentation. For instance, if your planner recommends that you invest in a portfolio of mutual funds, her explanation should tell you which funds are recommended, why these particular funds were selected, and what income you can expect to receive from them. The planner should also put in writing how often you will receive a written review of your investments (usually quarterly or semiannually) and what the charges will be to manage your investments. It is important to understand exactly what you are doing before you do it.

No. 17: It's OK to Make Mistakes

All of us, but particularly widows, are concerned about making mistakes. Even if you follow all these rules, you still may make some decisions that don't turn out as well as you had hoped. Keep in mind you don't always have to be right (see Rule No. 4). If you make a decision that later you regret, don't let this prevent you from moving ahead. Instead, identify what was wrong with the decision you made and then move on. Difficult as it is to accept, it is important to realize that making mistakes is part of your learning process.

Summary and Conclusion

We think these guidelines should help you when you are investing. Take the time to reread them periodically because as you gain more experience, they will mean even more to you than they did initially. After a while, you may find you actually enjoy monitoring your investments. It is a great feeling to be in control of your own financial future.

Diane

Reactions to the Basic Investment Guidelines

Diane had implemented Dorothy's earlier investment recommendations to invest her insurance money into a portfolio of mutual funds, but she had never really understood why these investments had been selected. Dorothy had told her the money would be divided equally into five different mutual funds: a bond fund, a balanced fund and three different stock funds. She had asked her father to review Dorothy's investment proposal and he had approved it, but Diane now wanted to have a better understanding of what she had done and why.

Dorothy had told her that if she invested all of her money in bonds she could receive an annual income of 5 percent. However, currently interest rates are rising. When interest rates rise, bonds usually decline in value. Therefore, if she invested all her money in bonds, her portfolio probably would not increase in value and in fact might lose value. For this reason,

Dorothy recommended that Diane invest in a diversified mutual fund portfolio that included both stocks and bonds. Dorothy explained that she thought that Diane's portfolio would have a better chance of growing if she was invested in stocks as well as bonds.

Diane did not understand why it was important for her portfolio to grow in value. Dorothy explained that although her mortgage payments would remain constant, her other living costs would probably increase each year as a result of inflation. If in the future, the companies in her portfolio increased their earnings, it is likely they would grow in value, increase their dividends, and thus enable her to cover her rising costs. With bonds, the income she received would be fixed and would not increase even if the company did well.

In addition, Dorothy told Diane that many pundits were predicting that there was a good chance someone her age might live to be 100 or even older. If she wanted her money to last as long as she did, then Dorothy thought she should invest at least part of her portfolio in stocks where there was the possibility that her portfolio could grow.

After having this discussion with Dorothy, Diane began to understand why investing all of her money in either the fixed annuity or bonds would not have been a good solution for her.

Next Dorothy suggested she transfer the retirement account she had at Mark's firm into an IRA account which she would manage. Because Diane would not retire until she was at least 62 and would not be receiving current income from this account, Dorothy suggested that she invest this money somewhat more aggressively than her personal portfolio. However, she still would invest this money in well-established mutual funds with good long-term records.

Although Diane's risk tolerance initially had been very low, now that she had a better understanding of her financial situation and was working full time she thought she was ready to take some risk. The time had come to be more aggressive with her retirement money, as Dorothy had suggested, because she did not expect to need it for many years. Dorothy had not led her astray thus far, and besides, they would review her investments on a semi-annual basis. Dorothy pointed out to her that they could move to more conservative positions at any time if she became concerned about the stock market.

Diane was pleased with this approach and decided to move the pension plan assets to Dorothy. Just a year ago, she realized, not only would she not have understood what Dorothy was talking about but also, as her personality profile at that time had indicated, she would have lacked the courage to make this decision on her own. What a long way she had come!

Susan
Reactions to the Basic Investment Guidelines

In an effort to become more knowledgeable about investing, Susan had taken the adult education course on investing that Bob O'Brien, her stockbroker, taught at the local community college. She had read some of the investment books from his recommended reading list and also had subscribed to a monthly personal finance magazine.

Feeling more confident about her financial knowledge, she met with Bob to discuss the money Lance had invested with him. Bob reviewed the portfolio with her. He said that Lance made all his own decisions in this account. He had told Bob he was more aggressive with this account because his retirement account at the firm was invested so conservatively. Lance had bought some of these stocks based on "hunches" and unfortunately, his hunches weren't always good ones. Further, these companies didn't pay any dividends.

After Susan had paid off her stepchildren, the portfolio was worth about $150,000. It was invested all in companies based in the United States. She was adding $50,000 from the sale of the lake cottage. Bob suggested she sell some of Lance's hunch stocks and use some of the money to diversify the portfolio somewhat by adding some international stocks and some real estate investment trust (REIT) stocks. Specifically he would invest 15 percent ($30,000) in international stocks and 10 percent ($10,000) in REITs. This would still leave 75 percent in US stocks.

Susan was somewhat concerned about investing outside the United States as she had heard stories about people losing money by investing overseas. He explained that just like making any investment there were both advantages and risks. However he tried to reduce these risks as much as he could by recommending that Susan invest in mutual funds with diversified portfolios managed by experienced portfolio managers rather than individual stocks. He would do the same with the REITs, investing in funds rather than individual stocks.

These seemed like reasonable suggestions, and she told Bob to go ahead with his recommended changes. Now she thought it was time to focus on Lance's pension account ($500,000). She had left Lance's retirement fund at Lance's firm to be managed because she had been overwhelmed by making the other decisions about selling the cottage, investing the trust assets, and dealing with her mother's care.

He suggested she choose among two different approaches for investing this money. The first approach would involve his selecting an outside money manager who met a certain number of predetermined criteria, which he would discuss with her. To have this manager handle the portfolio, which would be invested in individual securities, would cost her 1.5 percent of the assets a year. Bob was quite open with Susan, telling her that he would receive part of this fee; however, his job would be to monitor the money manager's performance. If, after giving the manager a reasonable amount of time to perform, he thought she should change managers for any reason, he would recommend she make a change.

An alternative approach would be for Bob to buy shares in a group of funds managed by different money management companies. When Susan invested in these funds, she would pay no initial commission to buy the shares although they would charge management fees. If she chose this approach, Bob would charge her one percent annual fee of the assets managed to supervise her portfolio of funds.

Although fees were important, how well the investments had performed in the past was even more important. Susan studied the records for the past five years of the proposed outside money manager as well as the fund groups Bob had recommended to her. Bob had told her that past records were no guarantee of future results, but you had to start somewhere! She did note that it appeared that the same managers who had created the records of these funds were still managing the same funds.

After considering the two approaches, Susan decided to go with the second one. The first approach did not appeal to her. It was not the cost that bothered her, but rather she didn't like the idea of an outside manager buying individual stocks and bonds without her involvement in the decision-making process. She felt she wouldn't learn anything that way.

She liked the alternative approach, because Bob's fee would be based on the value of the account. That way, if the portfolio did well he would share in the profit, and if the account didn't do well he would not. She also liked the fact that he would be free to choose from different fund management groups. This way she would not have all her eggs in one basket. She would be invested in funds that invested in different companies, and then she would be invested with different fund groups. If diversification was a way to reduce risk, she would be in good shape!

She preferred to have a financial advisor such as Bob select and monitor her funds, and she was willing to pay him to do it. After all, this was his business, and his job was to make sure that the investments continued to achieve competitive returns. Susan signed the appropriate papers to transfer the pension account to a self-directed IRA account at Bob's firm.

Susan still had the $25,000 in her 401(k) from her previous association, which she was rolling over into a self-directed IRA. She decided to invest this money in the balanced fund that Bob had suggested to her. This fund would be invested 40 percent in bonds, 45 percent in U.S. stocks, and 15 percent in international stocks.

Bob also reviewed her investment choices for the 401(k) plan at Susan's new association. He recommended that she invest the maximum amount possible and divide it between two stock funds.

Susan felt much better about her financial situation. She had full confidence in Bob given his long years of experience in the investment business as well as the fact he took time to explain to why he made the recommendations he did.

Audrey

Reactions to the Basic Investment Guidelines

Audrey realized her current financial situation was not complex. She had sold her house. Because her gain was less than the IRS exclusion, she wouldn't have to pay any tax on the gain. She paid cash for her new townhouse which enabled her to pay for some new furniture, curtains and rugs and she still had some money left over for a cash reserve. Mr. Silver had recommended that she put this money in a money market fund where it would earn interest and she would have it available.

He also suggested she consider selling at least half of John's stock. He pointed out that the stock had not increased in value since she inherited it a year ago. This was cause for concern because both the best-known stock indexes (Dow Jones Industrial Average and Standard & Poor's 500 Index) had risen considerably during the same time period. If she was going to successfully combat inflation, she needed it to increase in value. Further, the company had not raised its dividend in the past three years.

Mr. Silver suggested that Audrey invest the proceeds from this sale of shares into a balanced mutual fund. This meant that it would be invested about 40 percent in bonds and cash, and 60 percent in stocks (both US and international). In addition, it would pay a dividend that was higher than the one John's stock paid.

Selling the stock would be a big step for Audrey to take because of their long years with the company, but she could not allow this type of feeling to govern monetary decisions that would impact the quality of her life. Audrey appreciated Mr. Silver's sensitivity to the fact that she might be emotionally attached to the stock because it was John's company stock. Actually, she realized she personally no longer had a sentimental attachment to the stock. If the stock wasn't doing well, then she thought she should sell it all. Since Mr. Silver had consistently given her good advice in the past, she thought she would be wise to listen to him this time.

When she called Mr. Silver to tell him her decision, he was surprised but pleased. When he reran her income/expense statement with these new investments, it appeared that she would have more than sufficient income to cover her expenses. He told her that if she wanted to give some more money to her children and grandchildren and/or charities, she could do it out of her current income. However, he suggested she wait to make additional gifts until she had a better idea of what her expenses in her new home would be.

Audrey thought Mr. Silver's recommendations made sense. He assured her that the funds she was buying were good quality with good track records and, therefore, he thought they should grow in value over time. This was important to Audrey because she wanted to be in a position to continue contributing to her grandchildren's education as well as give some more to her pet charities without curtailing any of her other expenses. That was a good feeling!

Although Audrey was very pleased with the investment program Mr. Silver had put together for her, she decided she really would like to learn more about investing. One of her friends from the golf club, Janet Pine, told her about an investment club she belonged to and how much she enjoyed participating in the monthly meetings. Apparently, members of the club didn't have to invest that much money—$100 a month. This group of 15 women met on a monthly basis at lunch to discuss their shared portfolio. The club had been in existence for five years and had purposely stayed small, but one of their members was moving to Florida.

Audrey thought she would like to participate in such a group but wondered how the members would feel about having such a novice join them. She decided to ask Janet if they would consider letting her replace the person who was leaving. Janet suggested she attend the next meeting as her guest, which would give her an idea of whether she would like to join.

Audrey attended the next investment club meeting and found she was fascinated. You could not be a passive bystander at this meeting! The money you invested was the smallest part of the commitment. The group started by reviewing the ten stocks they currently owned and discussed whether they should make any changes. Next they reviewed the amount of cash they had and considered what they should buy. They had selected an industry they thought held potential for growth, and five of the members had prepared reports on the primary companies in the industry. After a long debate, they finally picked a stock they liked and decided to buy 100 shares. Should you ever decide to leave the club she could liquidate her share.

Audrey was concerned that she might be overcommitted with her other activities which included the symphony, Reading Is Fundamental, the grandchildren and golf, but she knew it was hard to find one of these clubs to join, and she really wanted to learn more about investing. It looked like a fun way to increase her investment knowledge in a non-threatening environment. Besides, it seemed like an interesting group of women.

She reflected back to the weekend she had just spent with Lionel. He had done everything he could to please her. He had bought her a beautiful plant and had complimented her on the way she had decorated the home. They had gone out to dinner alone on Friday evening. On Saturday night, they had joined the Lyons, her oldest and closest couple friends, for dinner at a restaurant. She could tell they liked Lionel a lot. The evening went very smoothly with no awkward moments. The men split the bill when it came, and it was like old times.

When they got home, Lionel took her in his arms and told her how much he liked her and her friends. She understood by his body language that he wanted to sleep with her. Her instinct was to say no, but another side of her thought she really ought to see how she felt about having sex with a man other than John, and she was attracted to Lionel. She allowed herself to walk upstairs to her bedroom with him, still feeling indecisive but lulled by the wine, the dinner, and the comfort level of the evening. It had been so long since she had been held and kissed by a man. She did miss that type of physical closeness.

Lionel was very considerate of her sexually, which she appreciated. It was easier than she had imagined. However, she slept fitfully and spent a good bit of the night thinking. If she were going to attach to someone, it would be Lionel. By morning, she had reached a conclusion. She knew she had to talk to Lionel and share with him her feelings. She told him he was the first man she had slept with since John's death. Certainly, it wasn't anything Lionel had done, but she wasn't ready for this kind of relationship right now and maybe never would be. She acknowledged to him her recognition of his need for a permanent relationship with someone and her respect for this need. It was just that at this point in her life she was not interested in a relationship of this sort. Lionel, the charming Southern gentleman that he was, said he was disappointed but assured Audrey that he appreciated her being honest with him.

The remainder of the weekend was very pleasant and smooth except that Lionel slept in the guest bedroom and gave her a warm, friendly kiss on the cheek before retiring for the evening, in contrast with the long, passionate kiss of Saturday night. By the end of the weekend, Audrey was convinced that she valued her current lifestyle and wanted to maintain it rather than become involved with a man, even one as nice as Lionel. She realized that aspect of her life was over, at least for the present. Right now, she wanted to concentrate on her volunteer work, her female friends, her golf, and, above all, her children, and grandchildren. She thought that most women would jump at the opportunity for a relationship with someone as considerate and warm as Lionel, but for her it was not right. She had bittersweet feelings, but in her heart of hearts she knew she had made the right decision.

Elizabeth
Reactions to the Basic Investment Guidelines

With each person she spoke to, Elizabeth grew closer to making a decision about moving to Florida. Mrs. Greenfield, her accountant, had told her that the retirement community was financially sound and that she had adequate income to cover her expenses. Mr. Grossfeldt, her attorney, had reviewed the legal aspects of the move, and there seemed to be no obstacles there. Mr. Winthrop, the real estate agent, had told her she should be able to sell her home easily. In addition, she would have the proceeds from the sale of the Vermont property, which had just been sold.

Elizabeth was still reluctant to sever her ties with her church. She thought she should discuss these feelings with Pastor Appletorn. He had always been there for her. When they met, he assured her that, while they would miss her at the church, their loss should not be the primary consideration as to whether or not she should move to Florida. From the information she had given him, it seemed that this move would be good for her. After all, Florida was not so far away that she couldn't come back to visit.

While she was meeting with Pastor Appletorn, Elizabeth asked him about a brochure she received from the church a couple of months ago. It described something called a charitable gift annuity. As she understood it, she could transfer some money to this charity, and in return the charity would pay her income for the rest of her life. She could set it up so that if she predeceased Abigail, Abigail would receive the same amount of income from this annuity for the rest of her life.

Pastor Appletorn told Elizabeth that the charitable gift annuity was quite popular with retirees. They liked it because they could receive a competitive level of income for their lifetime and then a designated beneficiary could receive it for her lifetime. Ultimately, the church would benefit. He emphasized that this was an irrevocable gift. In other words, once Elizabeth invested in the charitable gift annuity, she couldn't change her mind. He explained that part of this income would be tax free initially. Then after a certain period of time, the income would be totally taxable. She would also get an initial charitable tax deduction equal to about one-third of her investment. Because she and Abigail would receive lifetime income, this deduction would not be as high as it would be if she donated the money outright.

He suggested she review the idea with her accountant and/or her lawyer. He said he'd be glad to answer any questions either of them might have. He also mentioned that her friend Lucy had invested in the charitable gift annuity and, as far as he knew, was pleased with her decision to do so.

Because Elizabeth planned for the church to ultimately inherit part of her estate, she thought why not give it now so she would have the benefit of a tax deduction and higher income? It appeared she wouldn't need all the proceeds from the sale of her home even after she paid the Northern Palms entrance fee. In addition, she had money from the sale of the Vermont lot. It looked like she would have more than enough cash available to finance her move and anything she wanted to buy for her new apartment.

Elizabeth took these statements to Mr. Grossfeldt and asked him for his opinion about the idea of buying the charitable gift annuity when she sold her home. He liked the idea but recommended that she move more slowly. Instead of giving it all to the Church, how about investing $10,000 in the annuity after she sold her home and giving $10,000 to Ben's university after she had settled in her new apartment in Florida. He was sure that the university would be able to offer a similar type of annuity. In this way she wouldn't put all her cash in one charitable basket.

Mr. Grossfeldt reminded Elizabeth that if she predeceased Abigail, Abigail would receive income from the trust as well as from the charitable gift annuity. When Abigail died, the trust assets would be split equally between the church and Ben's college. Because Elizabeth had already planned to split her estate between the two charities, it would be logical that she invest equal amounts in charitable gift annuities with the two charities.

Elizabeth liked Mr. Grossfeldt's approach to the gifting. After all, there was no urgency to do everything at once, and this way she kept her options open. She would talk to the people at Ben's university once she was settled. In fact, she remembered that the nice young man from the university with whom she had spoken had mentioned that he visited Florida regularly to see alumni, so perhaps he could see her there.

CHAPTER FOURTEEN

Establishing Your New Identity

Typically, the need to cope with the immediate demands of widow-hood does not allow time or energy for reflection on where you are on a personal level following this traumatic event in your life. In most cases, such reflection does not occur until several years later. By then, the passage of time has softened the acuteness of the pain you have experienced, and a number of important decisions have been made. You have reached the point where you are beyond simply responding to one demand or another. You have caught your breath and are now able to focus more on long-term planning.

For some of you, major changes will have taken place, and you will feel you are living a life quite disparate from the one you shared with your husband, whereas for others of you the changes will be much less dramatic and more subtle. You are ready to give some thought to where you are on a personal level today and where you would like to be in the future. What steps need to be taken to enable you to achieve that which you desire to achieve? What, if anything, do you want to change? Are you content with your present lifestyle, or do you feel you have resigned your-self to just existing?

Regardless of your previous behavior patterns, it is likely you have become more self-reliant. Usually with self-reliance comes improved self-confidence and a better self-image. You are undoubtedly familiar with paying your bills, tax forms, estate matters, and other aspects of life in our changing times. If you had feared making mistakes in the past, you should now be well beyond that stage of your widowhood. We hope that you have mastered the handling of various unfamiliar tasks.

Establishing Personal Goals

Widowhood has changed your life in many ways. Most likely by this time you have refocused and are considering your personal goals for the future.

Are there areas of your life you would like to explore that you have never dared to consider? This may sound trite, but it's never too late to try to realize a dream. Obviously, your future plans will be affected by your health, age, financial status, and family situation. However, the time has come to think about yourself and your personal goals.

If you had thought it would be fascinating to explore a certain subject, take a chance and enroll in a class in that subject. Investigate a sport you've always wanted to try. Consider a hobby. Take a trip. Perhaps you had wanted to get involved in some volunteer work but were reluctant to express an interest because you anticipated a negative response from your husband. Now is the hour for you! If you are in a position to focus primarily on yourself, allow yourself to do so—place your own needs above those of others. If you are someone who grew up believing it was your responsibility to always put the needs of others before your own, this may be a foreign and uncomfortable role. Your old beliefs may have worked for you in your married life, but they are not constructive in your present state, which requires you to make and implement decisions for yourself.

All too often, at this point in your life, you will have time to think about the choices you made and possibly the choices you didn't make. Were you an active decision maker, or were the decisions you made in response to what you thought was expected of you or accepted by others as the appropriate path for you? Was your attitude towards money determined by your childhood experiences and reinforced by your husband?

Remarriage: Issues To Consider

For some of you, embarking on a new path will bring a new relationship. If so, give some thought to the way in which you would like to see this relationship evolve. Would your first choice be marriage? If so, what do you need to consider? It is likely that the man with whom you may become involved has previously been married and that his marriage ended either in divorce or with the death of his former wife. What are his family obligations? Does he have children for whom he is financially responsible? Does he have debts and, if so, to what extent? There are innumerable questions to be asked and answered in order for you to make the best determination for yourself.

If remarriage is your objective, you need to be aware of the following. According to one study by National Institutes of Health, only 5 percent of widows over the age of 55 remarry. In addition, second marriages are even less likely to survive than first marriages. The probability of separation and divorce in a second marriage varies according to which study you review. In general, the majority suggest that at least 60 percent of second marriages end in divorce. These statistics do not mean that your particular situation will end in divorce—they are merely something to consider when considering remarriage.

If you decide to remarry, you might want to sign a prenuptial (or antenuptial) agreement, which outlines how your existing assets are to be handled after you are married. It should include provisions defining how future income and assets are to be treated and what your financial rights will be once you are married.

If you have established a committed relationship with someone, you will want to evaluate the pros and cons of either maintaining your present single state or remarrying. Before making this decision, you need to weigh a number of factors. Whether or not you ultimately choose to live together, one or both of you may feel it is preferable to maintain your single status for legal or tax reasons. Other considerations include your emotional state, your view of the role of a wife, your religious or spiritual beliefs, your age, your finances, and your health. Also important are your personal or financial responsibilities for a child, children, parents, or another relative.

In today's world, an individual has several choices as to how to establish and maintain a relationship with a new significant other. There are few givens. What is important here is for you to make a decision about what feels right for you at this point in your life. Do not allow yourself to be persuaded that there is only one course of action.

Whatever your decision, examine your motivations. Although there are many factors to consider, we would like you to pay attention to your motivation to reattach—if such is your inclination. Your need might be healthy and appropriate, but some women choose this route out of habit and fear of being alone. If so, reattaching to ease the pain of your loss may only lead to new problems. You may anticipate that by remarrying, you can return to the familiarity and safety of your previous lifestyle. This is not possible. Your new potential mate is undoubtedly an individual in his own right, with his own set of habits, patterns, needs, and expectations. You cannot replace your husband, but you can establish a new, rewarding relationship.

If you are uncertain about your reasons for reattaching or in any way are insecure about your motivations to reattach, seek help from a mental health professional. If you saw a professional at the time of your initial loss, consider some additional sessions with this person to help you clarify and understand what you are now feeling and experiencing. If you did not see anyone then, consider doing so now. Ask a friend, your spiritual advisor, or your physician for an appropriate referral.

If you participated in a widow support group and have developed new solid friendships, discuss with these friends your feelings about your new relationship. Sometimes these people have a different perspective of you and can provide you with insights about yourself that may be helpful, given their current impressions of you. Remember: you are not the same person you were when you lost your husband.

Do not hesitate to discuss the decision to marry or live with someone with an appropriate relative, sibling, child (or children), or even a parent. Also, consider discussing this with long-standing close friends. It is hoped that these people will be honest with you and respond with consideration and compassion to your questions and concerns. They will not be able to make the decision for you, but they may share with you some personal experiences and make observations that will help you decide.

Whatever you decide, your choices run the gamut from a valued, platonic friendship with a man to a physical and emotional relationship in which you maintain separate households, share a household, or make the commitment to marry. Again, the key is to select the best path for you.

Work: Volunteer or Salaried

For those of you whose situation and age preclude the need to find salaried employment, there are a host of worthwhile volunteer activities to which you might like to devote some time. These range from volunteer work at a hospital or other medically related facility to organizations such as the Red Cross and civic and cultural groups. Some communities have foster grandparent programs that many individuals find to be a most gratifying experience.

Most areas have volunteer service bureaus you can find on line under volunteer activities. Organizations are always looking for volunteers. Some even have a category for those wishing to volunteer over 50. They tell you which nonprofit groups are looking for volunteers and describe the work of the organization. You may also contact American Association of Retired Persons (AARP). Perhaps most surprising is that LinkedIn also provides information with regard to volunteer activities. You need to be clear about what you would like to do if you know, your past areas of expertise if appropriate and the geographic distance you are willing to travel. It is unclear as to whether or not you are able to meet with someone at a volunteer bureau to discuss volunteer opportunities or if it is all conducted on line.

On the other hand, if you need or want to have a salaried position and have never worked or have not worked in a long time, consider beginning this activity gradually. For some of you, now is the hour to become recertified in the field in which you had been previously employed. If you are able to locate a part-time position in this field, take it and see if it works for you at your present stage of life. The job exposure may allow you to better identify what you might like to do. While working, you may be able to obtain some training that will enable you to get a better job in the same field or in a related field.

At almost any age, you can find entry-level employment in retail sales or as a receptionist. The term entry-level means no previous experience is required. Training is usually provided on the job. This type of work appeals to many widows as a means of reentering the job market as well as socialization.

Since this is a time of transition for you. This may present an opportunity to obtain some training in a field in which you are interested and where there is the likelihood of employment at your age. For example, if you had done secretarial work before or earlier in your marriage but have not worked in ten or more years, you would need to brush up on your existing skills and acquire new computer skills to be employable. You can obtain information about training programs in your area from a number of sources such as a community college or a university or online.

Programs and information for women desirous of returning to the job market are varied. Some universities that routinely offer guidance to their graduating seniors have expanded these services to their alumni. Graduates also might have access to the school's job fairs. This is a case by case situation.

In addition to colleges and universities there are other resources available. Path Forward *www.pathforward.org* and I Relaunch *www.Irelaunch.com* are two reentry organizations that assist individuals who have been out of the work force getting back to work. They might help you find a "returnship" which basically is an internship for adults.

Other on line sites include Apres *www.apresgroup.com*. This group offers coaching classes and a community of support including an individual session designed to help you clarify your objectives and needs. The National Career and Development Association *www.ncda.org* is a non-profit organization that provides information about Certified Career Counselors as well as a directory of service providers. Certified Career Counselors have many tools at their disposal. They will work with you to match your skill set, interests, and previous work experiences to the current job market.

To identify employment areas that are expected to grow in the future, consult the U.S. Department of Labor's *Occupational Outlook Handbook* at your library or online at *www.dol.gov*. Also read books and recent magazine articles on the topic. Another useful resource is Women Work!, a nonprofit organization that works to assist women achieve financial self-sufficiency through job training and employment programs. You can find further information on the programs it offers by visiting its Web site at *www.womenwork.org*. The internet also offers a wide range of tools in the area of employment. You can search job listings and post your resume on sites such as *www.Indeed.com, www.monster.com* or *www.career-builder.com*. With the aging of America, there is an increasing need for individuals who are willing to work with our older population and possess a wide range of skills.

If you are not eager or willing to return to the workplace but need some additional income, there are other routes to consider. It might be possible for you to perform a service from your home, such as general clerical work, childcare, pet walking, or home sitting. You might decide to rent out an extra room in your home or garage space. These are some suggestions, but we'll leave to you the task of identifying what might work for you. If you have an idea, ask questions, make calls, follow leads, and see what comes of it! Many widows have found the book *What Color Is Your Parachute?* helpful in identifying heretofore unrecognized talents and interests that can generate income.

Location and Relocation

At this point, you should reconsider your living space—if you haven't already done so. Some of you have already moved, but for others this is the time when you should review your long-term living situation. Has your home become too difficult for you to handle? Should you downsize? Do you eventually want to make a move to one of a growing number of retirement facilities? Should you consider moving back to the town or region where you grew up? Should you move closer to your adult child or children? Should you move to a warmer or drier climate? You should consider the advantages and disadvantages of any potential move. We recommend when considering a move, rent before buying in order to keep your options open.

Depending on where you are currently living and what your long-term goals and needs might be in relation to your lifestyle, now is a good time to investigate alternative housing as well as location. For example, if you have friends in Florida and children in St. Louis, you should visit both places to see what is available for you and which location appears to offer the most support. In the final analysis, you might decide to stay where you are.

Some people decide to move in order to save on taxes. While not having to pay state income tax can be appealing, you should also consider estate and inheritance taxes, sales, and real property taxes. A good source for this information is *kiplinger.com/kpf/50states-taxes*.

If you do move and, after a reasonable amount of time, find you are not as happy in your new environment as you thought you would be, do not feel that you have to stay there. Make whatever changes you need to make, including returning to your previous locale.

If you have committed to a new relationship, you and your new partner may want to establish a home in a new location after disposing of your individual homes, condominiums, or apartments. In this manner, you will be creating a new beginning and giving your new relationship its own identity. For others, the preferable decision may be to combine resources and maintain one of the existing households. If you choose this approach, whichever person does not own the home might consider buying part of the home on the basis of a current appraisal. That way you avoid the "my home" conflict!

Summary and Conclusion

Again, depending on where you are in your life cycle and individual circumstances, allow yourself to identify where you hope to be in the future and how to get there. Whatever you decide, be clear about the degree to which the decision is your own and one that is right for you.

Diane

Reactions to Establishing Your New Identity

As Diane cleared the dishes this Wednesday evening, she realized that in a few days it would be three years since Mark had suddenly died. She couldn't believe how much her life had changed since that fateful day.

She was working full time as a paralegal for a law firm. She viewed her job very differently now than when she had previously been employed, which felt like eons ago. Now, work was important to her, whereas earlier her job had been something to occupy her time before having children and staying at home. She took pride in the skills she had developed in estate planning. This type of work had personal meaning for her. She knew she made a contribution to the clients with whom she met because of her own life experience. The job was not just a way to pay the bills; she felt she was actually helping people.

Diane was also able to acknowledge that she provided meaningful assistance to the estate lawyer with whom she worked. He counted on her and often asked for suggestions on ways to approach a particular client given her knowledge and experience as a widow. Sometimes he asked her to share with a client the danger of ignoring a particular issue based on what she had personally gone through. She felt valued.

She recalled how difficult it had been for her to think about working when Dorothy had made her realize that it was essential for her to be employed. She had reluctantly agreed to take the paralegal refresher courses.

Diane had dreaded the thought of having to let go of the lifestyle she had enjoyed so much as Mark's wife. Yet here she was three years later, somewhat resentful of the various demands made on her time because of the need to work but feeling good about being productive and appreciated by her employers and her children. She took pride in the way she handled her work and knew she had a reputation as one of the firm's best paralegals. It was common for her to overhear one of the other lawyers commenting to her boss about how lucky he was to have Diane working

317

for him. The various raises and performance evaluations she received reflected the firm's recognition of the contribution she made to the firm.

Diane told Alice she would finish the dishes by herself tonight. Alice was delighted, but Diane was not just being considerate of her daughter. She really wanted a few minutes to reflect on her life without interruption. The end of the year seemed to lend itself to this process.

Erin had begun her first year of college this past year and was thriving in this new environment. Diane had to be mindful of costs when going through the college selection process. Together, Diane and Erin had decided that she would attend a state university. Since the costs at this institution were lower than at a private college, they were able to afford tuition as well as room and board. She was enjoying college, had made many new friends with a broad range of economic backgrounds, and was doing well academically. Her strong private-school education had definitely helped her get off to a good academic start at college.

Jeremy was now in eighth grade, in middle school, and Alice was in fifth grade, in elementary school. Both of them attended the neighborhood public schools. They too seemed to be making satisfactory progress academically.

Of the children, Jeremy had the most difficulty initially dealing with the loss of his dad. Diane had not been surprised by this given that Mark and Jeremy had been very close when Mark was alive. Jeremy particularly missed their time together when they participated in Boy Scout activities. Mark had achieved Eagle Scout status and had encouraged Jeremy to follow in his footsteps. When Mark died, Jeremy dropped out of his troop despite repeated calls from his friends. Finally, the scoutmaster came over and coaxed him back into attending meetings. The scouting activities had been a great help to him as he adjusted to life without his father. The other day Jeremy told Diane that he wanted to become an Eagle Scout. Mark would have been so proud!

Alice seemed to love being in public school. She could walk to school with her friends. She was in the drama club and Girl Scouts, both of which took place at school. She was also a crossing guard, a rather prestigious assignment for someone her age and grade.

All in all, Diane was comfortable with the way the children were developing. The most striking difference from the days before Mark died and after Mark died—which was how Diane viewed her life—was the way they functioned as a family. They were now a unit; any important decision was discussed. Diane carefully weighed the children's expressed feelings before arriving at a family decision. She knew with certainty that this aspect of their lives was healthier and the bonds between them were stronger than at any time when Mark was alive. Diane hoped they would carry the present mode of problem solving into their personal relationships in the future.

Tomorrow evening Robyn was coming over to dinner so they could discuss the three-day weekend they were planning together. She made a list of things she needed to buy for dinner on her way home from work tomorrow. As Diane completed her jobs in the kitchen, she realized that the weekend she was about to spend with Robyn would be the first weekend she had spent in her adult life going someplace without her parents, her spouse, or another family. She supposed that now, at the age of 45, she was finally growing up.

She glanced at herself in the hall mirror as she was about to go upstairs to see how Jeremy and Alice were coming along with their homework. She felt pleased with herself for managing to keep the home. She loved it, and its decor represented her major accomplishment in life before Mark's death. She had agonized over every piece of furniture she'd purchased and spent hours debating between this wallpaper pattern or that and whether or not she had selected the perfect fabric. She could hardly relate to the former Diane. She couldn't imagine having the time now to spend in this manner. What a luxury!

She also thought she was in better physical shape now than she had been in those days, thanks to Robyn's insistence on her joining a health club. Robyn practically dragged her there in the beginning, but now it had become a valued part of her weekly routine. Diane made a point of going to the health club at least two times a week and often was able to get there three times a week.

She smiled to herself as she walked upstairs, for it was at the health club, about three months ago, that she met Tom. They had gone out several times, mostly informally, and had really gotten along well. She remembered a co-worker telling her, when she had said she worked out at the health club, that health clubs were a great place to meet eligible men. She had laughed at the time and said, "Not if you saw what I look like when I'm working out." Yet here she was dating someone she'd met at the club. She hoped things would continue to go well between them. She and Tom talked so easily. She also found herself very attracted to his quiet strength. She thought in a kind of disbelief that she'd had more significant conversations with Tom in three months than she'd ever had with Mark. She was now a different person. She was at a different place in life. She would always wish the tragedy of suddenly losing her husband and children's father had not occurred, but she was able to readily acknowledge that she liked the Diane of today better than Diane, Mark's wife.

There was no way to compare her present and past levels of understanding regarding financial matters. Before Mark's death, she had comprehended nothing and, in addition, chose to have it that way. This was one area for which she held her parents—or at least her father—responsible. Her parents had indirectly encouraged her to believe such matters were truly best left to men to handle. She now viewed herself as childlike in the way she had asked Mark if she could spend money on this or that, and she didn't like that image at all.

As she had gained financial knowledge, she had been very clear with her dad about his role. She usually had him review Dorothy's recommendations, but she made the final decisions. This was an adjustment for him because, like Mark, he was accustomed to making all the family's financial decisions. But Diane knew her dad had greater respect for her now than he had in the past, and consequently their relationship was stronger. There was no question that she liked herself better for taking charge of her financial life. "Taking charge" was probably not quite accurate. She still relied heavily on Dorothy for guidance, and finances were clearly not her favorite subject, but she no longer abdicated responsibility when it came to decision making.

Susan

Reactions to Establishing Your New Identity

Susan reflected on how much her life had changed since she had last found herself on a flight winging her way to Minneapolis for an American Society of Association Executives (ASAE) convention. The previous ASAE convention in Minneapolis was the first one she had attended after Lance's death. At that time, she could never have imagined how much her life would change. The self-assured executive of today could not have been glimpsed in the frightened, uncertain, menopausal widow of three years ago.

Today, as the plane carried her toward Minneapolis, she was the director of a relatively small association that had grown under her leadership. The therapy she had undertaken with Dr. Coleman to help her deal with Lance's sudden and untimely death had resulted in her exploring many aspects of her own psyche. She never would have sought therapy for herself because she had no conscious awareness of needing to do so. However, looking at those aspects of her personality had provided her with a much greater understanding of those factors that had impacted the way in which she viewed life, made decisions, and interacted with others. Why had she had readily accepted what her dad had communicated to her about taking total responsible for her mother? She and Dr. Coleman had spent a good bit of time on this topic, which had been most helpful.

When Lance died, she suffered a major loss. There would always be an empty place in her heart for him. However, she rarely dwelt on her loss anymore. She was alive and leading an active, productive life. She understood her financial position and was satisfied and comfortable with the accountant, attorney, and investment advisors she had selected. She had renewed her social contacts with some of the friends she had lost touch with when she had been married to Lance. She had formed new friendships that were important to her. Perhaps most significant and gratifying was her relationship with Sean.

About a year ago, at a local ASAE meeting in Seattle, she had met Sean, an attorney who had made a presentation to the group. During the social hour that followed the meeting, Susan found herself talking at length with him about a problem she had at work. She was particularly concerned about the potential legal ramifications. She asked if he would be willing to consult with her further on a professional basis about the matter. He had indicated his willingness to do so, and they had exchanged business cards. Susan's secretary had contacted his office and scheduled a meeting with him for the following week. At the conclusion of their business meeting, Sean had surprised her by asking if she would have time to join him for lunch. She did and proceeded to take the longest lunch hour she had ever taken—three hours.

Sean was an interesting man. Dissimilar to Lance in appearance, he had been a widower for the past three years, attempting to raise his daughter, Melissa, a freshman in college. Although she didn't like to admit it, Susan saw him as more open and somewhat warmer than Lance, particularly when he described his relationship with his daughter. By the time they had finished lunch, it was clear to both of them that there was a degree of attraction between them, and they arranged to go out to dinner the following Saturday. In the course of the evening, Sean was very up-front about his worries about getting into a relationship with a woman because of a bad experience he had had with a woman following his wife's death from cancer. Susan was equally honest with him about her doubts as to whether or not she could ever allow herself to have a relationship with a man who had an adult child. She described the personal pain she had experienced as an outgrowth of the rejection she felt from Lance's children both while he was alive and after his death. Just remembering the way Adam and Leslie had treated her made her shudder. Sean was quick to pick up on her feelings and suggested they allow themselves to continue to date and see what materialized.

In the course of the next month, she saw Sean about twice a week. She was pleased to learn that he, too, was a committed cyclist. He had not taken any long bicycle trips as she and Lance had done, but he was equally enthusiastic. He owned a small motorboat, which he used on a lake not far from where she and Lance had had their cottage.

After seeing each other regularly for about six weeks, Sean asked Susan to have lunch with him and Melissa the following Saturday. Melissa was very interested in contemporary art and had prevailed on him to accompany her to the current exhibit in a particular downtown gallery. He thought it was important for Susan and Melissa to get acquainted. With considerable reluctance and trepidation, Susan agreed. Their relationship was progressing, they were increasingly enjoying the time they spent together, and both knew this was a critical factor in whether they should allow themselves to maintain and pursue their present path.

Susan was amazed at the openness with which she and Sean communicated in view of the limited time they had known each other. When she was being totally honest with herself, she realized she and Sean were better able to share ideas, feelings, and thoughts with each other than she had ever been able to do with Lance. She recognized this sharing was, in part, an outgrowth of her work with Dr. Coleman. Sean, too, had had some psychological counseling and was good at identifying his feelings and expressing them. They had explored so many ideas and feelings in such a short time.

She remembered how she had agonized over her first meeting with Melissa. She couldn't even decide what to wear and must have put on and discarded five different outfits before she settled on a silk blouse, slacks, and a scarf. She expected the worst but hoped they would respond well to each other. Melissa was of medium height with relatively long blonde hair and large deep brown eyes. She had a warm smile and an openness that Susan found very appealing. She could see how fond father and daughter were of each other and how comfortable they were with each other. Susan didn't ever remember the same level of comfort between Lance and Leslie, although perhaps at that point in her life she was less aware of interpersonal relationships.

Lunch was pleasant, and conversation didn't lag. Both women were relieved that they didn't instantly dislike each other. Both were aware of the importance to Sean of their responding positively to one another. Susan was surprised at Melissa's ability to mention her mother in a way that caused no discomfort to any of them. Melissa asked Susan many questions about her work and her background. At this juncture in her life, Melissa was unsure of her own professional goals and had not even selected her undergraduate major. Susan had astonished herself when she suggested to Melissa that perhaps she'd like to spend a day with her at the association getting a firsthand idea of what work of this nature was all about. Melissa was truly pleased by the invitation, and they arranged to do so within the next two weeks. At the conclusion of the lunch, all three of them were aware of just how pleasant everything had been.

Susan smiled to herself as she recalled that it was on the occasion of her next date with Sean following the lunch that she allowed herself to sleep with him. She had been so fearful of this aspect of their relationship not working out and of failing to meet Sean's expectations. She thought she was more nervous about this than her first sexual experience. Perhaps it had something to do with her feeling less feminine because she viewed herself as being in the midst of menopause. She had heard horror stories about women having a variety of difficulties with sex, from a loss of a sense of sexuality to being non-orgasmic. She had been a wreck thinking about introducing this dimension into her budding relationship with Sean and had delayed addressing it with him. She rationalized that she was worried about becoming attached to a man with a child. However, after that critical lunch, she knew she could no longer avoid her own anxieties and would have to address them. When it actually happened, it just felt natural and wonderful.

Sean had taken her to dinner and talked her ear off about how positive Melissa was about her. Susan was very pleased but also felt good about her own positive response to Melissa. All of this was so different from her experience with Lance and his children. Adam and Leslie had never allowed themselves to get to know Susan as a person. They acknowledged her as their father's wife but knew very little of what she did or how she felt about things or what she thought. Melissa probably knew more about her after one lunch than Leslie and Adam had known about her in the 12 years she was married to their father. Maybe it had something to do with their loyalty to their mother.

Later that evening, when Sean took her back to her condominium, he held her in his arms and kissed her gently as he had before. This time Susan allowed herself to respond. She was unprepared for the strength of her body's response to Sean. She didn't know if it was what she had read about menopause, her fears about Sean's daughter, or Lance's memory that had prevented her from allowing herself to respond physically to him before that night. Whatever it was, it melted away as she found herself responding to him. She no longer felt the need to work everything out in advance and was ready to explore this relationship on all levels.

Within the past year their relationship had developed into a very solid one. They had a mutual respect and an acceptance of each other as equals. They shared some common interests and enjoyed participating in them with each other. Above all, they were able to talk to each other in an open and frank manner that was new to Susan. Just this past week they had made the big decision to marry. Susan was so excited she could hardly believe it was real!

She realized the plane had begun its final descent and roused herself from her musings. She wondered if Andrew, her friend from Chicago, would be here. If he was, he'd be surprised to see how much she had changed and grown. She'd have a lot to tell him.

Audrey

Reactions to Establishing Your New Identity

It was well past midnight when the chauffeur-driven car John Jr. had hired pulled up to her front door following the 65th birthday dinner the children had arranged for her. It had been a wonderful evening. She always savored these moments as times to reflect on where she was in life. She seemed to view the present in relation to the past and also the future. She was pleased with her decision not to pursue her relationship with Lionel, even though it would have been so nice to have had him as an escort this evening.

She knew her decision not to move forward with Lionel was right for her, but she did question her motives. Part of it was the geographic distance between them, but it was more than that. Basically, Lionel met all of her requirements: He was charming, in good shape, physically attractive, and financially secure. Yet she had been reluctant to move the relationship forward in the manner he would have liked. Something was missing for her. She continued to feel it was connected somehow to the way she felt about her marriage to John. Was she simply afraid to try marriage again? In her present widowed state, she felt less encumbered than when she was married. It was a feeling she valued. Her experiences growing up and in marriage had led to her meeting the expectations of others instead of her own. This now felt like a trap. Many excuses came to mind, but Audrey was honest enough with herself to admit she enjoyed the companionship of men but did not want to remarry and risk falling into old patterns.

She enjoyed all of her present activities and couldn't imagine giving any of them up, although she knew she was losing weight again. She was certain when she saw Dr. PaPadisio next he would scold her about doing too much and not eating properly. She knew she had to pay more attention to her eating patterns. It was just that when she got caught up in an activity, it was common for her to forget about eating. Audrey was clearly in danger of being overcommitted. Asking herself why she had allowed herself to take on so much was really unnecessary. She knew the answer: it was primarily a reaction to everything she had not been able to do when she was married to John. For the first time she was doing what she wanted to do, not what a good wife was supposed to do to help her husband. There was so much out there to choose from, and she enjoyed so many different things. It wasn't that she hated all of the entertainment she had done for John. It was just that her current endeavors represented her own choices, and that meant so much to her.

Her work with Reading Is Fundamental was particularly gratifying. Audrey found herself giving more and more time to this organization. As she watched her grandchildren develop, she knew how much time Joanne spent reading to them, playing educational games with them to expand their verbal skills, and encouraging them to explore computer games to increase their knowledge. She doubled the hours she gave to her work with Reading Is Fundamental. She felt so badly for those children less fortunate than her grandchildren. She loved seeing the way their faces lit up when the volunteers from Reading is Fundamental came to their school to give them a book of their own to take home!

Sometimes Audrey wondered if she kept herself so busy because she didn't want to think about anything or be alone. This thought didn't seem valid to her. If anything, she spent too much time evaluating what she was doing and the reasons for it. She wouldn't change anything about her relationship with her children and grandchildren. She felt fortunate and thought that few women had the kind of substantive ties she did with her family—ties of mutual respect. All of them felt comfortable living their individual lives, yet there was a richness to the quality of the times they spent together. When possible, they rotated the celebration of major holidays among the three homes. Keith's parents usually joined with her in celebrating the holidays, but her daughter-in-law's family was large and had long-standing holiday traditions of their own, so John Jr. usually alternated spending the holidays between the families, which was fine with all concerned.

Her financial situation was very stable, and Audrey was grateful for that. She met regularly with her advisors and was pleased with the way her money had been invested and managed. She had joined the investment club and remained active in it. In fact, she had been elected secretary this past year. She had learned so much on a financial level and done so many different things on a volunteer basis she could hardly believe it.

She wondered how John would respond to the Audrey of today. If he were still alive, she knew she wouldn't be the person she was now. Perhaps these were strange thoughts, yet she wondered if he would like her in her present mode. She really believed he would prefer her as she had been and would have something negative to say about women who committed themselves to all these outside activities. All in all, at 65, she was very positive about the quality of her life.

Elizabeth

Reactions to Establishing Your New Identity

Twenty months after Ben had died, Elizabeth found herself ready to make a decision about her living situation. Fall in New England was always beautiful to her, and this morning it seemed exceptionally so. However, with fall came the thought of winter, and Elizabeth didn't know if she was up to facing another winter in Boston on her own.

Last winter there were times when she could not leave her home for days because of snow. The neighborhood was changing, and the young boys she had counted on to mow the lawn and shovel snow were now off at college or launching careers and living on their own. The few homes that had been on the market had been sold to young couples with young children not yet ready to take on these jobs.

She had spoken at great length with Pastor Appletorn, the Weatherlys, Lucy, and Mabel about relocating to Florida. Being in the same retirement community with Abigail was really appealing. She had visited Abigail in Florida three times, and each time it seemed more desirable. She had met so many people with whom she enjoyed spending time. There were so many things to do—she was rarely by herself.

Elizabeth also questioned her purpose in life. The majority of her life was behind her. Was she being foolish to look forward to something—sort of a new beginning? Who needed her anyway? Did she have anything to give to anyone, and did it matter? These were grim thoughts that made her feel empty and hopeless. At the same time, she wasn't ready to sit around and wait to die. What would be gained by settling on a retirement community in Boston? She would still have the cold weather to deal with it and would miss Abigail's company.

On her last trip to Abigail's community, Elizabeth had met two women in their eighties who enthusiastically described their recent trip down the Amazon River. Another woman, who was in her nineties, told her of a recent bridge game she had played on the Internet with partners in Hong Kong, Australia, and Washington, D.C. Still another resident in her seventies spoke to her about her interesting experiences with online dating. Their enthusiasm for life was contagious. She was eager to get to know these people better. Most important, she thought, was how good she felt when she visited there. She had no dependents, so it didn't matter where she lived. There was nothing wrong with wanting more out of life at her age. Pastor Appletorn had stressed to her the appropriateness and positive aspects of a productive life. She no longer felt guilty about those feelings or disloyal to Ben for having them.

Elizabeth looked at the kitchen clock. It was already 10:30. Where had the morning gone? She was beginning to get somewhat concerned about her feelings of fatigue. She felt tired a great deal, was sleeping more, and was having a harder time mobilizing. She didn't like feeling this way. If she stayed in Boston, she thought she might become more of a recluse. When she was in Florida, she felt more alive and more willing to participate in the activities available to the residents of the community. From a health standpoint, the move would also be a good idea. She could always come back to Boston in the summer and visit friends.

Her only reluctance about moving to Florida was the finality it represented. It would be closing the door on her life with Ben. She remembered that Mabel had visited her husband's grave site on a weekly basis the year after he died. She wondered if a loyal wife was supposed to do that? She hadn't thought that she would want to do that when Ben died. Did that make her disloyal? She didn't think so. She thought she had been a good wife. Yet Ben was dead now, and she was alive. What did it say about her marriage to be facing a Boston winter and feeling alone and afraid to leave her home with only Mittens to keep her company? Did it make her less of a wife to Ben? She didn't think so. If she moved to Northern Palms at this point in her life, when her health was relatively stable, she would be eligible for their lifetime continuing care program. This would take a great burden off her shoulders. If she became incapacitated, she had no one to care for her the way she had cared for Ben.

As an outgrowth of her visits to Abigail, Elizabeth had developed several new friendships and maintained these contacts online and even by telephone after returning to Boston. Her new friends were trying to persuade her to relocate, citing their own experiences in weighing the pros and cons of the move. None of them seemed to have any regrets, and all encouraged her to move to Florida.

As Elizabeth looked around the familiar kitchen with its somewhat faded wallpaper, she realized that there really was not enough available to her in Boston to warrant staying through the winter. She had basically had a good life with Ben in this home, but it was time to move. Mittens appeared by her side from his favorite corner in the living room as though he knew she needed him to be near her and rubbed against her leg, and she absentmindedly scratched his head. A tear slid down her cheek as she realized she had made the decision to close this chapter of her life. She decided that the Lord would approve and not look at the move as being disloyal to Ben.

Elizabeth felt fortunate knowing she had no financial concerns. She had already spoken with Mr. Samuels, the trust officer at her bank, and learned she could maintain the management of her trust account there or transfer it, should she so desire, after getting settled in Florida. For the present, she would leave the trust in the hands of Mr. Samuels because she felt comfortable with him. Too much change at one time would be unsettling.

Elizabeth couldn't wait to tell Abigail that she had finally made the decision to join her at Northern Palms. Elizabeth knew exactly which apartment unit she preferred. She intended to start the purchase process immediately. She thought she would like to be able to leave Boston no later than December 1. When she reached Abigail on the phone and told her of her decision, she talked so much that Abigail could hardly get a word in edgewise. Abigail was thrilled that at long last her sister was coming south!

Next, Elizabeth called Pastor Appletorn and told him of her decision to move to Florida. She also told him that she had finalized her estate planning with Mr. Grossfeldt, her attorney. She had designated the church as the ultimate beneficiary of half of her trust after she and Abigail died. Meanwhile, she intended to put $10,000 in the charitable gift annuity offered by the church as soon as she sold her house. That way she could ultimately benefit the church but receive more income now. Pastor Appletorn was most appreciative of her generosity and thanked her profusely.

After talking with Pastor Appletorn on the telephone, Elizabeth felt ready to move to Florida. She felt blessed that she was capable of living on her own. Many women her age were not in as good shape physically, financially, or mentally. Although she was somewhat nervous about all the changes she was about to introduce into her life, she found herself looking forward to it.

When she allowed herself to think about it, she realized she acted differently in Florida than she did in Boston. She participated in many more activities there. The trips available to the community seemed like fun, and she couldn't wait to have the opportunity to take some of them. She knew she would join the sewing club as soon as she had her furniture in place. She had attended a few meetings and enjoyed them immensely. The members had all been welcoming and fun. Who knows, perhaps she would try learning more about how to use a computer. She was tired of hearing about the many things you could do on your computer and not knowing what people were talking about!

Most surprising to her was her present correspondence with Abe, a member of the community she met through Abigail. He was nothing like Ben. He talked a great deal, played a lot of golf, and seemed to love to take trips. Their mutual interest in travel led to their initial conversation. She couldn't believe he had taken the time to email her, but he had, and he always included the latest community trip information. He told her he was sure these trips would help convince her to make the move.

She felt a little disloyal to Ben for being attracted to this casual, relaxed lifestyle, but what harm was it for someone going on 77? In fact, if anyone had told her she would be excited about embarking on a new phase of life at 77, she would never have believed it.

She would contact Mr. Winthrop in the morning and tell him she was ready to put the home up for sale. Her life and identity as Ben's wife had officially ended. She was ready to be what she now was—a widow by the name of Elizabeth who was ready to start a new life. If not now, when?!

Epilogue

Undoubtedly, you have had many experiences since the death of your spouse that have contributed to the person you are today. However, the loss of your spouse was one of the most painful experiences of your life to that point. There will be times when you reflect on the range of emotions you experienced during that traumatic time in your life as if it were yesterday—the tangible pain, the agony, the fears about the present and the future, the sense of being bereft of purpose, the vulnerability, the loneliness, and the anger, to name some of the more common feelings. But, most important, you should now have a sense of having experienced on a personal level the rhythm of life: birth, childhood, adulthood, and death—a growth process in which all living things participate. As a widow, you have firsthand knowledge of this life process—its forming, molding, reforming, and remolding.

Few of the widows with whom we have spoken felt they were the same person ten years after the loss of their spouse. Many were more pleased with the person they were today than they were with their former selves. Others acknowledged that they had coped as best they could with their loss but never felt quite the same or as if life held much pleasure for them following this event. You had no choice in determining when your spouse would die, thereby leaving you on your own; however, having by this time coped with the emotional upheaval and the financial responsibilities that accompanied your loss, you have grown. One has the opportunity to grow from all of life's experiences. We therefore encourage you to be all that you can be. Following an appropriate recovery period after your loss, move forward. Life progresses for all of us, including you, and you need to allow yourself to drink of its waters.

Diane
Ten Years Down the Road

Diane, now 52, found herself daydreaming while the family watched with intensity the latest efforts of the Washington Commanders in their bid to play in the Super Bowl. She had been reminiscing about the time five years ago when, after considerable thought, she had decided to accept Tom's proposal of marriage. For several reasons, she had initially found herself ambivalent about his proposal. To her surprise, she had realized she enjoyed being independent and wasn't sure how she felt about giving up this independence. Also, although responsible when it came to most matters, Tom's attitude with regard to money management could best be described as casual. He didn't have nearly as much ambition as Mark had, but he did well and was well thought of by his company. In addition, she wasn't sure how his two grown children would blend with her three children in a combined family unit.

She remembered conspiring with Dorothy about various approaches to involve Tom in the financial planning process. She didn't want to alienate him, overwhelm him, or suggest that she didn't love him, but she knew she would not marry without a premarital agreement. She and Dorothy had finally decided that a straightforward, nonstrategic approach was best. After all, Tom was 55, and it was time for him to pay some attention to retirement planning. As Dorothy had said, they might be retired for 25 or 30 years, and Diane wanted to make sure they had enough money. Even now, five years later, Diane smiled to herself when she recalled that conversation. It certainly had been a reversal of roles. There she was, convincing her fiancé that financial planning was important, when five years earlier she didn't even know what financial planning was.

Tom had agreed to meet with Dorothy because what Diane had said about planning for retirement did make sense. When they met, he liked Dorothy but was a little overwhelmed by everything that was involved in a premarital agreement. However, he knew how important the children were to Diane and realized that both the shock of unexpectedly being widowed and her financial circumstances at the time had made her very much aware of the need for financial planning. As for himself, a recent round of early retirements at his company had made him more conscious of retirement issues. Although his job had not been affected, he had some apprehension about the future he had not had before—since he had worked for the same company for 30 years, he had thought his job was secure. He was no longer confident that was true. He had come to truly appreciate Diane's concerns about their financial future.

She had been thinking about the time, following their first meeting with Dorothy, when they had drafted a joint budget as well as an asset statement. There had been surprises for both of them. Diane discovered that Tom had accumulated little in the way of assets other than the equity in his home and his retirement account. On the other hand, Tom was taken aback by Diane's financial situation. Looking at her asset statement, he realized that she had a substantial amount of money for which she was responsible. Dorothy and Diane had done a good job of managing this money for the past ten years. Now he understood why the premarital agreement was important to her.

In putting together the budget, they were able to determine what made the most sense for them as a couple. They had decided it would be best for them to live in Diane's house at least for a while. In this way, Alice could complete high school with no disruption. Tom suggested that he sell his house. Once his house had been sold, then they could come up with a budget that would include his contribution to the household as well as to his retirement account. Planning in this way had been the first step in a truly joint endeavor. It had represented growth to both of them and felt symbolic of their future together.

She roused herself from her musings. It was almost halftime, and Diane was going to put more food out for Tom and the assorted guests, which included Alice's friends as well as a few of Tom's co-workers in the football pool. She could hardly believe Tom was almost 60. She had a hard time accepting that Erin, now 25, had not only graduated from college but also had earned a master's degree. Jeremy, now 21, was in his junior year of college majoring in economics, and Alice was a junior in high school. She didn't feel the way 52 sounded.

Diane valued her marriage to Tom. He treated her as an equal, was loving, and tried to be sensitive to her needs. Their ability to communicate with one another was excellent, and they shared mutual interests. He had no problem with her doing things with her women friends or co-workers. The female friends with whom she was close meant a great deal to her. Before Mark's death, she had not had these types of friendships, and after she remarried, she worked at maintaining them, as did her friends.

Diane thought she was as extroverted as she had previously been, although better organized. Juggling work, her marriage, the children, her parents, and friends was not easy, but being able to handle it all gave her a great deal of satisfaction. She regularly used the stress-reduction techniques she had learned in the special class offered by the health club. The deep breathing and visualization techniques she had learned had been particularly helpful. She tended to practice what she had been taught and found these techniques helped her to solve problems better and, in fact, to function better in all areas. She thought they had also enabled her to gain better control of her emotions. She didn't think she'd ever cry at the drop of a hat the way she once had, nor did she think she "wore her heart on her sleeve" anymore. Sometimes she could hardly recognize the Diane of ten years ago. She was so much more self-sufficient now. She had been through the worst type of personal tragedy she could envision for a woman and had not only survived but had thrived.

Susan
Ten Years Down the Road

Susan and Sean were now enjoying their seven years of married life. They both valued their relationship and felt lucky to have found each other. Neither had expected to find another person who would provide the pleasure and closeness they clearly shared. For both of them, the relationship was different from the one they had with their former spouses. They worked at not making comparisons and were successful at it.

The aspect of her present life that surprised Susan the most was her relationship with Sean's daughter, Melissa. Their initial positive response to each other had expanded. The two women genuinely liked spending time together and had grown to love each other. Susan had never dreamed of being so close to a stepchild and so was unprepared for the rewards of such a relationship. Melissa had graduated from college with a combined graphic arts/business major. While in school, she became involved with a wonderful young man to whom she was now married. She and Susan had planned the wedding, thoroughly enjoying the experience and their collaboration. Melissa had married during her senior year and had just had her first child, a boy. Susan adored her grandson. She proudly showed pictures of him on her phone to all her friends, co-workers, and acquaintances. They all teased her about being a grandmother but tolerated her enthusiasm fairly well. She enjoyed every minute of it.

The deterioration in Susan's mother's Alzheimer's condition had resulted in her needing full-time nursing care. They had moved her to the Memory Care wing of the retirement community in which she had been living. Much to Susan's surprise, her brother had married his longtime partner and appeared to be quite content. Ron had maintained his involvement with their mother and over the years had increasingly assumed responsibility for her. He had made small purchases for her and driven her to various doctors' appointments and the hairdresser when he was able to do so. He had even introduced her to his spouse. Susan was pleased that her decision to involve Ron had enabled both Ron and her mother to have a closer relationship in her declining years than they had had previously. Susan thought this had been beneficial for both of them. She wondered what would have happened if she had not modified her behavior and encouraged Ron to become more active with their mother. Both of them would have lost something that had become meaningful and special to them.

Susan realized that the Susan of today was a much softer woman than the Susan of ten years ago. Although she continued to be organized, efficient, and dependent on list making to prioritize what she needed to do, she felt she was less rigid and more in touch with her feelings than at any other point in her life. She was also more tolerant and accepting of others, more secure, and less intense. She didn't feel 60, but that was in fact her current age. On rare occasions, she would find herself musing about her life with Lance and the person she was at that point in her life. She wondered if the Susan of today would have been attracted to Lance, and yet she would have described herself as happy with him. It was just that now she realized both she and Lance were uncomfortable with expressing their feelings and thus had never adequately shared them with each other. So much had happened to her in the years since Lance had met his tragic death. If Lance had not died, the Susan of today would not exist. It was a sobering thought for Susan. Without any reservations, she liked herself better today.

On a recreational level, bicycling had been a favorite activity for Susan when she was married to Lance. She had many fond memories of these excursions with Lance and had been very uncertain about how she would feel sharing the same activity with Sean. As with everything else, they talked about it and, for starters, decided to try it out, not revisiting the places she had frequented with Lance. This worked well, and most recently they had combined a camping-and-bicycling trip in Canada, which both of them had thoroughly enjoyed. Sean had a great deal more experience with camping than Susan had, but she was a willing student and had come to truly enjoy it.

On a professional level, her association had grown under her direction. She had received appropriate recognition for her accomplishments and had even been approached by a larger association to assume the same role with them for more money. She had gone back to Dr. Coleman for a few sessions to discuss the advantages and disadvantages of the new job offer. She had turned the offer down because she felt comfortable managing the various aspects of her current life and at this time was not anxious to take on any more responsibility.

Over the years Susan had increased her investment knowledge. She continued to work with Bob O'Brien, who gave her sound advice. They had built Lance's pension assets to a nice amount. This account, together with her retirement plan from the association and Sean's assets, should provide them with a comfortable income when they retired.

Sean and Susan had been thinking more and more about their retirement. They had even considered moving to a warmer climate, but because they really liked the Seattle area they had decided not to move. They felt the apartment where they lived was ideal for the present as well as the future. Susan and Sean had even attended a retirement lecture Bob O'Brien had given and had started to complete the worksheets he provided. They weren't ready to retire yet but wanted to be prepared when the time came.

It was hard to believe how content Susan was only ten short years after Lance's death. Back then she had trouble envisioning life without him. Now here she was with a better job, physically active, financially secure, and emotionally content. She was truly a fortunate woman.

Audrey

Ten Years Down the Road

Audrey took a long, luxurious bath before dressing for the Reading Is Fundamental gala scheduled for this evening. She was one of the honorees in recognition of her contributions to the organization over the past nine years. She had done such an excellent job of chairing her chapter's fund-raising luncheons in the past three years that it had raised more money than at any time in its history. She didn't feel that she had done anything extraordinary, but the numbers spoke for themselves. Everybody with whom she worked was impressed.

She was glad her children and grandchildren would be present. J.T., now 24, was in graduate school working toward a master's degree in business administration, and Casey, age 22, was in a combined master's and doctoral program in environmental sciences. Both had told her they would make every effort to attend this event in honor of their very special "Gran Gran." Of course, it was no problem for Joanne's children to attend because they were all still living at home.

Audrey looked in the mirror and thought she looked pretty good for a 72-year-old woman. She was slim and paid meticulous attention to her appearance. It was now ten years since John had died, and she had a hard time remembering how it felt when she was married to him. She had done so much in the past ten years.

She also felt lucky to be alive. Almost four years earlier, during her routine physical, Dr. PaPadisio had identified what he thought was a small lump in her left breast. The mammogram she had the next day confirmed his fears. She had a biopsy shortly thereafter, and Dr. PaPadisio had told her that it confirmed a malignancy. However, he was quick to assure her that the type of cell identified was a slow-growing type and not at all comparable to John's situation. She really didn't believe him about the prognosis but was determined to go along with the recommendations of the surgeon to whom he referred her. The surgeon recommended that Audrey undergo a mastectomy and breast reconstruction immediately thereafter. Audrey reviewed all of this with John Jr., who agreed with the treatment plan after looking at the X-rays and lab reports and talking to both of her doctors. Everyone had been very supportive. She had had the surgery, and things went well.

Audrey was fortunate because her recuperation was smooth. She had heard nightmare stories from her friends about their experiences with breast reconstruction. In fact, for whatever reason, her weight stabilized following her surgery; even Dr. PaPadisio had commented on it. She had not had any health problems since that time, and she had regular six-month checkups.

She was totally committed to her walking routine. Achilles had died of old age, and she had debated for some time about replacing him. She didn't know if she wanted the responsibility of a new dog but missed the companionship of Achilles. Finally, she broke down and bought an irresistible German shepherd puppy that she called Zeus. She had decided she was more likely to maintain her walking routine if she had a dog to walk. Zeus was a handful, but she really got a kick out of him; he was just adorable. Joanne's children also loved to have him around.

After her initial visit with Joanne to the spa so many years ago, Audrey had purchased a stationary bicycle for use at home. She used it regularly and thought the combination of the bike and her walking kept her in good physical shape. She had actually enjoyed the spa so much she made it a practice to go every year with her daughter. Both mother and daughter valued these trips. She sometimes wondered why she hadn't done anything like that before John's death. It was just one of many things she had never thought about doing when John was alive.

Going to the golf clinic with her married friends had also become an annual event. Only now she was not the only widow in the group since another woman had lost her husband. Actually, she had run into Lionel again at one of these clinics. He had remarried and told her that he was happy with his new wife. He went on to say she would always be very special to him, and he held her in the highest regard. Their brief relationship was a good experience for both of them. Both knew what might have been, yet both were satisfied with their present lifestyles. Audrey was so glad their paths had crossed again. It confirmed for her the correctness of her decision to remain unattached, yet it reaffirmed her fondness for him.

She had also taken trips with various groups. She was still active in the investment club and had attended a couple of their international meetings. She had gone to London with Heather and had also taken some trips with her friends sponsored by the symphony. Her horizons had widened considerably. Audrey had her annual visit with Mr. Silver last week and was very pleased with the current status of her portfolio. Her mutual funds had more than doubled in value over the past ten years.

Although she certainly maintained an active lifestyle, Audrey had not had any difficulty keeping within her budget. She had been able to maintain her gifting program with John and Joanne and felt it had helped stabilize Joanne's marital situation. Keith had finally found a job he liked and had been working for the same company for five years. Now that the children were in school full time, Joanne had gone back to college to get her degree and was teaching in a local elementary school.

As she put the final touches on her makeup this evening, Audrey thought she was fortunate to have had a husband who provided her with the financial resources to develop a life of her own after his death. He could not have related to the Audrey of today, yet he had contributed to her creation.

Elizabeth
Ten Years Down the Road

Elizabeth smiled as she opened her mail. There was the familiar anniversary card sent to all the members of the retirement community to recognize the number of years they had been in residence. My, my, eight years! It didn't seem that long, and yet it seemed even longer. This certainly was not a new feeling; so many things seemed both forever and yet fleeting. If she had been in the retirement community for eight years, that meant it had been ten years since Ben passed away. She didn't think about him that much these days, although she did have fond memories of her married life. It was a different time and place, and she was different.

Mittens brushed against her leg on his way to sitting in his favorite spot of sun in the morning. My goodness, if Ben had been dead 10 years, that would have made Mittens about 13 now. One would never know it. He was still very peppy and loved to sit in her lap, purring away, when she had settled in for the evening. She always thought of him as a little piece of Boston that had moved with her. She was glad she had decided to take him in, although she didn't rely on him for companionship the way she had in Boston.

She often thought about her present life at Northern Palms in contrast to her life with Ben. She could accept that her present life was now a much fuller one. She continued to be an active participant in the sewing club and had joined the bridge club. Fortunately for her, she had experienced very little memory loss and didn't have a hard time keeping track of the cards at bridge games—except when her mind wandered and she allowed herself to daydream, usually about an upcoming trip. Elizabeth was continually surprised at how important travel had become to her. She never thought she would be so interested in going to different places. She always took at least one trip a year, and she especially enjoyed the cruises. She guessed this wanderlust was an aspect of her personality that lay dormant throughout her marriage to Ben because he had no interest in travel.

She had better stop daydreaming and get moving. She had to attend a meeting of the welcome committee, of which she was the past chairman. Over the years the committee had incorporated some of her suggestions into the standard welcoming package presented to all new residents. She was pleased with her contribution and derived considerable satisfaction from it.

She also wanted to stop and spend some time with Abigail before the meeting. Abigail had suffered a mild-to-moderate stroke several years ago and had limited mobility. She had residual partial paralysis of the right side, which particularly affected her right leg. She was therefore somewhat of an invalid and could really get about only in a wheelchair. Elizabeth was pleased that she could be with her now. She knew it meant as much to Abigail as it did to herself.

While getting dressed to see Abigail, Elizabeth listened to the morning news. According to the weatherman, Boston had just gotten six inches of snow. She certainly didn't miss those winters. The warm Florida weather really agreed with her. Initially, she had been concerned about the humidity, but it had not turned out to be a problem. Last summer, when she had visited Boston to attend Pastor Appletorn's retirement dinner, some of the parishioners told her she was more animated than when she left Boston eight years earlier. She never got tired of hearing, "My, that Florida life certainly agrees with you. I've never known you to be this talkative."

It had been good to see so many of the church members. Unfortunately, Mabel and some of her other acquaintances had died. She missed them, but she enjoyed reminiscing about them with mutual friends. On behalf of the congregation, Pastor Appletorn expressed appreciation for her generosity to the church. She was able to stand and smile when she was asked to do so in recognition of her contribution. Ten years ago, she would have wanted to hide under a table if so recognized, but now, although she was somewhat embarrassed, it posed no problem.

She had affiliated with a church near Northern Palms. She enjoyed it and the people, but this affiliation didn't feel quite as rewarding to her as that with her church in Boston. Perhaps this was the result of all the support she had always felt was available to her there. In fact, the only void in her life as a result of the move was the loss of Pastor Appletorn and other church members, such as the Weatherlys. In the overall scheme of things, she thought this was a relatively small price to pay for her otherwise presently happy life.

One of the first things she had done when she moved to Florida was to establish residency. This required getting a new driver's license and plates for her car. As part of the process she also met with a local estate planning attorney recommended to her by Mr. Grossfeldt. It was important that all her legal documents including her trust conform to Florida law. Once established as a Florida resident , she no longer had to pay local income tax. This was a real advantage compared to the taxes she was paying in Massachusetts.

Thanks to Ben, she had no financial worries. About four years ago, after talking to several friends in her new location and listening to a lecture by a trust officer from a local bank, she had decided to transfer her trust account to Florida. It seemed to be the right thing to do given her current residency. As always, Mr. Samuels had been very helpful and reassuring to her regarding the advisability of this decision. She was especially thankful to him for never making her feel stupid or unimportant. She wanted to express her gratitude in person.

In her new setting, she had developed many rewarding friendships. She thought it was the first time in her life people related to her for herself. She had a hard time expressing this feeling to anybody, including Abigail, but she thought it was true. Abe, the man with whom she had corresponded eight years ago before deciding to relocate, had become a valued, special friend. They really enjoyed each other's company. They both loved to travel and always took the same trips offered by the retirement community. They had structured their lives so they could spend time together every day. Neither she nor Abe ever openly discussed it, but what they shared was comparable to married life. At the end of the community activities each evening, they would retire to her apartment, she would prepare something to drink, such as lemonade, and they would have a snack. They would watch TV and talk. She thought he seemed to have more respect for what she thought than Ben ever did, but she didn't allow herself to dwell on such thoughts. Abe was also very complimentary, always remarking on a new outfit or her hair or something. Back in Boston with Ben, she had sometimes felt she was invisible or a piece of furniture.

As she thought about her new life in Florida (now not so new) and the agony she went through in making the decision to relocate, Elizabeth wondered what her problem had been. The move to Florida had been very positive. It had been a wonderful idea, and she was so pleased she had acted on it. She had no regrets. She was more self-confident and more outgoing than she had ever been in her life. She had discovered things about herself she had never imagined were there. She discovered that she truly enjoyed people and was more adventurous than she had realized. She had a hard time fathoming that now, in her eighties, she was still discovering facets of her personality that had been dormant all of her adult life. But such was the case. There was no question in her mind: Her present life was fuller and more rewarding than most of her previous existence.

Psychological Bibliography

- AARP has several useful publications available free of cost.

- Albom, Mitch. *The Five People You Meet in Heaven*. New York, NY: Hyperion 2003.

- Amatuzio, Janis. *Forever Ours: Real Stories of Immortality and Living from a Forensic Pathologist*. Novato, CA: New World Library 2007.

- Beattie, Melody. *Journey to the Heart*. San Francisco, CA: HarperCollins 1996.

- Bolles, Richard Nelson. *What Color Is Your Parachute?* Berkeley, CA: Ten Speed Press, 1999.

- Brabant, Sarah. *Mending the Torn Fabric: For Those Who Grieve and Those Who Want to Help Them*, Amityville, NY: Baywood Publishing Co. 1996.

- Caine, Lynn. *Being a Widow*. New York, NY: Penguin Books, 1990.

- Colgrove, Melba. *How to Survive the Loss of a Love*. Los Angeles, CA: Prelude Press, 1993.

- Curry, Cathleen. *When Your Spouse Dies*. Notre Dame, IN: Ave Maria Press, 1997.

- Didion, Joan. *A Year of Magical Thinking*. New York, NY: First Vintage International, 2007.

- Feinberg, Linda Sones. *I am grieving as fast as I can; How young widows and widowers can cope*. Second Edition, Armin Lear Press, 2022.

- Felber, Marta. *Finding Your Way After Your Spouse Dies*. Notre Dame, IN: Ave Maria Press, 2000.

- Ginsburg, Genevieve Davis. *Widow to Widow: Thoughtful, Practical Ideas for Rebuilding Your Life*. Tantor & Blackstone Press, 2021.

- Grollman, Earl A. *Living When a Loved One Has Died*. Boston, MA: Beacon Press, 1997.

- Klaus, Silverman, and Nickman. *New Understanding of Grief*. Taylor & Francis, 2014.

- Kubler-Ross, Elizabeth. *On Death and Dying*. New York, NY: Simon and Schuster, 1997.

- Lord, Janet Harris. *No Time for Goodbyes: Coping with Sorrow, Anger & Injustice After a Tragic Death*. Sixth Edition. Compassion Books, Inc. 2006.

- Rando, Therese A. *Grieving: How to Go On Living When Someone You Love Dies*. Lexington, MA: Bantam Books, 1991.

- Schiff, Harriet Sarnoff. *Living Through Mourning: Finding Comfort and Hope When a Loved One Has Died*. New York, NY: Viking, 1987.

- Staudabacher, Carol. *A Time to Grieve: Meditations for Healing After the Death of a Loved One*. New York, NY: HarperCollins, 2011.

- Tomkin, Lois. *Growing Around Grief*, Green Fuse Limited, 2018.

- Trusty, Sharon, Corkern, Barry M. and Crisp, Sally Chandler. *Widowed: Beginning Again Personally and Financially*. Little Rock, AR: August House, 1999.

- Viorst, Judith. *Necessary Losses*. New York, NY: Fawcett Fireside, 1998.

Miscellaneous Bibliography

How to comfort others who have lost their loved ones:
- Florian, Amy. *A Friend Indeed: Help Those You Love When They Grieve*. Chicago, Illinois: Corgenius, Inc., 2017.

Financial guidance for your children and grandchildren:
- Lieber,Ron. *The Opposite of Spoiled: Raising Kids Who are Grounded, Generous, and Smart About Money*. Harper, 2015.

A workbook for listing all your personal information:
- Pauper, Peter. *I'm Dead. Now What? Important Information about my Belongings, Business Affairs, and Wishes*. White Plains, NY: Peter Pauper Press 2015.

Financial Bibliography

- Aliche, Tiffany. *Get Good with Money: Ten Simple Steps to Becoming Financially Whole*. Rodale Books 2021.

- Bach, David. *Smart Women Finish Rich*, Third Edition. New York, NY: Broadway Books 2018.

- Doviak, Peggy. *52 Weeks to Well-Being: What a Woman Needs to Know to Become Queen of Her Finances*. Norman, OK: Centerboard Press, 2023.

- Hay, Tina. *Napkin Finance: Build Your Wealth In 30 Seconds or Less*. Dey Street Books 2019.

- Housel, Morgan. *The Psychology of Money: Timeless Lessons on Wealth, Greed, and Happiness*, Hampshire, Great Britain: Harriman House, Ltd., 2020.

- Lam, Bourree and Carpenter, Julia. *The New Rules of Money: A Playbook for Planning your Financial Future*. Clarkson Potter/Penguin Random House, 2023.

- McArthur, Virginia A. *Let's Talk about Estate Planning; Conversations about real-life missteps in providing for loved ones*. Cambridge Studio Publication, 2020.

- Savage, Terry. *The Savage Truth on Money, Third Edition*. New York, NY: John Wiley & Sons, 2019.

- Snow, Ted D. CFP®, MBA, *Investing Quick Start Guide: The Simplified Beginner's Guide to Successfully Navigating the Stock market, Growing Your Wealth, & Creating a Secure Financial Future, Second Edition*. ClydeBank Media LLC 2022.

Psychological Resources

The following are some suggested organizations that may be able to assist you:

American Association of Retired Persons
Grief and Loss Programs
888-687-2277
www.aarp.org/families/grief-loss

National Hospice and Palliative Care Organization
703-837-1500
www.caringinfo.org

Widow support groups

Modern Widows Club
www.modernwidowsclub.org
Virtual community and support group, they have multiple chapters around the country

Sisterhood of widows
www.sisterhoodofwidows.com
An online support group

Soaring Spirits
www.soaringspirits.org
Their mission is to connect widows to each other and to provide information on numerous programs and resources

Widow Connections
www.widowconnections.org
An online group created by widows for widows to find a trusted community of others in a similar situation

Financial Resources

To find an estate planning lawyer in your area, contact:

The **state bar association** located in your state capital
(ask for a list of estate planning lawyers)

American College of Trust and Estate Counsel (ACTEC)
202-684-8460
www.actec.org

To locate a tax advisor in your area, contact:

American Institute of Certified Public Accountants
www.aicpa.org/states/info/index.htm

National Association of Enrolled Agents
www.Taxexperts.naea.org

To locate a financial planner in your area, contact:

Certified Financial Planner Board of Standards
www.letsmakeaplan.org

The Financial Planning Association
www.plannersearch.org

National Association of Personal Financial Advisors
www.info@napfa.com

For filing claims for Social Security and Medicare:

Social Security Administration
800-772-1213
www.ssa.gov

Medicare
800-633-4227
www.medicare.gov

For help with health insurance forms:

> **Alliance of Claims Assistance Professionals (ACAP)**
> 888-394-5163
> *www.claims.org*

For help paying your bills:

> **American Association of Daily Money Managers**
> *www.aadmm.com*

If you want to join an investment club:

> **National Association of Investors Corporation (NAIC)**
> 877-275-6241
> *www.better-investing.org*

About the Authors

Alexandra Armstrong, CFP® was one of the first women in the United States to obtain the CERTIFIED FINANCIAL PLANNER™ professional designation. She is Chairman Emeritus of Armstrong, Fleming & Moore, Inc., a national financial planning firm based in Washington, D.C. which she started in 1983. Recently retired, she focused her career on advising single women, dual income couples, retirees and those close to retirement.

A native Washingtonian, Ms. Armstrong also found time to take leadership roles on several nonprofit boards. She served as president of the Financial Planning Association, the Boy Scouts National Capital Area Council, and the International Womens Forum of Washington DC. She previously was Treasurer of the Reading Is Fundamental board and the DC Police Foundation. Currently, Ms. Armstrong is a board member of the Foundation for Financial Planning and Chair Elect of the Foundation of the Boys and Girls Club of Sarasota and DeSoto Counties. She was inducted into the "Washington Business Hall of Fame" and has received the Alumni of the Year Award from Stone Ridge and the Award of Excellence in Commerce from Boston College Alumni Association.

Ms. Armstrong has written a financial planning column for *Better Investing Magazine* for over 40 years. She is the co-author with Doctor Mary Donahue of *Your Next Chapter: A Woman's Guide To A Successful Retirement* (published in 2020). She has been quoted in virtually every major U.S. financial publication and has appeared on numerous national television programs including, CBS This Morning, Good Morning America, and Wall $treet Week.

Mary R. Donahue Ph.D. was suddenly widowed and left with two young children at a relatively young age. Throughout her professional life she led a successful psychology practice in the Washington D.C. metropolitan area. Her practice was focused on women's issues across the life span. These included career development and relationships as well as family related matters such as separation, divorce, domestic violence, and loss

Dr Donahue's commitment to women's issues has led her to speak with regularity to both professional and lay audiences. These included educating the judiciary and professional groups such as the American Bar Association, local County Bar Associations and the Association of Family and Conciliatory Courts. In addition she has testified before the State of Maryland Legislature. She has been a contributor to the Washingtonian Magazine and spoken on both radio and television shows including CBS Good Morning America.

Dr Donahue is a member of the American Psychological Association and the Maryland Psychological Association. She is the co-author of a children's book entitled, *What's My Job* as well as *Your Next Chapter: A Woman's Guide To A Successful Retirement.*

Index

Made in United States
North Haven, CT
21 June 2024

53911128R00232